The FULLNESS THEREOF

Making decisions for *Kingdom Living*
in the here and the hereafter

Advantage
INSPIRATIONAL

LEONORA AUSTIN, D.MIN.

The Fullness Thereof by Leonora Austin, D. Min.
Copyright © 2005 by Leonora C. Austin
All Rights Reserved
ISBN: 1-59755-102-3

Published by: Advantage Books
www.advbooks.com

This book and parts thereof may not be reproduced in any form, stored in a retrieval system or transmitted in any form by any means (electronic, mechanical, photocopy, recording or otherwise) without prior written permission of the author, except as provided by United States of America copyright law.

Unless otherwise indicated, Bible quotations are taken from The Holy Bible King James Version.

Library of Congress Control Number: 2006935109

First Printing: October 2006

06 07 08 09 10 11 12   9 8 7 6 5 4 3 2 1
Printed in the United States of America

This book is dedicated to God the Father, God the Son, and God the Holy Spirit. Thank you!

It is my prayer that everyone discovers that happiness can only be found when you give yourself totally to Jesus Christ.

Leonora Austin

Table of Contents

Introduction 7

Chapter One 27

Chapter Two 81

Chapter Three 111

Chapter Four 141

Chapter Five 181

Chapter Six 193

Chapter Seven 207

Chapter Eight 213

Leonora Austin

Introduction

"Grandma, I just called to say I love you. What are you doing?" said Maggie. She heard the squeaking sound of the rocking chair, and she knew her grandmother was rocking back and forth, just like she has always done since she was a little girl. She has many fond memories of her grandmother singing old hymns in that very rocking chair. She would often sing, "By and by Lord, when the morning come, all the saints of God are gathering home, we will tell the story of how we overcome, and we'll understand it better by and by." "I am sitting here reading my Bible, let me read this to you baby. I love Psalm 50. Reading this constantly has kept me throughout the years. God took care of me! Do you hear me?" She continued talking and did not give Maggie a chance to answer her. Maggie learned years ago that it is best to allow Grandma to say whatever she wants to say. Besides, she believes that Grandma lived long enough to earn that right, although she must admit that she is sick and tired of her grandma always talking about God. It is as if she does not remember anything else. Every time something happens, this woman can see God in it. She sneezes and Grandma says, "God bless you child." She misses the bus trying to get there early to get into the club, and her grandma will say something like, "Only God knows what would have happened if you caught that bus." To her, most old people talk about God too much. "Why can't she talk about something juicy, something about someone she knows every now and then?" she thought to herself and she has enough sense to not reveal to Grandma what she is truly thinking for fear of dying before her next birthday. Grandma might be old, but she knows for a fact that Grandma does not play.

"God is still taking care of me. Listen to this," she said. She read aloud to Maggie, *"The mighty God, even the LORD, hath spoken, and called the earth from the rising of the sun unto the going down thereof. Out of Zion, the perfection of beauty, God hath shined. Our God shall come, and shall not keep silence: a fire shall devour before him, and it shall be very tempestuous round about him. He shall call to the heavens from above, and to the earth, that he may judge his people. Gather my saints together unto me; those that have made a covenant with me by sacrifice. And the heavens shall declare his righteousness: for God is judge himself. Selah. Hear, O my people, and I will speak; O Israel, and I will testify against thee: I am God, even thy God. I will not reprove thee for thy sacrifices or thy burnt offerings, to have been continually before me. I will take no bullock out of thy house, nor he goats out of thy folds. For every beast of the forest is mine, and the cattle upon a thousand hills. I know all the fowls of the mountains: and the wild beasts of the field are mine. If I were hungry, I would not tell thee: for the world is mine, and the fulness thereof. Will I eat the flesh of bulls, or drink the blood of goats? Offer unto God thanksgiving; and pay thy vows unto the most High: And call upon me in the day of trouble: I will deliver thee, and thou shalt glorify me. But unto the wicked God saith, What hast thou to do to declare my statutes, or that thou shouldest take my covenant in thy mouth? Seeing thou hatest instruction, and castest my words behind thee. When thou sawest a thief, then thou consentedst with him, and hast been partaker with adulterers. Thou givest thy mouth to evil, and thy tongue frameth deceit. Thou sittest and speakest against thy brother; thou slanderest thine own mother's son. These things hast thou done, and I kept silence; thou thoughtest that I was altogether such an one as thyself: but I will reprove thee, and set them in order before thine eyes. Now consider this, ye that forget God, lest I tear you in pieces, and there be none to deliver. Whoso offereth praise glorifieth me: and to him that ordereth his conversation aright will I shew the salvation of God."*

Grandma paused for a moment, as if she was taking in what she had just read, and then she started praising God and thanking Him for what He has done for her. She has been through a lot, and she knows that it was God who protected and took care of her. As if she remembered that she was on the phone, she said, "Baby, you know how I am. I love the Lord, and I get excited every time I think about Him. What I had just read is powerful, and I am here to tell you that God is not playing with us child. We have to get it right down here before we get up there. I don't care what anyone says, if you can't love down here, you are not going to live up there. I thank God that this is not our home, and I told you this before, you better live a life that is pleasing to God, child. I know you are young, and want to have fun, but think about what I just read to you. Our home is in Heaven, and we will live with God forever. Think about that! Everything belongs to Him, and for those who do not want to live a life that is pleasing to God, will one day realize that they should have. It's not too late, but the minute you take your last breath, it will be. I just hope and pray that all of you young people realize that you can have fun down here if you do things the way God wants you to do them, rather than having ya'll type of fun."

Maggie did not want to hear this again, and because she did not want to disrespect her Grandma, she decided to just listen. She has good sense, for she knows that if she disrespects her grandma, she will lose her full set of teeth. She was told long ago that a wise person would listen to those who have experience things that they will experience soon. Her mom told her that she did not listen, but wished she did and what she found out was that the old people were right. It's hard to imagine it.

She did not fully understand the scriptures that her Grandma read, and because she did not want to appear dumb, she did not ask her grandma to tell her what it all means. It really does not matter anyway, because she has already decided that she is going to live a life that is pleasing to her, and will think about pleasing God when she is old and gray like Grandma. Obviously what she read meant something important to her, especially since she was so emotional, but it is just words to her. Words that will probably mean more when she is old, but right now, she really does not feel she needs to fully understand them. She is still young, and plans to live for a very long time. She feels that she has so many years ahead of her, and for now, she does not want religion, especially Grandma's restrictive religion.

When she thinks of the fullness thereof, it means living life to its fullness, which is what she and her friends intend to do to do from now on. She cannot understand how religion will cause her to live to the fullness thereof. It does not make sense to her. What makes sense is to do whatever you like, when you like to do it, and as much as you want to do it, and not having anyone trying to tell you not to do it. She does not want to continue to live a life that has so many restrictions; she just wants to have some fun before she gets too old to have fun.

Sure she loves God, but she wants to serve Him after living a little. She knows enough about the Bible to know that it speaks against almost everything that she wants to experience at this moment. She does not understand why God created so many things, and not want his creatures to enjoy all of them. How could He give us the desire to dance, but restricts that dancing to only the music that glorifies Him? She does not understand Him, and she does not see anything wrong with dancing to the so-called, devil's music. Why is it his music anyway? The music she listens to does not say it is worshipping the devil.

Grandma would read the Bible to her all of the time up until a few years ago. She knows enough scripture to be dangerous, but there is so much she does not know and understand. What she just heard her grandma read made it obvious that she does not know much.

Grandma always talks about the world to come, but she just wants to enjoy this world right now, since God forced her to live down here. She wants to have her mansion down here on earth, and if God heard her prayers, she believes He will allow her to make a good income so she can purchase one down here, or at least marry a rich man who is able to meet all of her needs. "Grandma can have hers up there if she wants to," she mumbled to herself, and she heard Grandma say, "What did you say?" "Grandma, I plan to make lots of money, and when I do, I will buy you a mansion if you want me to," she said. She told her grandma this so many times, and she always got the same answer. "God built me the perfect place child. He knows exactly what I want, and I will not have to pay any mortgage or utility bills, but thank you anyway," she told her granddaughter with a big smile on her face. She loves the fact that her granddaughter is a loving and caring person. How many young adults will buy their grandparents anything? Her friends always tell her that she is fortunate to have a granddaughter that will even call her every now and then. Their grandchildren do not call them at all. She feels sorry for them, but when they tell her things, she just does what she does best, which is to encourage them. She does not want her friends to give up hope that their grandchildren will one day call to say they love them. "If you change your mind, just let me know," she said to Grandma. Grandma considers herself blessed and highly favored, and she is not going to apologize to anyone because of it. God is good to her, and she plans to be one of His best servants. God has truly blessed her throughout the years with good health, and a sound mind. She has several homes, and all of them are paid for. They are not mansions, but they are beautiful, and she keeps her home clean and tidy. She knows that she has to take care of the things that God has blessed her with.

"Maggie, I want you to promise me something," she said and waited for Maggie to respond. "Okay, what do you want me to do?" asked Maggie. "I want you to promise me that you will get to know Jesus," Grandma said. Maggie did not know what to say, so she decided to be cautious. She feels that she loves Jesus, but she admits that she does not know enough about Him. She totally believes in Him, and was baptized years ago, but she does not want to commit to a lifestyle like her Grandma's

The Fullness Thereof

yet, a lifestyle that will not allow her to have fun while she is still young. She can envision herself in a long dress with a Bible under her arm, which causes her to believe that she will look just like a mini version of her Grandma. "What a nightmare," she thought to herself with a huge funny looking frown on her face. She is young, and she wants to still look young. Being a Christian, to her, is looking unattractive because of the hats and long dresses, and other articles of clothing that hide the figure. She wants to wear her dresses short and tight, just like the other young people she hangs around. No matter what, she knows that Jesus loves her, and that He died so she can live forever. She also believes that He got up out of that grave just for her and the other sinners in this world. She believes that Jesus is perfect, and knows that she is not, and if He were a young adult just like herself, He would want to have some fun too. She plans to get perfect in her old age, but for now, she plans to live life to its fullness. She decided that she will say yes, and will commit to the lifestyle when she is old and no longer able to have fun. "I promise," she told her grandma using her best convincing voice.

Grandma was not fooled, and remembers that she did the same thing when she was Maggie's age. She knows exactly what her grandchild is thinking, and said, "I know you plan to live a life that I don't agree with child, so don't think that you are fooling your grandma, but I want you to know that I will continue to pray for you until the day I die. I already know that you will be a preacher because God already revealed it to me. I was not always saved child, and I have done a lot of things that I am not proud of, so I want you to call me when you need to talk," Grandma said. "Okay Grandma, I promise to call you," Maggie said realizing that her grandma is a special lady.

This was not the first time that she was told that she would be a preacher. As a matter of fact, she hates hearing it. She hopes that everyone is wrong, correction; she prays that everyone is wrong. She wants to be bad for now, and maybe if she is bad enough, God will not call her into service. She wants to experience worldly things because they look fun. She knows that God gave her free will, so she can just say no to becoming a preacher. "Baby, I have to go now. I love you," Grandma told Maggie. "I love you too Grandma," said Maggie and hung up the phone.

Maggie grew up in a house that she felt had too many rules. She is grown up now, and can now do whatever she thinks she is big enough to do, and she does not have to worry about what her mother and grandmother thinks. She plans to break all of the rules, and if she is careful enough, her family does not have to know about all of the bad things that she vows to do. She wants to live a life that has no limits. She feels that she is an expert when it comes to the things of the world. According to her, she knows so much more than most adults, so she will have her fun and do not have to fall into some of the traps that her friends found themselves in. She does not plan to do some of the things that some of her friends are doing, she is too smart for that. She does not want to do the things that will cause her to go to jail. She wants to be bad, but not that bad.

You are known by the company you keep, was the saying that she heard since she were a child, but she does not believe it is true. Some of her friends are criminals, and just because she enjoys their company, it does not mean that she is also a criminal.

She is glad that she talked to her grandma, and decided that she would be honest with her from now on. She and her grandma have always been close, but she did not want to tell her everything from fear of being judged. She heard about some of the things her grandma did when she was young, but she did not believe them. Her grandma was rebellious and according to some of older family members, she did some things that even she would not dare do. Her grandma has changed, and it is obvious to her, but it is a shame that most of the older family members still talk as if she is still doing them. If you would hear them talk, you would think that they were perfect and never did anything, and they wonder why the younger generation never talks to them. She plans to keep all of them out of her business.

To her, Grandma was a saint. Grandma would listen and give her good advice, which would be straight out of the Bible. She remembers talking to Grandma about something and after she made her read the answer right out of the Bible, she decided to talk to her after she commits the crime. Reading the Bible always made her aware of what she was about to do was wrong, so she could not do it because each time she tried, she heard scripture. It was as if God was talking to her. "Ignorance is bliss," she said out loud and wondered if that statement was true. She decided that it depends. Pleading ignorance because you are not aware of the changes in the law is not a valid defense, so she decided that it really is not bliss. She plans to become wise one day, but not today, this year, nor this decade. She believes she has plenty of time to get it right with God.

She does not want to be like her mother. Her mother, to her, is so weak. She always did what she was told, and is still doing what her man tells her to do. She does not understand why God said the man is the head of the family. It is as if God does not trust the woman. She agrees that women are too emotional at times, but she knows men who would put women to shame by their girly outbursts. She remembers a woman coming into the club and killed her husband because she thought he was cheating on her, and come to find out, the man was innocent. Too bad she found out the truth after he died. She allowed her emotions to totally rule her to the point of becoming unstable. "So, that is it!" she thought. "Then why did God make us so emotional? It is His fault then, not ours," she thought, and them immediately, she remembers a man doing the very same thing, and said, "God, please forget what I just said. I need to think more clearly before I speak, I guess."

In some ways, she respects her mom. Before her stepfather came into their lives, her mom worked three jobs to provide for them. She provided a good home for them, and managed to save enough money to put them through school, and went to school herself. She constantly told everyone to get a good education before getting married and having children, but Maggie decided that she does not want to go to school yet. She graduated from high school, and wants to take a break for a couple of years. She wants to enjoy what this world has to offer, and if there is learning to be done, why not go to the school of hard knocks first was what she believed.

She definitely does not want to get involved with someone like her biological dad. He left them years ago, and refused to send money. He is a high school dropout and his major occupation appears to be selling drugs out of the neighborhood club, which she frequents every now and then, but usually her dad is too high to recognize her.

Her stepfather is the type of man who is always in the church, and he expects his new family to love the church just as much as he does, which is unrealistic. She still can't believe how he made them go to church every time the doors were open, and every time she complained to her mother, she sided with him. "You are so weak," she often said under her breath, and if her mom ever heard what she said, she knows that her mom would have killed her. "Why didn't I get a strong, independent mother, God?" she would often ask, and one time she thought she heard a soft voice say, "Stop complaining Maggie," and it was at that moment that she realized that it could have been worst. At least her parents loved her. Her stepfather was the one who always came to her rescue when she needed a male figure. He was the one, who taught her how to ride a bike, perform minor repairs, taught her how to do algebra, and so many other things that she forgot about. She knows that he is a good man, and her mom did well. But, she still feels that she is church out. She decided on her 18th birthday, that she will not step foot in church again, because she does not want God or anyone else telling her what to do. She was free at last, and now it is time to live it up. "No rules and no restrictions. I am free to do whatever I want, and even God cannot stop me," she shouted in front of her family and friends the day she moved out of the house. She felt bad after she had said it, although it was what she felt.

Maggie and Sophie found jobs in this very depressing economy, and what they do not know is that God was the one who touched the employer's heart, and caused him to offer them the jobs. Their mothers prayed and asked God to help them to find a job, and God answered the mothers' prayers. They have been working at the deli for more than a month now, and although they are earning a little more than minimum wage, Sophie is able to maintain her high maintenance lifestyle by picking the right man or woman to pay for whatever she needs done at the time. Maggie disagrees with Sophie's choices and decided to try to make it on her own, even if she has to do without some of the things her heart desires.

Right now, they are on top of the world, because they believed they pulled themselves up by their own bootstraps. They believe they can conquer the world without help from anyone and anything. Their parents wanted them to go to college, but Sophie believes she can do well without getting a higher education, even better than her mother is doing right now, and without working as hard as she does. They know others who are living on their own without depending on their parents, so they believe they could do the same thing. They also have friends who moved out of their parent's home, but still go home to eat. At least they do not plan to do this, so their parents should be grateful. They have more material things than most of their friends because of their parents, and although they still do not have everything they want, they have what they need. According to them, they are still young and healthy, and because they do not have children, there is nothing to prevent them from doing what they want to do.

Both of them found an apartment in a building that looks like it should be condemned by the city, but the rent was within their budget. They decided not to become roommates because they believe that true freedom is to live completely on your own, and although they do not have all of the luxuries that they had at home, for now, it is okay because they plan to have everything they want in the near future. Sophie will have what she wants quicker because she uses both men and women to get what she wants. Maggie has the bare necessities right now, and plans to get what she wants slowly.

"Let's go to the club tonight," Maggie said. "Okay, I want to get my groove on with every fine man there tonight. It has been a tough week, so I want to reward myself, and reward others, if you know what I mean," said Sophie. "Girl, you say that every week," laugh Maggie. "And I mean it every week, besides, we are out on our own, so why not celebrate!" said Sophie. They picked out their most provocative outfits, got dressed, and headed towards the club.

Both of them began to reminisce about the party their families threw for them that ended at 10:00 p.m. It was dull because they were not allowed to have alcoholic beverages. They believe their parents are still a little upset by their remarks after the party ended, and they reminded them that they were not raised that way. Sophie refused to apologize to them that night because she felt equal with all of the adults, including the parents. They decided they would never apologize to anyone again, because they do not have to answer to anyone, especially their nosey godly parents. As they continued to think about that night, Sophie still does not believe she was in the wrong, but Maggie knows she was.

After the party, their parents made them clean up. It took them an hour to clean up all of the mess. They did not want to do it, but their parents made them, and besides, their friends also sided with their parents. Maggie and Sophie could not believe it. These are the same friends who told them that they should behave as if they were adults by doing what they wanted to do. These same friends are the ones who go shopping at their parent's house when they run out of groceries, instead of going to the grocery store. These are the same friends who talk about their parents behind their backs. At least they are saying what they want to in their presence. That day, one of Maggie's friends pulled her in the kitchen and told her that she needs to respect her parents. She reminded her that she grew up in the church, and because she was moving out, it did not mean that she should lose her mind. She talked to Maggie for over an hour, and Maggie agreed that she was right that night. She went to her parents and apologized for her behavior, and they accepted her apology, then Maggie explained to Sophie why she should do the same, but Sophie refused. She said, "I am grown, and that is that. I don't have to apologize to them!" Everyone in the house heard her, but she did not care. She still does not care, and unfortunately, Maggie admired her for her unwillingness to compromise her beliefs. She wished she were as strong as Sophie, although she sometimes thinks she is missing some of her brain cells because she will do and say anything without first thinking about the consequences.

After everything was clean, everyone said goodbye to each other. Maggie hugged her family and friends and thanked them for the gifts. Sophie also thanked everyone for the gifts, but it was obvious that she was ungrateful. Sophie hugged a couple of her friends; the ones who she felt did not betray her.

When they got outside that night, their friends stopped them to explain why they should always obey and honor their parents. Maggie listened but Sophie said she does not have to listen to that garbage. She told them that honoring thy mother and thy father was for those who believe in God, and she no longer does. Someone told her that one day she would get back what she had done to her parents, and the others agreed. Maggie felt bad and ran into the house to ask for her parent's forgiveness again. They told her that they forgive her, and they prayed a short prayer together. When she went back outside, she heard Sophie cursing out their friends. They decided to end their conversation with her after they finally realize that it was not doing any good. They were dealing with a fool, and it is so unfortunately that the fool does not realize that she is one. "What a pity," one of their friends said. Some of them did the same thing years ago, and after witnessing what Sophie's is doing, they saw their old selves, and thanked God for His grace and mercy. They are so glad that they changed, and all of them hope that Sophie will change one day. She has so much potential, and if she joins the right side, God could use her and make her big someday. It is funny that she is the very type of person He uses. Sophie is someone who will not compromise, especially if she believes that she is right.

They were glad to be heading towards the club as they continued to talk about what happened at the party their parents threw for them, and then they decided to change the subject. They vowed to stay friends forever, and Sophie went further and said, "Let's go to my church this weekend. I am going to introduce you to paganism, where we worship more than one god." "I don't think so! I tell you what, when it comes to that, you and I have to go our separate ways. I know enough to know that there is only one God, and I believe I will stick with Him. My biological dad does not believe in God either, and I refuse to be like him," Maggie said with so much disgust that it appears that everyone around her felt it. "Well, I got news for you, you are already like him," Sophie said. "No I am not. I do not do drugs and I at least go to church," Maggie said. "I thought you said you are no longer going to church," said Sophie. "Yes, I did. But, I still believe in Jesus, and I will continue to believe until the day I die, so lets drop it!" shouted Maggie and she stared at Sophie daring her to say anything. "Other than religion, you and your dad are alike. You will see," Sophie lied. Maggie thought for a moment, and decided to let it go. Fighting with a fool is not worth it. She knows that she is dealing with someone who was not all there, and for the first time in a long time, she came to terms with it. How could she follow someone like this? To her, this is the case of the blind leading the blind, and she does not want to fall in the ditch. "The girl really needs therapy. Not just any kind of therapy, but Christian therapy. Someone holy needs to lay hands of her immediately," said Sophie to all of her friends.

Joseph got up early this morning and prayed for over two hours. He asked God to help him in his ministry, and to help him to reach more people. He wants to be just like Jesus, and he cannot understand why his brothers in the ministry have a hard time ministering to the needs of the people at the shelter. He loves talking to them about Jesus, and seeing their eyes light up when they get what he is saying. He loves it, but Cory and Stephen express their displeasure in being around homeless people, they said it makes them feel dirty, and it makes Joseph sad to the point that he prays for them all of the time. Joseph understands the need, and he believes it is God who helps him with explaining Himself to others, and because of it, the people open up to him. He loves being used by God, and finds enjoyment in helping people, especially those who want to know why this and why that in the Bible, but it saddens him when he notice that others do not have the same zeal as he does.

He never takes God's credit when the other members of the church tells him what a wonderful job he is doing, and because of his efforts, more people are being added to the church. Joseph quickly tells them that it is the Holy Spirit who adds to the church, and it is He who is doing the work. Those who are spiritual understand exactly where he is coming from, but the others do not. He finally started thanking them to avoid trying to explain spiritual things to unspiritual people. He remembers reading a verse in the Bible that lets him about the carnal mind cannot discern the things of the Spirit, and it was at that point that he knew he was wasting his time, and besides, they mean well.

He remembers the Sunday when He, Cory, and Stephen went up to the front of the congregation and announced their call into the ministry. He did not want to do it, and kept arguing with God the entire time, but God was not hearing him. When he heard the Holy Spirit telling him to go up front and announce his call, he told him no, he was not going to do it, and he meant it. He has been telling the Holy Spirit for almost a week that he does not want to be a preacher, and asked him to pick something else, to please pick something else. He felt that he is doing enough for God to be left alone. He was singing in three choirs and working in the Finance Room, so why should God put that awesome burden on him! He knows that being a preacher is serious. That is the highest position, and he felt that God should look out at the other members of His church and choose a more qualified candidate. There were so many to choose from, so why should He reach down into the bottom of the barrel and choose him? He felt that he does not know enough to do a good job although he completed his Doctorate of Ministry degree. He felt dumb as a rock. He understands that the Holy Spirit would teach him, but that did not matter. The more he resisted, the more God insisted, and God won the battle.

God knew exactly what to do to get him to submit. A normal person would know when to throw in the towel, but not Joseph. He felt he could win this battle and outsmart Almighty God. He should have known that he was defected when he felt God pulling all of the life force out of his body. Joseph refused to give up. He was dying, and quickly he temporarily surrendered to God, and told him that he would do it, and to let him know when he wanted him to go down with the thoughts of still trying to defer until next week. He was still trying to outsmart God. Well, God let him know that it was time to go down by squeezing his life force out of his body once again, and he quickly walked down from the choir stand and set on the chair. He felt better, and once again, he was able to breathe normally. He felt the Holy Spirit hands on his shoulders as he waited for the Pastor to come to him. He was glad that the Holy Spirit did not leave him alone while he sat in the chair. Joseph is still grateful. God won after all, and he is happy to say that he is truly happy that God chose him.

Each time he remembers that whole ordeal, he laughs. He actually tried to outsmart God, who is able to take his life, and to give him life again after He takes it. A God that is so powerful that He can do whatever He wants to, who rules and super rules, and who created everything that was created, including him. A creature trying to outsmart the creator!

He is so glad that he serves a God who is so compassionate and understanding. God knew that he was foolish, but chose him to preach His gospel anyway. God knows all of his weaknesses, and promises to help him, and he knows enough to know that God will do more than keep His promises. He knows without a shadow of doubt, that he serves a beautiful, wonderful, and most powerful God. He worked for the devil for many years, so he can at least work harder for God, especially after he realized that it was Jesus who died for him, and because he believed that Jesus lived, died, buried, and rose on the third day according to scripture, that he now has everlasting life. God gave him life, and Satan wanted him to have everlasting death. He thanks God for God, and that is the very reason why he is now working so hard for God. When he thinks back on the things he used to do, and how messed up he was and still is, it causes him to work harder for God. He is so glad that he finally accepted his calling. What a privilege to work for the only Almighty God!

He is looking forward to going to church tomorrow morning, and because he was so busy this week, he forgot to study his Sunday school lesson. He wants to be prepared, and because he has a hunger for learning God's truth, he wants to fully understand what God is telling him through the lessons, and he also wants to be aware of any mistakes in someone's teaching. He is aware that there are many false teachers, and unfortunately, he knows that there are some in the church he attends. Just because a person says God calls him, does not mean that God actually called him. He is fully aware that one of his friends was not called by God to preach because he told him so. His two friends constantly brag about going to the club, drinking alcohol, chasing women, and other things that ministers of God have no business doing. He was out there in the world before he allowed God to change him, and now since he is now filled with the Holy Spirit, he has no desire to do those things that he used to do, and he thanks God for it. He knows that change is something that takes a long time to complete, but at least Cory and Stephen should try to do things according to the way that God demands them to do them. They don't even try, and it bothers him because he believes the new converts can be led astray because of some of the things that so called leaders in the church are doing.

He just got off of the phone with Cory a few minutes ago. Cory wanted him to go to the club with him and Stephen tonight, and he quickly declined his invitation. Cory accused him of being the Pastor's pet, and for almost an hour, he tried to explain that he was not his pet, but he has to do what the Bible tells him to do, which is to live a life according to God's rules, and to obey their spiritual father.

He is sick and tired of his friends, who are constantly telling him that he thinks he is this and that, and it was after he hung up the phone that he realized that for the past two years, he was trying to please man rather than God. He tried to blend into the background, and downplay his education because he wanted them to feel good about themselves, and because he did not want anyone to focus on him. He did not want them to be jealous of him because they have the same opportunities as he does. They can go to school just like he did. When God bless him with a higher position, he wants to be able to walk into his blessing, rather than settling for something smaller because he did not prepare himself. School has taught him that he needed God, that he must rely on God, and that without God, he would surely fail. Education taught him that he does not know much at all. Compared to the amount of knowledge available to all those who are interested in learning, none of us know much. He wants to know the secrets of everything, and because of so much knowledge out there, the amount that he knows is so insignificant. For that very reason, he continues to seek knowledge and understanding. He read in Proverbs that the fear of the Lord is the beginning of knowledge.

He is fearful each time someone calls him doctor, and for the first time today, he realizes that he should not be fearful because it was God, who told him to go to school, and it was God who helped him through school, and it was God who caused him to become a Doctor of Ministry. It was nothing he did, so why should he fear the reaction of others? Fear does not come from God, and although he knows this, he felt he was doing what was right, which was to be humble by downplaying everything that God has blessed him with. God has blessed him with good looks, and he even tries not to look his best so he could better become less noticeable. He simply does not want people to think that he thinks that he is better than they are, because he does not feel that way at all. He notices it when someone acknowledges something that he did how the brothers' expression changes and that is the reason why he tries to downplay everything so they can feel comfortable. He knows that he will need assistance from God to help him to overcome this weakness, which he now knows is a fear of rejection.

"Listen Cory, I cannot go with you man," he said. Cory still tried to convince him to come by trying to explain that they are brothers, and should fellowship from time to time, and at various locations. He even went as far as saying, "God's children also frequent the club from time to time, so it is okay with God to fellowship at the club." Joseph knew that the devil was talking, but he felt sorry for Cory because he was not aware that an ungodly spirit was leading him. "Cory, I am not going to the club tonight, tomorrow, or in the future!" said Joseph. "Okay, but I thought you would at least want to join your fellow brothers of the Gospel from time-to-time. Just because you got an education does not mean that you are better than we are," said Cory trying to make him feel bad on purpose. "I don't think I am better than anyone! Besides, you said that God told you to go to school! I chose to be obedient to God, and it was He who helped me through school, and you chose to be disobedient, and now you are claiming that I think I am better than you are?" asked Joseph and because he was screaming, it make Cory pull the phone about two inches from his ear. "I think you think you are better than we are because you refuse to hang with us. You did before, and now it is as if you decided to be like those other people. We just want you to be our friend, and do the things that we used to do from time to time," said Cory hoping that he could make Joseph curse. "I have changed, and I cannot do the sinful things that I used to do in my past. Once I accepted Jesus, and allowed the Holy Spirit to lead me, I am a new creature. I cannot please you and please God if you and God are not one. You and Stephen are choosing a life that leads to destruction according to the Word of God, and I want to live a life that is pleasing to God. I remember the things that we used to do. I did not realize that I was miserable until I left that lifestyle, and now since God wiped my slate clean, I vowed not to go back into the world in which He pulled me from. If it means that you and I will no longer be friends, well, so be it," Joseph said with a calmness that frightened Cory. "So, you are saying that you are not going to hang with us?" said Cory not willing to give up just yet. "That is what I am saying," said Joseph who realized that he has to end this conversation. "I need to understand this man, you said you valued our friendship and felt we needed to come together every now and then to fellowship with each other. I am giving you the opportunity to have fellowship with your brothers, and you are turning your back on us? Am I understanding what you are saying?" said Cory. "I cannot meet you at a club, but we can have fellowship in a place that is acceptable to God, but if we are to meet in the club only, then your answer is yes. The Bible tells me that because I am light, I am not to have fellowship with darkness. The club is where darkness meets and I have no business there. If you are unwilling to meet in another place, then I cannot have fellowship with you," explained Joseph who is now ready to hang up the phone. These feelings are new. Before today, he never wanted to hurt Cory's feelings. He wanted to be loved and accepted by his brothers, but for the first time, he does not feel that it is possible under the circumstances. Cory told him to have a nice life, and slammed down the phone, and Joseph knew that he pleased God, which is very important to him.

It has been a couple years ago when he stopped going to the club with them. He knows that he will miss them, but he has to be about his Father's business. He has to stop pleasing man. He wants to be totally used by God, and if he is constantly holding himself back because of his fear of rejection, he will never be able to be fully be used by God. He knows that it will take time to overcome, but he knows that God will help him. He knows God to be a friend that will stick closer than a brother.

He feels sorry for Cory and Stephen. They know the truth, but choose not to live a life that is pleasing to God. To him, they are unclean. They act as if God is not aware of what they are doing, and as if He will not do anything to them. The God he knows is full of love and compassion, but God is also a killer! If he had not gone down and set in the chair when God wanted him to, he would have been dead. They have attended Bible study just like him, and they are aware of what God did to His enemies in the Old Testament, thank God for His mercy and grace.

He got on his knees to pray for them, and as soon as he began, God told him to stop. God does not want him to pray for his two friends anymore. God will deal with them Himself, in His own way, and He is not accepting intercession from him on their behalf. He was allowed to pray for them up until this very moment, so he got up off of his knees, grabbed his Sunday school book, and began to study tomorrow's lesson.

Stephen and Cory decided that they would meet at the club to minister to lost souls and to come up with a plot to punish Joseph. They felt he needs to be punished for something, and unfortunately, they cannot come up with the reason. After a few drinks, they believe they will come up with a good plan. They agreed to meet at the club around 10:00 p.m. tonight.

Stephen knows that God called him, but he is unsure if it is to preach the Gospel of Jesus, because for over a year, he is having a hard time trying to get anything from God. He heard other preachers explain how God gave them their sermons, and he remembers God giving him the first two sermons, but He has not given him any since then. He asked Joseph for advice, and he was telling him that he has to live a life that is pleasing to God. He does not want to stop doing everything all at once, but he knows that Joseph is right. He felt that God knew what he was doing when he called him to preach, so why should God expect him to change at that very moment. He did change a little because he does not enjoy the club as much as he did in the past. If the truth is to be told, he goes because Cory convinces him to go. He knows that he should not be there and that he is not pleasing God by being there, so each time he goes, he gets on his knees and asks God to forgive him. He plans to do that tonight, and after hearing what he heard in Bible study, he knows that he has to stop allowing Cory and other people to convince him to do what he knows to be wrong. He has to ask God for help in doing this because he wants to start doing what is right, starting tomorrow, just prior to Church.

He often prays that God intervenes to make Cory not want to go to the club, but he believes that God is not listening to him because every week, Cory convinces him to meet at the club. He tries to discourage him by taking so long to get ready, but unfortunately for him, Cory still wants to go. He and Cory are cousins, and he was taught that he should put his family first. Cory is a few years older than him, and they grew up as brothers. Both of their dads were pastors, and because of it, they were expected to preach. He witnessed his dad and uncle doing bad things when he was a little boy, and as soon as one of their church members came over to the house, they would act as if they were holy and righteous. He remembers them saying they were human, and that God understands that they have shortcomings. He believed them until his pastor preached about some of the things that he witnessed as a child, and now he is convinced that he was not told the truth by his dad and uncle after his pastor backed up what he said with scripture.

He enjoys going to different churches preaching because he gets to sit at the nice table, is waited on hand and foot, and because he is a man, he gets treated better than the women preachers. He loves it! It makes him feel like a king, and what he does not realize is that Satan is constantly whispering in his ear, and is causing him to daydream about becoming one of the best preachers in the world. Satan told him that once he gets his own church, he can have fame, fortune, women, and be treated like this every day of his life. He would exalt him above his pastor, and if he wants, he would give him this church. So Stephen began to have dreams of owning his own church, and he must admit, he loves the thought of being in charge and getting paid extremely well.

He does not want this church because it is not big enough. He desires so much more than what his pastor has. A larger church with a large congregation will ensure that he gets everything his heart desires, including his pastor's daughter and wife. He has everything planned out, and he sees himself announcing his desires from the pulpit after he preaches one of those feel good messages, just like his dear old uncle did. He decided that he would become one of those prosperity preachers like the ones he sees on television. They know exactly what to say to get people to come to church when they are desperate for a financial miracle, and keep them in church because they will do whatever he tells them in hopes of becoming wealthy. He believes he has it in the bag, and because he is hearing voices confirming his thoughts, he believes it will happen. Besides, his god is telling him so.

He has his eyes set on a church that is down the street from the church he is currently attending. He believes that he will get it because he knows a couple of the partying elders there, and he plans to talk to them tonight at the club. His dad would not be happy with the path he chose. Sure, he would have been overjoyed when he announced his call, but he knows that his plans would cause him some concerns. His dad was an upright man, although he still was a sinner saved by grace, but his uncle was crooked as crooked could be. He made so much money. Everyone, including members of their family, treated him like royalty. That is why he wants to be like him. He feels a struggle going on inside of him because he knows that the thought he is having does not coincide with the Bible, but for tonight, he will push forward. He does not fully understand what is going on, and he is tired of being confused. One moment he wants to do what is right, and then five minutes later, he is dreaming about becoming famous and wealthy in an ungodly way.

Cory is looking forward to going to the club. It is at the club where he feels at home. He loves interacting with other party goers, and although he is a preacher, he does not believe that God will be mad at him for living it up as long as he does it right. The Bible said to render unto Caesar what belongs to Caesar, so as long as he is in this world, he is giving Caesar his do by behaving in a way that is pleasing to Caesar, and when he is at church, he will behave himself for a few hours. The only reason he became a preacher is because his dad wanted him to be one, and after seeing his dad being worshipped as if he was a god, he wanted to be treated in the same manner. His dad's desire, before he got sick, was to have his son co-pastor his church, which was one of the largest churches in the area.

He always wanted to be like his dad, and because he saw how his dad used to live, he wanted to do whatever it took to get some of the same things his dad had, such as several new cars each year, new suits, jewelry, and whatever his heart desired. His dad never paid for any of it because his congregation always made sure he and his family was taken care of. When his dad wanted a big-ticket item, he would preach one of those sermons that made people believe that God would still love them no matter what they choose to do, and God would overlook everything because of it, and the people would shower him with material wealth. How could he not be a preacher after witnessing his dad getting everything his heart desired, which included women, which seem not to bother his mother.

He remembers telling his dad that he does not hear God talking to him, and his dad confessed that God does not talk to him either. His dad became a preacher because his dad was one. His great-granddad was the one who started the church that his dad was the senior pastor in for over 25 years, but if anyone saw his dad now, he would see a horrible sight.

His dad started preaching the next day after he got out of high school because his dad told him to. He never worked a day in his life, so at an early age, he knew that preaching was the right choice because to him, it requires very little effort. The only problem now is the church, which his dad was the pastor burned down the day before he announced to his friend's church, that he was called to be a preacher. He felt he was called, but the one who called him was self. This church is not as big as his dad's church was, but it has to do for now. He feels that he will be an asset here because his dad taught him how to preach meaningful messages that the congregation loves to hear, and messages that will motivate them to put more money in the love-offering basket. His dad was accused of preaching to those with itching ears, but his dad did not care because it was those sermons that kept his bills paid and provided for a great living for him and his family. He felt his dad was a very smart man.

Cory took out of his best suit, the suit he believes that will allow him to pull the finest women in the club tonight. He is out to score tonight. For some unknown reason, women are attracted to him, and he thanks God for making him a tall attractive man. His good looks have always been an asset, and are what made the men in his family so great. He believes women will do anything to have a good looking preacher marry them, and he believes he is the best looking man in church, with Stephen being a close second, and for this reason, he believes they will do well in their ministry.

He decided to call Stephen to find out what time he will be leaving his apartment because Stephen takes too long to get ready, and if he were in charge of creating humans, he would have made him a girl. It takes him an hour to brush his hair, so he decided weeks ago to remind him to call him when he walks out of the door. He wants to arrive early so he can look at all of the women who come through the door, and his plan is if he sees one of the people that attend his church, he and Stephen will slip out before that person sees them. He knows the club is not a place for a minister, but because he called himself, it is okay as long as some of the people do not see him, and besides, they should not be there either.

He called Stephen and he picked up after the first ring, and said, "Hello." "Steve, this is your cousin man, are you ready?" he said hoping to hear that his wait is over, and soon he would be talking to beautiful and drunk women. "Yes, I am ready, and after we hang up, I will walk out of the door, if it is okay with you? I'm not staying long because I might have to teach Sunday school tomorrow morning," Stephen said. "Whatever man, I will talk to you at the club, later," Cory said and they hung up their phones and walked out of their apartments.

Chapter One

Sunday

"At last, we are here!" said Maggie with lots of excitement in her voice. Traffic was bumper-to-bumper all of the way there, and everyone appears to be out tonight in their Sunday best. Usually, traffic in Atlanta is not like this in the wee hours in the morning, but both of them felt it was worth the wait, because there were so many good-looking men standing in line to go into the club. Some of them were with their partners, and the others appeared to be alone, but it was okay. At this club, anything goes. "There is a mixture out tonight," said Sophie hoping to find another sponsor to help her buy the things she wants. "Yeah girl, I see men with men, women with women, and the rest with I don't know what," said Maggie looking at all of the made-up faces. All were there to have a good time and it was obvious to her. It looks like a great big Halloween ball, except no one was wearing a store-bought mask.

The line was extremely long, so they decided to talk to the people who were in line ahead of them to pass the time away. The man in the brown suit was named Thomas, and he is tall and nice looking, and the best thing is he works for a brokerage firm. He looks like he has lots of money, and when he smiles; he looks like an angel with a full set of teeth. The other man name is Eric who constantly tells everyone that he is unhappily married, and as he puts it, "I am married while I am at home, but as soon as I walk out of the house, I am a single man." He is very handsome too, but he was also cocky.

He told Maggie and Sophie that he and his wife have an agreement that allows them to live separate lives, but they cannot take their other partner to their home. He has no intentions of getting a divorce, but he will not tell women this. The reason for this is he wants relationships with no strings attached, and if he is interested in a beautiful woman, he will tell her that he is married, and will reveal to her that he is not happy at home. Women fall for it every time. He will never tell her that he will never divorce his wife, because that is what men like him do, but at least he tells the potential victim about his wife. If he has to lie to get what he wants, he will do it, no matter what it is, and in this case, it is worth it.

His last extramarital affair lasted a little longer than two years. He convinced her that the divorce was in the works, and he did not care what his lies were doing to her because he was getting all of his needs met, but when she found out the truth, she broke it off and is now telling all of his friends that Eric is scum. Eric threatened her by telling her that he would kill her if she continues to talk to his friends and family.

Maggie found herself wondering if she had made a mistake. This is not uncommon for her because she grew up in the church, and is constantly hearing her grandmother say, "You should not go anywhere where Jesus is not welcomed honey. Time is winding down, and if you don't get yourself right, right now, you will find yourself not making it in." She knows that she will make it in, but she also wants her mansion and other treasures when she goes up there. Her grandmother told her that because she believed on Jesus, she is saved and that will not change. Her pastor talked to all of them about salvation, and she believes the Bible is correct. But for now, she is not interested in building up treasure in Heaven because she is young, and according to her, she has plenty of time to do that later. Her plan is to start laying up treasure when she is her grandmother's age because that is the time she plans to act right. But, she feels a struggle going on inside of her. One minute she wants to get right at the very moment, and the next minute, she wants to wait until she has one foot in the grave. She acknowledges the fact that she does not fully understand the Bible, but she knows more than most of her friends. She believes she loves God, but for now, she wants to love him by saying it rather than doing things to prove it. She knows that God knows everything about her, and can listen to her thoughts, so to her, He understands her. She wishes that she could concentrate on one thing rather than flip-flopping.

Lately, she has been seeing strange things. She cannot determine if they are real or imaginary, and each time she sees one or more of them, they became clearer. At first, they were blurry, but now, she is beginning to hear them, and because they are clearer, they are becoming less and less imaginary, although they are very hard to describe. The last time she saw them; they were hideous and were really jumping to the music just like everyone else in the club. After she blinked a few times, they would disappear. "Maybe, I was drinking too much," she often thought and decided to make an effort to control the amount of alcohol she consumes tonight. She wants to enjoy herself, and wants to see things that are real tonight. She has an active imagination, but this is ridiculous! If she sees them tonight, she will consider making an appointment to see a psychiatrist. "Wait a minute, I have a psychic girlfriend!" she thought wondering if this girl can really help her. "I will talk to her first thing tomorrow, if I see things tonight," she mumbled to herself and hoped no one noticed.

They were now inside the club. Boy was it crowded! "There is a table," said Sophie trying to determine if it was the best table. They ran over to the table. They knew from experience, that if they did not get to the table quickly, someone else would grab it. There were a few empty tables, but this particular table has the desired view because they want to see everything. The angle allows both of them to see the door and everything else, which allows them to check out everyone and everything. They are in the center of the room, and they want to be at the center of things. Their new friends, Thomas and Eric came over and asked if they could sit at their table. They said yes, hoping they could charm the men into buying them drinks throughout the night.

It is understood by all that everyone is free to dance and socialize with the person of their choice, and no one should take offense if no one from the table in which you sit, does not ask a member at the table for a dance. This is one of many unwritten rules. At this particular club, it also applies to married couples.

Although she is younger than Maggie by a few days, Sophie believes she is wiser, because of her views and experience. She considers herself to be a free thinker who likes everything, and likes to experience everything, especially those fun things that are considered immoral by society. For instance, she does not see a problem with dating a transvestite. Maggie would gag at the very thought, but for some reason, it excites her. Nothing and no one is off limits to her. She has done more things than most fifty-year old people have done. She feels that she has been on her own since thirteen because her dad died when she was young, and her mother worked all of the time to provide for her and her two brothers, which is the reason why she felt she was on her own. She often stole money from her Mom and justified it by believing it belonged to her anyway since her mother was working to support her and her brothers. If her mom did not have enough money to make ends meet, then it is not her fault. Maybe Mom should have worked a couple more jobs to bring more money into their house, then she would not have to steal her last few dollars all of the time, besides, her mom always gave money to the church. The preacher is living better than they were, so why can't the preacher give some of the money back.

After years of stealing from her mom, her mom finally had enough and told her to leave after she graduates from high school. Her mom told her that she would continue to support her if she goes to college, but she will have to leave home and move on campus. She never apologized to her mom for stealing because she did not feel that what she did was wrong, and she feels the same way now. Her mom used to have nice jewelry but she managed to steal that too without a second thought. She sold them to the highest bidder, and now, she still does not regret anything she did. Her mom put a down payment on the apartment she now rents. Everyone in the family told her that she is selfish and that one day, she will have to answer for everything she did, but she is not worried about that. She told all of them that stealing what she wanted are required to survive, and that is how the European settlers got the United States, and no one is saying that they were wrong.

Sophie never understood why her mom continues to quote Bible scripture to her. It did not do any good because she no longer believes in her God. She remembers attending a conference a year ago at her high school, and the lady explained to them that everyone and everything is god. The strange thing was that none of the people in the community was invited to attend this conference, although it was conducted in the school's auditorium. The speaker said god exists in all things, which made sense to her because she explained how some people had more power than others. People can get more power by stealing it from nature. She constantly said celebrate yourself because you are god. What she heard was very convincing, and because the lady described how everything created itself because god exists in nature so thoroughly, she plans to attend another New Age conference soon. She wants to know how to harness the power that is found in nature in hopes of gaining more power, and just maybe, she can harness enough power to rule the world. She was also told that women are the true rulers, and not men, unlike the Bible, that little piece of information made her the happiest. What she heard was what she wanted to hear, regardless of whether or not it is the truth. She does not believe everything, but believed she can work with what she heard thus far. What she heard justified her reckless lifestyle, and Christianity does not.

She told her mom about the conference and her mom told her that they are trying to recruit them, and said they were a cult. Her mom called the school to find out about what her daughter was talking about, and for some reason, the school would not give her any information about the organization that came to talk to the students, but they invited her mom to come to their next conference after her mom pretended to express an interest in joining that particular religious organization. Her mom went to the meeting and was thrown out because she told them that they belonged to the devil.

Sophie has a talent for picking out the most generous person from out of a crowd. She will never worry about paying rent because she finds multiple partners to pay for it each month. Maggie, to her, is stupid because she does not allow anyone to pay her rent. "How can a woman be so stupid? If they are willing to pay for my service, why not let them? How can this be wrong?" she often says. The other thing that made Maggie stupid in her eyes was that she would always talk about leaving the club early, knowing that there would always be nice looking victims there.

Sophie does not feel church is needed, and lately, Maggie has been hinting about going to church with her grandmother. All of the people she knew that went to traditional churches always turned their nose up at people who went to clubs. She considered all of them to be hypocrites, and would often see some of them who claim to be preachers out there on the dance floor partying with her. They talk about her lifestyle, but did the same things under the cover of darkness. They better be glad that they believe in what happens in the club should always stay in the club, which is one of many unwritten rules.

She had affairs with all types of people, including deacons and preachers. Some of them went to the club with her, and would attend church early Sunday morning. They were sinners Monday through Saturday night, and sometimes Sunday morning, but around 10:00 a.m. they miraculously turned into saints. She knew enough about their Bible to know that she should not play with God, just in case He really does exist. To her, that proves that it is possible that the Christian God does not exist, and the lady from the New Age conference was telling the truth because it appears that deacons and preachers are not living a godly life, then why doesn't God punish them? Why does God allow them to attend church on Sunday? How can they sit in church on Sunday, and put down everyone who has a lifestyle that does not fit the ideal lifestyle that they said Jesus said they should live? They are not living the life that they say everyone should live. And they say I am confused?" she thought to herself.

She recognized one of her lovers sitting at the table next to her. He was with a woman that was not his wife, and she knows that he will attend church tomorrow morning, and will sit in the pulpit with the rest of the ministers. She also sees two other people who said they are preachers sitting at the table next to him. Looking at them makes her wonder if God is truly real. How can Christians claim that what she is doing is wrong when she sees those who claim to be His servants at the club partying and drinking with those who they call the lost? She attended church the day two of the men announced to everyone that they were called to be preachers. They are leading double lives, and she believes if the senior pastor knows it, he would not allow them to sit in the pulpit with him. By day, they are self-proclaimed saints, and by night they belong to their real father the devil, which is very obvious at this very moment. If God were real, people like them would turn those who are searching for God away from Him. Obviously, they do not believe in the lifestyle they preach about. They do not believe it because they refuse to live a life according to God's rules; they are hypocrites and should be punished. She wished she would be the one who was put in charge to punish them.

If God is so perfect and require His followers to be perfect as well, then why do the people He calls are out with her and the other sinners partying in the clubs? She does not understand why God does not strike these men down. She believes the real reason why Cory announced that he was called to preach because his dad and grandfather were preachers. She knows he thinks being a preacher is an easy gig. She dated him a few years ago, and he told her his plans. She ended the relationship because she did not want to be a preacher's wife, and she did not want to be one of those women who wait for their husband to come home after visiting one of their mistresses. Cory is just like his dad and granddad, and she knows that he would never change.

Maggie's grandma told her that she does not believe that God called Cory to preach after hearing what Sophie told her. She said if God did not call him then he would be working for the devil. She believes that Grandma has a point, and although she does not want to accept the fact that Christianity is necessary, she will acknowledge that Grandma walks the walk, and talks the talk. Grandma is peculiar and appears to look at the person's soul, and she seems to have the ability to see what is really there, so she believes that if Grandma were not a Christian, she would make a powerful pagan god. She cannot stay around Grandma too long because she always feels uncomfortable. Every time Maggie wants to take her along to visit her, she tries to come up with an excuse. When she was young, Grandma would hug her, but ever since she accepted paganism, Grandma would talk to her as if she was casting out demons. She was always nice, but she was all of a sudden so different and every remark she made to her about what pagans believe, she would respond with scripture from the Holy Bible. Every time she sees her, she also mentions the name of Jesus several times; it was as if Grandma saw something in her that is evil.

Her current minister lover felt pressure from his mother to go into the ministry. His mom would constantly tell him to announce his call before she dies, which could be at any moment. She is the type of person who is always crying that she is sick, and goes overboard with acting out a particular illness. Her performances were very amusing, and if you listened to her, you would discover that she has every illness known to man. When he would talk to her about God, she would often tell him, "Why would I want to serve your god that does not have the power to heal your mother? Your mother always saying how God is good to her, but a moment later she is complaining about her life of pain and suffering. Go ahead and convince me by telling me why I should serve your God." He could not say anything, and he was fully aware that Sophie knew about his mom's addiction to drugs and alcohol.

She wanted to go over to say hello to him, but decided not to. She plans to invite him and his mother to their next meeting. She doesn't know how many people they are fooling, but she knows that they are not Christians. They are already pagans, but they do not know it.

Maggie could not take it any longer, so she decided to dance, even if she has to dance by herself. As soon as she stood up, Eric asked her to dance with him. He grabbed her hand, and they walked to the dance floor.

They were moving to the beat of the music, and as she listened to the music, she recalled something her grandmother said to her last week. Grandma called her the next day after she had one of her visions, and said, "Maggie, I need to share something with you. Remember I told you that you should not go to the club because secular music does not glorify God? Well, God gave me a vision. We were in Church, and all of us were singing, dancing and glorifying God. God lifted me up, and I looked down on the drum and other musical instruments. Then I went through a dark tunnel, and because I am used to God doing this, I was not afraid so I kept my eyes open. I thought He was going to take me up in a whirlwind again, but He did not do that this time. He took me to a place where a beautiful lady was playing a piano. I could not hear anything in this location, but when I was in the church, I heard music, well anyway,

God took me closer to her, but I still could not hear her nor could I read her lips although we were face to face. I told her that Jesus loves her and closed my eyes. God wanted me to keep my eyes open and I felt something that felt like an electrical current, so I opened my eyes. The lady changed into a devil. Baby, the devil is behind secular music, and I mean all of secular music. I once believed that jazz was okay, but now I know that it is not." Maggie remembers telling her that she does not see any harm in it and that they only go to the club to have fun. Her grandma told her the story about Jesus casing out demons, and she really could not understand what her grandma was talking about until now. She thinks she is seeing something right now, but does not understand what it is. As she remembers the story, she believes that Jesus was able to see the demons in that person, and it appeared that He alone was able to see them and no one else, but the question she has is why does she see them? She remembers her grandma reminding her that just because it looks good, does not mean that it is good, and something that appears innocent may not be innocent at all. She told her that she needs to look through the outer shell, and to the core of the person, but this is ridiculous. Is she seeing the inner core of people or is what she is seeing are demons? Grandma explained that Sophie is a pretty girl, but she is controlled by a devil, but right now, as she looks at Sophie, she does not see anything unusual, so she must not be seeing the inner core of the person. She thought she saw things in the past, but she blew them off as something that was in her imagination because she knows the girl so well, but they were not like the things she is seeing now. These things are up close and personal. She believes Grandma does not understand Sophie like she does, but she also admits there is something in Sophie that causes her to seek after the occult, which is in her opinion, makes Sophie suspicious, and she wonders if Sophie is seeing what she is seeing right now.

All of a sudden, one of the things jumped up and landed right next to her and Eric! "Oh no!" she shouted, and would have ran if the dance floor was not so crowded. She tried, and bumped into someone. "What?" says Eric looking as if he was concerned about her. "Oh nothing, I guess I am seeing things again," Maggie said hoping fear did not show on her face. Eric thought she saw an old boyfriend or someone that she does not want to see tonight. So far, she has not had a sip of alcohol so what she is seeing is not imaginary. After blinking a few times, and he did not disappear but is still there on the floor appearing to be break dancing, and the rest of them are appearing to be coming closer. She looked around the room, and suddenly there were lots of them, and their numbers started increasing rapidly and no one appears to notice them except her. Some of them were dancing, and others are whispering in the ears of people! They are now coming in from the outside, and are dancing with each other, and with the people on the dance floor. They were all around her, and for some reason, no one is noticing except her. Is she crazy? Is she seeing things that are not there? Should she be admitted into a mental hospital? "What is wrong with me?" she thought and wanted to cry and run.

After the song ended, she, Eric, and a couple of the demons walked back over to the table. She whispered to Sophie, "Do you see anything in here that is not human?" Sophie started laughing, and said, "Girl, what have you been taking? You are kidding, right?" "No, I am not kidding!" she screamed looking at her with disbelief showing on her face. "What do they look like Maggie?" asked Sophie trying to sound as calm as possible. "They look human, and then they change into pinkish looking creatures that are hideous. Don't tell me you don't see them?" asked Maggie, who felt that because Sophie is a member of the occult, she could see them easily. "I guess because I am not taking the same medication as you are taking," Sophie said in a voice that could freeze a nation in 2 seconds flat. "For your information, I had not taken anything, not even a drop of alcohol tonight," she said returning her icy stare, but not with the matching voice and attitude. Because everyone at the table was staring at her, she felt foolish, and it was obvious to her that they do not see anything. She knows that if she continues, they will think that she should be locked up in the nearest mental institution, so she said, "Come on now, can't y'all take a joke. I just wanted to see if anyone saw his or her imaginary friends, you know the ones we talk to on a regular basis. All jokes aside, I do not see anything," she lied but on the inside, she is in paid because of the overwhelming fear. "I just want everyone to get excited and enjoy themselves while we are here," she said trying her best to hold back the tears.

Each time the door opened, another person turned into something that looked like a devil. "Oh no, Grandma is right," she thought and wanted to head towards the door. They were dancing, singing and drinking. Some of them were going in and out of other people. "Are you ready to go?" she asked Sophie hoping that she will bend a little and says yes. The reply she got from everyone at the table was no, so she decided to leave them, and told them that she was not feeling well. "I will talk to you tomorrow Sophie. I have to go now," she said and immediately got up from the table with her purse in her hand.

She walked quickly towards the door. She saw one of the demons trying to talk to her using sign language, and for some strange reason, she understood exactly what he was saying to her. He wanted her to walk up to one of the married men, and take him home with her. He said the man was rich, and would buy her anything her heart desires, and she told the demon no, and he continued to try to persuade her to do awful things like curse someone out, slap an older woman in the club, borrow the security guard's gun and shoot up the place, and to her amazement, the thing did not stop, but continued as if he could not understand what the word no means. She wanted him to disappear, but the thing was persistent, and he finally told her to dance with him, and that he wants her as his girlfriend. He was trying to get the others to help him woo her, and she could not believe it; these things are real because she knows that she is not dreaming now. She had an overwhelming feeling that she must reach the door as soon as possible, and if she did not reach it fairly soon, something bad would happen to her. She needed to get to that door right now. There are so many of them, and they were everywhere causing havoc and to her amazement, they were now controlling everyone in the room; and right now, there are approximately five demons per person. She finally made it to the door, and she looked back at the table that she was sitting at, and for a split second, she thought she saw Sophie turn into one of those things. She quickly turned around and noticed a huge one sitting on the stage, and from the way he behaved, she decided that he must be the leader. He did not want anyone to leave, and told the demons that were close to him to stop her from leaving by any means necessary. She quickly opened the door and slammed it behind her.

It was about 4:00 a.m., and it felt good to be outside and away from those things. She looked behind her and did not see anyone or anything. That was the most frightening thing she has ever experienced, so she decided this was the perfect time to pray. She don't know how many times she called on Jesus while she was trying to leave the club, but she knows it was a lot, and obviously He heard her because she made it out of the club. "I don't need to wait until I get home, I need to talk to you right now God! You are a present help in the time of trouble, and I know that you have the power to change things and situations, and right now I need You to perform a miracle in my life. God I am asking You to change me into what you had intended for me to be. I am sorry that I had messed up and felt that I had outgrown You, and I need to say I am sorry. I love you Father, and I promise to dedicate my life to You. I heard about the spiritual world, but I did not believe it until today, so I need You to help me.

The Fullness Thereof

Father, please have mercy on me. In Jesus name I pray, amen," she prayed out loud, and did not care if anyone heard her. She continued to talk to God and asked Him to protect her, and thanked Him for allowing her to exit the club. She promised to attend church every Sunday for the rest of her life if He did not allow one of them to follow her home. For the first time in her life, she knows that the Bible is true, and she does not want to end up in hell. To her, she just experienced a small piece of hell. She saw devils, and she knows that she does not want to dwell with them forever and ever. She loves Sophie, but she loves Jesus more, so she decided that Sophie has to go, unless she decides to change her ways. She promised to do whatever God wants her to do, starting right now. She felt better now and decided to run home, but quickly remembered that she has on shoes with three-inch heels. She got home, and set her alarm clock for 8:00 a.m. so she could be on time for Sunday school and church service.

"What was your friend sniffing?" said Eric with a huge smile on his face and chuckling a little. "Nothing," said Sophie embarrassed because her friend left the club in a hurry, and as if she saw a ghost. "I believe she needs psychological help. I didn't see anything, and still don't see anything except people," she said actually feeling sorry for her friend and in a way, jealous because she did not see anything, or at least she does not believe she saw anything. "Where is Thomas?" she said turning around and trying to see if she sees him on the dance floor. "He left before the first song was finished," Eric said throwing both hands in the air. "I don't know why he even comes. He does this every time he comes to the club," he said shaking his head from side-to-side. "Don't tell me, he is one of those church going boys," she said looking at him to see any sign of disgust. "No. He and I are brothers, and our family do not attend anyone's church," he said. "Thomas is weird, and he is constantly searching for answers to everything, and unfortunately, one of the books he reads is the Bible, but my parents don't know it yet. I found out about it just before he moved out of my parent's house. If my parents knew, they would have killed him, and I do mean kill him," he said thinking that he should have kept his mouth shut. "He admitted that he does not understand the Bible, but he does not let that fact stop him from reading it anyway," said Eric who now has a frown on his face. "I love my brother, but he is peculiar," he laughs and shakes his head. "I really hope he finds what he is searching for soon," he said.

"Does he have a woman?" she asked and waited for him to answer in hopes that he will say no. "Oh yes, of course, he is weird, but he is not gay. She is beautiful girl and my parents like her a lot, and as a matter of fact, Thomas does not know that they were the ones who made sure they became a couple. They know what Thomas likes, as far as beauty goes, and they stepped in and made it happen because they wanted to find someone who shared the same values as our family does, and she expressed an interest in Thomas as soon as she saw him," he said. "Well, that explains why he does not stay long. He wants to be with her," she said wondering what it would be like to be his girlfriend. "Maybe, but I don't think so," said Eric and she noticed that he has wrinkles in his forehead. "I believe something else is going on with him, something that is bigger than her," he said. "Yeah, he and Maggie appear to have the same issues, except he did not leave because he was seeing things that were not there," she said. "Yeah, I agree," he said then he wonders if he saw something too. "Well, I take that back, maybe he thought he saw something because he left in a hurry. Thomas has always been a bookworm, and when he does not understand something, he constantly researches it until he fully knows everything about the subject. I believe he is wasting his time, but Thomas has always been that way, and he is not going to change," he went on to explain.

"My parents did not allow us to read the Bible because they believe there are many gods, instead of one big God, so they raised us to be open-minded. They told us that god exist in everything, including us, which made me feel special. Thomas also believes this, but still, he wants to know the how and why of everything. If my parents knew he was reading the Bible after he moved out of their house, they would have disowned him, and if they knew I know about it, they will disown me too. I am not going to say a word. As a matter of fact, you are the only one who knows about this, and if word gets back to my parents, I know who told them. I will come after you. I love my brother, so I will never tell them," he said looking at her in the eyes to make sure he meant every word. "I believe it will break their hearts if they knew, but my brother can take care of himself. He has a good job, he has money in the bank, a beautiful girlfriend, who was also my girlfriend, but he does not know it, or does he needs to know that piece of information, and he owns property. They wasted so much time trying to convince us that Christians are fools, but Thomas does not believe it, and the more they talk, the more he did his research. I don't know the results of it, nor do I care to know it, because I simply believe my parents. They taught us that we should hate all of them because they hate us. My parents said one day, our religion will be the main religion in America, and I for one am looking forward to that day. We eventually joined the new age movement, and they teach us to believe in its concepts, all of them. The goal is to usher in a one-world religion where there will be no rules and no laws to govern anyone. Can you imagine a world where I can do whatever I want to do, and I will not be punished for it. Where I can kill someone, and it is perfectly okay? I don't know how many people I have killed so far, so my behavior is fully acceptable by my religion. Society believes I am a bad seed, but I know for a fact that I am not, and the Christians are the ones who are the bad seeds," "Wait a minute, all Christians are not bad," Sophie said. "Yes they are because I believe they are bad. Both of us are right because no one is wrong," he said. "You mean that there are absolutely no rules at all?" she said, and he responded by shaking his head in a fashion that says yes. She can see problems, but right now, she does not want to address them because as he stated, everyone is right.

He paused for a minute to allow her to speak, but since she nodded her head and did not say anything, he continued to explain his religion to her by saying, "They sit in their churches and talk about the rest of us; they put us down every Sunday, and I will be glad when we are the rulers of the religious world. One of the first things I plan to do is to kill all of the Christians. I am going to go to each church and open fire, and because it is acceptable under my religion, I will not be punished for it," Eric said realizing that Sophie was hanging onto every word he was saying.

Since Eric knew about the religion that she is interested in, she decided it is the perfect opportunity to learn about it from an expert. She counted her lucky stars and believed the gods had sent someone to inform her about the things she was praying to her gods for, so she started saying the chant that she learned in one of the meeting, and he joined in. She does not know what the chant means yet, but she thanked her gods for sending his messengers to her, however what she did not know was that it was the devil that sent him to talk to her, and the chant was thanking and glorifying Satan, and asking him to be with her and become her leader.

Thomas was glad to see his bed. He feels out of place in the club, and he only goes to show his brother that he can hang out with him, and to prove to himself that he is just like everyone else. Deep down, he knows that he is not. "What is wrong with me?" he constantly asks himself after feeling like a fool each week. Everyone in the club appears to have a good time, but each time he goes, he feels empty, out of place, and lost. It is as if he is surrounded by evil as soon as he enters the doors of the club, and he notices that each time the feelings become more and more intense, and his stay becomes shorter and shorter. Tonight, he broke his all-time record by staying inside the club for only fifteen minutes, and as soon as he walked through the doors, he thought he saw something that was so hideous that even he cannot describe it. There were ugly beings everywhere, and as soon as they appeared, or when he was able to see them fully, he decided it was time to go.

Occasionally, he would turn the television on and look at a Christian program, and he remembers one particular day, about fifteen years ago, he turned on the television and watched a preacher talk about the end times. He remembers the preacher giving them scripture to prove his point about what the devil and demons will be doing because they know that they have a short time remaining, so their goal is to make sure all people are confused, causing problems, and doing all things that are wicked to prevent us from getting into the Kingdom of God.

He wrote down the information, and begged his dad to buy him a Bible, and as soon as he got the words out of his mouth, his dad yelled at him and told him that the information in the Bible is fiction, and that it was no such thing as the world ending. He told young Thomas that he would live forever in some form or the other. He told him that if he dies in the old body, he would be transformed into something else, such as a dog or cat. Thomas looked at his dad as if he was crazy, but remained silent and respectful. He heard this before but one of his teachers told him not to believe in such lies. His teacher and friends at school talked about the Bible often, and what they had to say made sense to him, so much so, that he does not believe anything his family has to say. He often wondered if he was adopted because he was like no one in his family.

After his dad refused to buy him a Bible, Thomas decided to go to his neighbor's house, and asked to borrow his Bible. The nice gentlemen said yes, but he could not risk taking the Bible home, so his neighbor told him to come over to read it anytime he wants to. He also offered to teach him, and invited him over for Bible study, and now Thomas still attends Bible study at Mr. Raven's house every Saturday night at 6:00 p.m. sharp. He is so glad that Mr. Raven no longer lives next door to his parents, because if they did, his parents would have known that something was wrong. Mr. Raven moved the day Thomas graduated from high school.

It was awkward at first, because after he would attend Bible study, he would go home to get ready to go out to the club with Eric, and immediately, he would feel as if he were turning his back on God. He often wondered how his parents would allow them to go to the club at a very young age, but would not allow them to step foot in a church so they could learn about the one true God. When he went to the club, he would never stay for more than 30 minutes, because he knew he did not belong there, and it made him feel uncomfortable because he felt that Jesus was coming back any time now, and he did not want Him to find him at the club or anywhere where children of God do not belong. He would rather be worshipping God when Jesus returns to rapture the Church, and not somewhere where the devil is being glorified by indulging in sin.

He prays constantly that his family will get to know Jesus, and he believes if his family had met someone like the Ravens, their religious beliefs would be different. He wished that his family could experience a little of what he feels now, if they do, they would surely change their ways, and would want to meet Jesus and be filled with the Holy Spirit. Meeting Jesus was the best thing that happened to him, and for this reason, he has not missed Sunday school, church, or Bible study in five years.

He started sneaking off to church when he became a senior in high school. He would tell his parents that he was hanging out with his friends; it was the truth, but not the whole truth because he did not tell them that his friends went to church, and he went with them. He never took his friends to meet his parents and he told them why. No one in his family knows about this, and Thomas preferred it that way, but he wanted so badly to tell Eric. He does not know how and he did not know if he could trust Eric to keep his secret. Eric, and the rest of his family will never understand because they truly believe the one and true God does not exist, and they also believe that everything evil is good.

When he was living at home, he remembers seeing spirits in his house, and because he was so young, he thought they were not real, but now since he knows so much more about the spiritual world, he knows they were evil spirits. He now knows that he will never go back to the club again, unless it is to tell someone about Christ. He decided that he never wants to walk alone again, and vowed to talk to God continuously. "Holy Spirit, it is you and me now. Please don't ever leave me, and please don't allow me to ever leave you. Okay?" he said to God with a humble heart. He got on his knees, and prayed to the Father in Jesus' name. He asked the Holy Spirit to help him pray, and as always, He did. What a mighty God he serves.

Stephen and Cory forgot about their plot against Joseph. As soon as they arrived at the club, they were in awe at the amount of nice looking women that were present there. Most of the women that fascinated them were the ones who were showing everything, and left very little to the imagination. These were the women who were not welcomed at their church, according to them. These were the women who they would love to date, but would refuse to marry because they were not considered virtuous by anyone, including themselves. These were beautiful and wicked women who know how to make a man feel that he is loved and hated at the same time. These are the women who could scare the devil himself if he makes them mad. These are the very women that they were attracted to, and now it is time to feast.

Cory and Stephen walked up to sisters, who they considered the prettiest women in the place. When Cory looked at their faces, he saw a beautiful painting of two women with red full lips, blush on their high creek bones, gray coloring above their bedroom eyes, and makeup that was blended together that made the both of them appear perfect. He and Stephen walked up to them and began a conversation with them, in hopes of making them their own. They found out that the women were single and available, so they decided to buy them drinks and they all sat down at the nearest available table. After talking for a couple of hours, they managed to get their phone numbers and address. They were glad that the women did not care that they were preachers. They were concerned because they felt that if they knew, they would not want to see them again, and they really wanted to establish a relationship with these women. Both of them admitted that they had never wanted anyone so badly until this very moment. The women have all of the qualities that they were looking for. Both of them were tall, beautiful, educated, have good jobs, and own their own homes. They invited the women to church with them, and both of them declined, explaining that they prefer not to go to church with a hangover, but they promised to attend Bible study with them, provided that they would be welcomed in their everyday outfits.

Maggie got up before her alarm went off, and got dressed for church. She was still sleepy, but she remembered her promise to God. She knew God heard her, because He did not allow any of the demons to follow her home this morning, and He allowed her to have a peaceful and restful sleep. Although she was only asleep for a few hours, it felt like she was in bed all night, and she thanked God for it.

Most of her church clothes are still at her mom's house. She regrets her decision regarding not attending church until she was old. "I was dumb Lord, so please forgive me," she said while smiling. She did not want to attend church in revealing clothes, so she decided to wear jeans and a white shirt. She remembers the Bible says to come as you are, so she decided to do just that, although from experience, she knows that some of the older women might say something about her clothes, but she does not care. They don't know what she just went through. She is going to church for the right reason, which is to glorify God, to feel His presence, and to let Him know that she totally belongs to Him, and she appreciates everything He does for her. What she saw last night made her realize that Jesus might come back at any moment because of mankind's wickedness, and what she knows to be true is that it is becoming more and more wicked moment-by-moment. Coming as she was is not waiting until she was perfect. She understands that she is in need of a Savior, and she will go to the house of God to worship Him in spirit and in truth.

She walked to church, which is around the corner from where she lives, and when she walked through the doors, she realized she got there just in time for devotion. They were singing, praying and reading scripture, which made her, feel so good. She remembers there was a time when she did not like devotion at all. She remembers the older deacons signing old hymns and praying. Some of them would pray those long prayers and she remembers wanting them to hurry up because she was getting tired and annoyed. She preferred the short prayers to God, which are straight to the point. God is patient, but I bet He thought the same thing was what she often wondered. It was a shame that she and her family could recite word for word what the praying deacons were going to say. They said the same prayer every Sunday, but today, she welcomed it. These are not the deacons she grew up with, but she believes they are wonderful substitutes. She is glad to be in the house of the Lord, and she is ready to hear His word.

Although she knew she saw demons this morning, she wants to know more about them, so she said a prayer. She wanted God to give her answers, and she felt that she is in the right place to get the answers that she is seeking. What she really wants to know is how to defeat them.

Sophie woke up, and discovered that Eric was in her bed. "Did I have fun?" she asked herself while glaring down at Eric's stink body. She does not know Eric, and he does not know her, but she had to admit that this type of behavior is not uncommon for her and some of her friends. They met each other for the first time this morning and now he is lying in her bed. She saw what she wanted, and went after it, and to her it is a win-win situation, but what was it? This man stinks, and the odor radiating from his body is making her gag, so now, she is questioning this win-win situation. "Is he diseased or something?" she asked herself because she believes no one can truly smell this bad without having something fatal.

She remembers him telling her and Maggie that he was married, which is okay, because she was not looking for a long-term relationship with anyone. She loved the club scene, and she believes Eric felt the same way, but as soon as he wakes up, she will send him on his way. She does not want him to become used to spending the night with her and stinking up her apartment.

She has a calendar, and she will not be able to squeeze him into her schedule. She has a total of six partners, four of them are men, and two are women, which is enough right now. They all have high paying professional jobs, so they are able to take care of all of her needs. Some of them have families of their own, but as long as she was getting paid, she does not care. She and Eric have a lot in common, which to her makes him undesirable as a potential partner. He wants to be taken care of, and she is not the type to take care of a man.

Sunday was a day where she slept in late to regenerate and to prepare herself for work the next morning. She cherished this quiet time, and she is unwilling to share it with someone who cannot support her lifestyle, so she decided it was time to wake up Eric, and send him home to his wife. She wants him out right now. The others she brought home left before daybreak, so she was really surprise to see that he was still here, but now, he got to go.

"Wake up Eric," she said while pushing him off of her bed. He complained, but she ignored him and continued pushing until he was leaning off of the side of the bed. "Hey, it is time to get up. I have things to do," she said trying hard to hold her breath. "What time is it? It is still early. Give me a couple of hours, okay?" he said trying to look up so he can see her face. "No, you got to go now," she said while coughing and gagging. The odor is beginning to become stronger as he moves. He reminds her of one of the Charlie Brown characters. He slowly rolled onto his back and stared at the ceiling. His armpits reveals dirt, grime, and something that she is not familiar with, nor can she figures out what it could be. He was trying to come up with a convincing plea but decided not to because he realized that she would not buy it. He got up, got dressed, and asked if he could use her bathroom. "Sure, but hurry up. Your wife is waiting for you," she said trying not to breathe in deeply. "No she isn't, we have an understanding, and I thought I explained that to you last night, "he said, and she is starting to feel sorry for his wife, and Sophie said" You did, but I must warn you, game knows game. You and I are alike." "Oh, so it's like that?" he asked, and continued by saying, "You really think you know me, don't you?" "Yes, I do. You are looking for someone to take care of you, and baby, I am not the one. You got to go now!" she screamed trying to convince him that he was in danger and she was about to go psycho on him. He grabbed his jacket, and walked out of the front door hoping that she would stop him, but knowing that she would not. He decided not to tell her good-bye or thank-you. She was right, and he hated to admit it. She is the first woman who recognized the game, and unfortunately, she was just like him, except she was better at this game than he was. "What a pity," he thought.

As he walked towards his apartment, he noticed a group of people in line to go into the church. "Well, at least the line is shorter than the line I was in early this morning at the club," he said out loud, as if he was talking to them. He noticed a difference in the behavior of the people in line. All of the people in the line he stood in last night had at least 20 times the people, and each of them paid big bucks to get in. The people in this line did not have to pay to enter, but the line is much shorter. "I guess salvation is free, but many people do not want it," he chuckled and wondered why people prefer to live life in the wild lane rather than living in holiness, whatever that is. "If this is a sign of what to come, then I guess that most people will be partying in hell with him, rather than going up to be with Jesus," he thought as he continued walking and remembering what some of his friends said about what Heaven is like. All of them told him that he would go to hell because of the things they see him doing. He still does not believe it, but just in case, if hell is where he is going, then it must be like the club, so he feels that he will be okay. He hopes the part he heard about hell fire is not true. He continued to look at the people in the church line and noticed that the people were hugging and greeting each other as if they were relatives, who had not seen each other in years, and no one appeared to have a problem with standing in line, nor was anyone arguing, fussing, or fighting. To him, this type of behavior was boring. He likes excitement and action, and as he remembers what the Christians told him, he will see lots of it in hell, except they will be screaming because of the pain. Seeing people arguing and fighting provided interesting entertainment for him and the people who are like him. "What type of world would it be, if everything was peaceful? It would be boring!" he thought to himself hoping that the Bible is not true.

"What if the Bible is true?" he thought to himself, and immediately one of the demons talked to him and told him that it was not.

The church is the last place he would ever want to attend. To him, Christians led a boring and unfulfilled life, which lacks excitement and adventure. Because of his unwillingness to take care of himself financially, he is always on the prow, looking for his next meal and victim, but a church woman is undesirable because she would bug him until he attends church, and plus, she is fed lies each and every week, which would influence how she sees him. Too him, life is one big game. The game is risky, but if he does not take risks, then he would just roll up and die. What is he trying to figure out if life is one big game, and if he is suppose to play by the rules in the Bible, then he is sure that he would lose, but his religion says there are no rules, but who are the winners if there are no rules. Who will decide who gets in, or stays out? "Too many questions, you are concentrating on the wrong things. You will be just fine," a very hateful voice said to him.

The church also talks about him all of the time, and it seems to him, all Christian preachers are doing it without fail. Every time he turns on the television Sunday mornings, one of them starts talking about what he is doing or not doing. He is forced to look at it because he is too tired to get up and turn the television to a different channel. The last one he saw talked about men not taking care of their wives and children, those who make their wives work, and they refuse to be the bread winner, and he had the nerve to say that he was no good and should be ashamed of himself. No, he does not have a traditional job, but he enjoys doing what he does, and he makes over a grand a day selling drugs. "How many men make over a grand a day? Are you, preacher man, making more than me a day? Just because I don't hand it over to the wife, and you do, and she spends all of your money, does not mean that I am a bad person? It only means that I am smarter than you," he shouted to the church crowd. They ignored him, and turned around and continued talking amongst themselves. His dream is to become a supplier because he will get to keep most of the money. Although he makes more than a grand in the first hour after he opens the door, he only gets about half of it because he has a few people working for him.

To keep his employees in line, he sometimes has to be creative. The drug business is very serious, and it is also dangerous, so he has to always be very careful. He sometimes see his customers come in and out of the club all of the time, but they do not notice him because when he is at the club, he always wear expensive suits, and when he is selling drugs in the neighborhood, he looks just like the people he sells the drugs to. He does not want to stand out, because if he does, the cops will be able to pick him out. He does not want to go back to jail.

He remembers an incident that happened two days ago involving one of his girlfriends who came into the crack house and made a scene. She saw his other girlfriend and decided to take off the jewelry that he gave her and threw it on the floor. She immediately changed her mind and decided to sit down, which was the right decision for her at the time, because if she took it further, he would have killed her. She decided it was better to have a good time, than to make him mad. Then one of his employees came in and he escorted him to the office while pointing a gun to his head. Although everyone in the house witnessed this, he did not care. He and the young man staggered into the office, which was located at the front on the house, opened the door, and went in. The big boss wanted to see this person immediately, and they removed the young man's clothing and tortured him for a long time. When he returned to the office, the young man and the object that he was tied to came crashing down to the floor, which surprised some of the people in the room. He did not know what was done to the man, but he knows that he does not want to be punished in the same manner. It is not uncommon to be punished in this manner in his world, which is a world where crime and drugs are king; a world where it is okay to seek revenge on the entire family for the crimes of one individual; a world where God is not welcomed, and where evil rules.

Eric believes that he may have to move to another country to make his dream a reality. He wants to be the big boss, and in his neighborhood, there is already a boss in charge, who rules with an iron fist. He wants the money and power that his boss, who just happens to be his hero, has. His hero does not allow anyone to come between him and his money. He witnessed his hero killing his three-year-old son because he cheated him out of ten cents after returning from the store with the merchandise he told him to purchase. He told him that business is business, no matter what. He is learning all he can about the business in hopes of becoming wealthy, but for now, he has to do whatever it takes to survive these mean streets.

The only reason he married Mary was because she was pregnant with his child and she was very pretty. During the time of their short courtship and early in their marriage, she had a good job, and was able to provide for him and the child, which also made her more desirable in his eyes. She lost that good paying job not long after they were married, and then she started working two jobs to feed him and their two children. Then about a year ago, she came home and told him that she can no longer work two jobs and take care of the children, so she decided to quit one of her jobs. He tried to persuade her to beg for her job back, but she refused, so now, she is bringing in less money into his house.

She told him that he was not a good man because he is not doing what a husband and a father is suppose to do, which made Eric mad. He does not consider himself to be a bad person because he helps out every now and then by giving the kids a few dollars at least once a year. He told her often that her first priority is to please him by doing what he tells her to do, and if she wants to remain in his house, she has to obey him, which was one of the conditions of their marriage. He constantly reminds her that she knew how he was before they got married, so she should never complain to him or anyone else.

He wants her to work for him, but she refuses. Once he moves up in the organization, she will not have a choice, he is the man of his house, and she must obey. Because she does not use drugs, he will allow her to keep his books. He is not able to do a good job with keeping the books because he is not able to control his drinking problem. He needs to be alert at all times, and if he ever wants to go to the top, he will need her to watch over his organization because she is always sober. For this reason, no one will be able to cheat her. They always cheat him, and he does not realize it until he sobers up. He does not even remember who most of the people were whom he conducted business with.

The two-bedroom apartment is too small for all of them, but they make do with what they have. The kids sleep in one of the bedrooms, and he and Mary sleep in the other one. The apartment is always noisy because everyone is always trying to talk at the same time. Because it is so small, everyone is able to hear each other's conversations no matter which room they are in.

While walking home, he hears a voice telling him that Mary owes him. He asked how, and he heard, "You take most of his stolen goods home that I have blessed you with, so at least she should appreciate you for bringing something to the table other than yourself. If it weren't for you, she would not even have children. Aren't you tired of her complaining about you not helping her with the rent, groceries, and the children? You are doing the best you can, but you can do so much more if she helps you sell drugs and you will be able to make more money if you become her pimp.

Besides, she should be grateful because she has a man, and a good-looking man at that. Do you remember what your mother said? Any man is better than no man at all, and your mother is always right because she is my servant," one of many demons that possess him told him.

His only outlet is to go to the club every night. At the club, he is king. He is very attractive, so it is not difficult for him to pick up lonely and desperate women. His smooth style allows him to win women over easily, until tonight. He met his match, and he wonders how this could happen. Tonight was still a success because he slept in a nice warm bed, and got most of what he wanted, which was companionship without much complaining about what a terrible person he was. Too bad he was thrown out. He hoped to stay a little while longer, or at least until she cooks him dinner.

He is now a couple of blocks from the apartment, and he believes he sees his wife and children walking down the street, so he yells out her name, and she turned around. "Where are you going?" he yells. "To church," she shouts back and kept walking. He runs, and finally caught up with her and the children. "Why are you going to church?" Eric said through clinched teeth. She explains that she needs help, and the help she needs only God can provide. She does not know what to do, and according to her family, she needs to start back going to church to gain power over the enemy that resides in her apartment. She told him she was sick and tired of being sick and tired, and wants to finally do something about it. She thought about suicide, and decided against it because of the children. She wants a better life for her family, and she knows that in order for her to attain this, she must have God in her life. "So, church will give you a better life?" he asked looking for any sign that will tell him that she is willing to obey him, but after not finding one, he continued talking, and asked, "If there is a God, then why things are so messed up down here? If there is a God, then why He made some people rich, and others poor? If there is a God, then why my parents did not worship Him?" He was angry, and his face and body language showed it. He could not understand why anyone would want to worship something that they cannot see or hear, someone who does not appear to be fair, who appears to favor one race of people over another. He was taught that the only person he should worship and praise is himself, and never worships something that he cannot see. "If there is a God, why would He even help you? You have been bad all of your life, and you and I know you have done awful things, so do you really think He will even acknowledge you?" he asked hoping his questions will convince her not to go. If she does not, he decided that he will beat her right there on the sidewalk, and he can care less if anyone watched. Mary started crying, and ran back to the apartment, and her children followed her. She is so tired of losing, and because she is not strong, she allows him to win. She knows that she is not doing what God wants her to do, but what could she do? She was taught to honor her husband, but she is finding it very difficult to do. She married a man who does not want to have anything to do with God, so what should she do? She knows that if she wants to be successful, she needs to find a way out of this relationship. She wants to be blessed, and she needs to find a way to find out what she needs to do to get it. She has to find a way, so she prayed and asked God to help her. "I need you Father, please help me

He is proud of the fact that he can easily control her every move. She was his woman, and she must do as he says, or he will beat her to a bloody pulp if he has to. One of the main reasons why he does not want her to attend church is because she will be around other people who would probably give her advice, and after hearing that advice, she may make plans to leave him. Over the years and even now, he relies on her for a place to stay and for a source of income when he has spent all of his money on booze, drugs, women, etc. Can he honestly say he loves her? He knows the answer is no. He does not love her at all, and to him, she is one of many necessary tools. His parents taught him, to love himself only. His mother told him to always control Mary and not to allow her to mess those children up by telling them about the Christian God which she believes does not exist, so that is also a reason why he must not allow her to attend a Christian church. He wants the kids to believe in the same things that he believes in. He also wants both of his daughters to go into business with him because he knows that men are good, but women are ruthless in the drug business. He would train them up to be miniatures of himself.

Maggie was glad to be in church again, and for the first time since being on her on, she felt safe. She did not know anyone there, but she still felt as if she belongs there. Most of the songs that were sung so far were old hymns. She remembers her grandmother singing some of them. For the first time in her life, she understands the meaning of "I want Jesus to walk with me." She wanted Jesus to walk her home last night. She needed protection from those evil things she saw in the club. She hopes she gets the answers she wants today. This is not her home church, but it is the closest church. So far, she is glad to be here.

The preachers are now walking out, and Maggie notices two of them were present at the club with her last night. She knows one of them because he dated Sophie for a little while, and she could not believe how they could party at the club, and then walk up onto the pulpit as if they were holy men of God. She chose to ignore them because they are not the ones who will deliver the message today. Regardless of their presence, she knows that she will hear a word from God.

The preacher is starting to preach his sermon, and she feels that she will hear something that will explain what is going on with her. He said to turn to Mark 5:1-10, and waited for everyone to turn to the proper section in the Bible. Then the church read in unison, "*And they came over unto the other side of the sea, into the country of the Gadarenes. And when he was come out of the ship, immediately there met him out of the tombs a man with an unclean spirit, Who had his dwelling among the tombs; and no man could bind him, no, not with chains: Because that he had been often bound with fetters and chains, and the chains had been plucked asunder by him, and the fetters broken in pieces: neither could any man tame him. And always, night and day, he was in the mountains, and in the tombs, crying, and cutting himself with stones. But when he saw Jesus afar off, he ran and worshipped him, And cried with a loud voice, and said, what have I to do with thee, Jesus, thou Son of the most high God? I adjure thee by God, that thou torment me not. For he said unto him, Come out of the man, thou unclean spirit. And he asked him, what is thy name? And he answered, saying, my name is Legion: for we are many. And he besought him much that he would not send them away out of the country. Now there was there nigh unto the mountains a great herd of swine feeding. And all the devils besought him, saying, send us into the swine, that we may enter into them. And forthwith Jesus gave them leave. And the unclean spirits went out, and entered into the swine: and the herd ran violently down a steep place into the sea, (they were about two thousand;) and were choked in the sea. And they that fed the swine fled, and told it in the city, and in the country. And they went out to see what it was that was done. And they come to Jesus, and see him that was possessed with the devil, and had the legion, sitting, and clothed, and in his right mind: and they were afraid. And they that saw it told them how it befell to him that was possessed with the devil, and also concerning the swine. And they began to pray him to depart out of their coasts. And when he was come into the ship, he that had been possessed with the devil prayed him that he might be with him. Howbeit Jesus suffered him not, but saith unto him, Go home to thy friends, and tell them how great things the Lord hath done for thee, and hath had compassion on thee. And he departed, and began to publish in Decapolis how great things Jesus had done for him: and all men did marvel."* "Brothers and sisters, what's in you, or should I say, what is controlling you? Could it by that you possessed with devils?" he asked everyone in church, and it was so quiet, that you could actually hear a pin drop. Maggie is not able to answer the question, but she doesn't believe she is possessed by devils, but she does not know for sure, because she has not been living a godly life lately. "How can I know?" she thought waiting patiently for the preacher to answer how, although knowing that he is not able to hear her. "Do you know that demons fellowship with other demons? Are you hanging out, or partying with demons? How can you tell? Since no one is talking, I will answer the questions for you? One way to tell is if the friend you hang out with does not have anything nice to say about anyone. You cannot reason with demons, and the reason you cannot reason with them is because you are dealing with demonic forces. If demons are in the midst, you will not have peace," the preacher said and it was as if he was looking directly at her when he talked. "So, they were demons," she thought but felt she already knew that they were, but she needed to hear it from the man of God. She remembered she couldn't wait to leave the club, and how uncomfortable she felt there. "What should I do?" she thought hoping that the preacher can hear her thoughts. "You cannot fight them because they are spiritual beings. They are fallen angels, and they have power that we humans do not possess, so you need spiritual power to fight them! Oh, the Bible tells us to resist the devil and he will flee, which is found in James 4:7. You need Jesus! He is the source of your and everyone else power. If you tell that devil to leave in the name of Jesus, he has to leave because there is so much power in the name of Jesus. If you tell him to leave, and don't say in the name of Jesus, that devil will beat you up. You don't have power!" he shouted at his audience. "They are everywhere, especially in places where God's children should not be. They love music. Remember, Satan started in the choir. When you young and old folks go to the club, and jumping to the beat of the music, there are demons jumping right beside you. If one person has a legion of demons in him, can you imagine the amount of demons in the club? A legion has at least 3000 members, and if you have 40 people with a legion of demons in them, you have from 120,000 to 240,000 demons in the club dancing to the same beat as you. All of you collectively are worshipping the devil, and I know some of you don't believe. You might say, well, just because I listen to secular music, it doesn't mean I am worshipping the devil. Ask yourself this question. Is the music glorifying God? I dare any of you to answer that question honestly. If you do, the answer will be no if you are listening to any form of secular music. When a child of God enters a club, he is in trouble from the start. If one person can put 1000 to flight, and two can put 10,000 to flight, then as a club going, partying Christian, you are coming up short. How many Holy Ghost filled partying saints do you think you will need to put 40 legions to flight? You are defeated as soon as you walk through the doors because God's children will not be partying in clubs with you. If you are partying at the club, will you claim to be God's child?" he said and made comical gestures although remaining serious. She is so glad that she made her way to the church because this is something she needed to hear, although she heard it before. It is so sad that things like this come to her remembrance when she is in trouble.

"I know some of you remember going to the clubs before you were saved, and I remember going too. I was not saved all of my life, and neither were you, but since you claim to be saved now, and for those who are still going to clubs, you are fellowshipping with demons. Just because you do not see them does not mean that they are not there. Unfortunately, some of you do not believe there are demons, so if you just happen to see them, you will think that it is just another partygoer because if you are drinking one of those so-called feel good drinks, anything will look normal to you. Read your Bible for yourself, and you will discover that they do exist. Don't let Satan fool you. Children of God are told to not fellowship with devils. For those of you who are not Bible readers, you can find this command in 1 Corinthians 10:20, I tell you what, lets turn there and read it right now," he said while flipping through the pages in his Bible.

Everyone in the congregation turned to the chapter. Maggie was not accustomed to this, but she did as she was told. All of the other preachers she knew always preached, and did not give scriptures, so this was a wonderful experience, and she knows that it is better for her to see it for herself. She read out loud with the others, *"But I say, that the things which the Gentiles sacrifice, they sacrifice to devils, and not to God: and I would not that ye should have fellowship with devils. Ye cannot drink the cup of the Lord, and the cup of devils: ye cannot be partakers of the Lord's table, and of the table of devils. Do we provoke the Lord to jealousy? Are we stronger than he? All things are lawful for me, but all things are not expedient: all things are lawful for me, but all things edify not. Let no man seek his own, but every man another's wealth. Whatsoever is sold in the shambles, that eat, asking no question for conscience sake: For the earth is the Lord's, and the fullness thereof."* "You cannot worship God while partying with the devil. When you are doing that which is not right, whom are you worshipping? When you go to a Prince concert, and don't tell me that you do not know whom Prince is. He was my favorite artist when I was out there in the world, but now God will not allow me to listen to him anymore, but whom are you worshipping when you go to secular concerts? It is certainly not God. When you go to the bar or a club, whom are you worshipping? Are you looking for Jesus in those places? Think about this. What if Jesus comes back Saturday night, around 2:00 a.m., while you are at the bar, and at that moment, whom would you belong to? Would you be raptured? If you are saved, you will be, but if you are not, you will not. Do you know the people you are fellowshipping with? Think about the person you went to the club with. When you hear this person's name mentioned by your friends, is it always associated with something negative? In other words, when this person is mentioned, do you constantly hear about the wrong things he is doing?" He asked, but no one answered. "When I was in the world partying, gambling, chasing women, and doing other ungodly things, I was not filled with the Holy Spirit. I didn't know that then, but I sure know it now," he said and she was surprised by his honesty. She is glad to know that he was not perfect, and that he understands.

"The Bible tells us that those who have the Holy Spirit know it. If you are filled with the Spirit, you will go to church to party, and not the club. There is no party like the Holy Ghost party, can I get an amen? If you want a high, there is no high like the one you get when the Holy Spirit comes upon you, don't you agree? I am talking to those of you who know what I am talking about! You will be drunk, oh what a holy buzz you will have! This buzz lasts for a long time, and you will never have to worry about the after effects that you get from alcohol, drugs, or other mind altering substances. The Holy Ghost will not cause you to have a hangover. You will be full of joy, and you will constantly look forward to that next high," he told the congregation with a look that lets you know that he was reminiscing, and she wonders when she can feel that high.

"If you go to the club, it is to pull one of God's children out, but you cannot stay there and party with devils that are in the club partying with the ungodly. If God tells you not to go, and you go anyway, you will leave the Holy Spirit behind, and you will enter without any spiritual protection. I don't know about you, I need my Help. Brothers and sisters, the Bible says He, who is God, will never leave you nor forsake you. It is you who leave God. The Bible tells us to pray without ceasing, and when I went to the clubs, I never fell on my knees to pray to God while I was on the dance floor, do you? When I went to clubs before I was saved, I never talked to God while drinking my alcoholic beverage, do you? When I went to clubs before I was saved, I never glorified God on the dance floor, and as a matter of fact, when I was getting my groove on, I did not even think about God. Oh, the spiritual world exists brothers and sisters! You read it," he said and scanned the room, and it was as though he looked each of them in the eyes, and at that moment, she knew she should have listened to Grandma rather than thinking that she knew everything because she felt she was grown.

Maggie was getting an explanation as to what she was seeing, but she is still unsure of what she should do next. She saw them in the club, but will she be able to recognize them in people while walking down the street? She does not ever want to see them again, so she decided to distance herself from her friends as soon as possible. It was not worth going to hell over. "Wow, if I do that, then I will become like members of my family," she thought shaking her head back and forth. She does not want people to think that she is stuck up. If she no longer goes to the club, party with her friends and associates, and drinking with unknown men on weekends at whomever house they end up at after the club, she would not have anyone to spend time with. This was the first time that she realized that she hung around undesirable people who are heading for hell and is driving towards it in the fast lane. She will be lonely, and she does not like being alone for long periods of time. She loves being surrounded by people; she loves being the center of attention, and she loves breaking most of the rules, up until now. She does not want to alter her lifestyle drastically, but she realizes she cannot continue with this evil lifestyle, and she must hang with the people that God thinks are good.

She knows the difference between right and wrong, but she does not like rules. The Bible has so many rules, and if she did not see those things, she would not be here today. "Why am I being punished?" she said aloud and hoped she could hear God answering her question. The people next to her looked at her. It was then that she realized that she spoke those words out loud, and everyone around her heard them. She now feels uncomfortable. The young lady that sat next to her grabbed her hand and gently squeezed it. She looked at her and smiled. Maggie felt better, and one of the reasons because the young lady was around her age, with gentle eyes. She came to the conclusion that she was not being judged by her outburst. The young lady reminded her of her grandmother, and she can envision her grandma saying, "Its okay honey, everything is going to be alright."

The preacher is now ending his sermon, and said that everyone needs to make up their mind as to whom they will serve. He said, "As to me and my house, we will serve the Lord. I love my friends, but I love Jesus more. I love my family, but I love Jesus more. I love all of you, but I love Jesus more. If you participate in a lifestyle that is not similar to mine, that is, if you want to have fellowship with devils, then I cannot hang with you, no matter how much I love you. I will continue to love and pray for you, but other than that, we will not fellowship and must part ways," he said and continued with remarks that made everyone in the service examine their lives. She got what she came for and she had to admit that she is happy.

She now knows what she needs to do, but she realizes that she needs help doing it. She saw demons on three separate occasions. The first time she saw them, it was only one of them. She felt it was her imagination running wild. The next time she saw them, there were probably six of them, but this morning, she saw lots of them. Because she was sober, she knows, without a shadow of doubt, that they were real. Now the preacher confirmed it. But still, she worries about how others are going to react to her decision about not going to the club again. That was the scariest experience she has ever gone through, which forced her to make up in her mind about not wanting to see those things again, and to do whatever it takes to prevent them from controlling her, so she decided to cut her friends loose. Should she tell her friends about what she saw in the club and what the preacher said? Will they think she is crazy? She remembers that her grandma told her that God hates a liar, and she showed her where it is located in the Bible, so she decided that she must tell the truth, but only if they ask. Otherwise, she will reveal very little for the sake of appearance. She is not strong enough yet, and she does not want them to spread rumors about her being crazy.

All three of the ministers heard their pastor's message, and knew it came from God. Joseph was the only one out of the three who was relieved that he stopped going to the club. He knew it was not right when he was doing it, and he also knows that his other brothers in the Gospel also know that going to the club is no place to be if you are a minister called by God.

Joseph looked at Cory and Cory rolled his eyes at him, but Stephen came over to him and told him that he wants to talk to him later. He looked as if he had lost his best

The Fullness Thereof

friend, and Joseph took his hand and began to pray for and with him. After the prayer ended, both of them said amen after Joseph asked God to give Stephen strength to do what is right, and to once again direct his paths. While Joseph was praying, he felt the Spirit all over Him, and he knew without a shadow of doubt that God heard and answered his prayer. Stephen hugged Joseph, and asked him if they could talk right now, and Joseph said yes.

Stephen walked Joseph to his car, and both of them got in and closed the doors because it was chilly outside. He explained to him that today's message hit him hard, and he began to cry and ask God to forgive him. He said he knows that he and Cory are cousins who are as close as brothers, but he cannot allow himself to be controlled by him any longer. He knows for the first time today, the seriousness of his charge, and knows that he is called by God to be His witness, and he must conduct himself as such. He continued to cry out to God in the presence of Joseph, who continued to pray for him as they were talking and crying.

After about an hour, their Pastor knocked on the window, and both of them got out of the car and hugged him. The pastor told Stephen that he is glad that he finally decided to do things that are right in the sight of God, and that God told him that He is pleased. It amazed both of them that they did not have to say a word, because the pastor told him everything that was going on with the both of them. He told Stephen that he turned him over to God as soon as he and Cory decided that they would not follow his instructions, and asked God to deal with them. He asked if he needs his help, and Stephen told his pastor yes, and he told him to come to his office, so he can counsel him and put him back on the right path. He turned around, and told Joseph that he was proud of him, and to continue to grow in the Lord, and Joseph thanked his pastor, got in his car, and drove home and Stephen did the same, praising God all of the way.

Sophie was alone at last. She hate lazy, sorry, and good for nothing men. She believes it is okay for a woman to be taken care of, but for women to take care of men is not right. "If a man doesn't work, than he should not eat," she thought to herself and truly believes the Biblical verse. I rather be alone than to have a man like Eric staying with me forever and ever. He is nice to look at but if you look deep, you will see that he is rotten at his core, but taking care of a grown man turns her off. He is worst than a skunk and an infidel, and she does not understand why anyone would want him, although he spent the night last night. "I guess those commercials are right, alcohol will make anyone look good, and I guess smell good as well," she said to herself while shaking her head. After saying it, she realized that Eric looks good sober too, but the odor is worst than anything she ever had the misfortune to smell.

She had a couple of hours to go before one of her partners come over. Karen believes she is a stewardess. Sophie believes in being what a partner wants her to be, so when she found out that Karen was attracted to stewardesses, Bob is attracted to candy stripers, Ted is attracted to loose women, and Melissa is attracted to nice girls, she decided to be what they wanted her to be in order to get paid, and she must admit, they pay her well. She has not told any of them that she works at a deli, and she does not plan to tell them either. All of them live in upscale neighborhoods, and the chances of seeing any of them in the deli is zero. She wished she could be as successful as they are, but right now, she will have to continue to pretend. They believe she is a rich girl who is abandoned by her parents. They give her money because she told them that it is what she has become accustomed to her parents do not want to allow her to work. She has lied so much, that she does not know what lie she came up with to cause them to empty out their pockets every time one of them came over. She doesn't remember the lie she told them that explained why she stayed in an apartment that looks like it should have been condemned years ago. The one thing she does remember is that the lie was good. Sometimes, she wished she could have been different, but unfortunately, this is the only profitable life she knows, and she plans to get what she can, while she can. Some may say this is the easy way out, but she believes it is hard work and it requires the skill of an actress, which she believes she has.

She would love to have children one day, but right now, she just cannot see it. A child would make her life a little bit harder. If she had a child right now, she would have to hire a baby sitter if she wants to go to the club, to the movies, or to anywhere where she does not want to take a child. Instead of spending money on herself, she will have to spend some of it on children. She knows she definitely does not want a child right now, so she decided that she would have to wait until she is ready to settle down. If she gets pregnant, she will just have to kill the child. Paganism allows this, so she will not have to worry about doing something wrong. As a matter of fact, if she sacrifices her newborn, she will go to a higher level, but she does not think she could do this. This type of thinking was sick, so she decided not to think about this again. The first thing she must do is to find a nice looking rich man, who does not have any issues. To her, that is the definition of the perfect man. The only thing she asks is he takes care of her needs, especially her financial needs, and be a good father to their children.

She looks out the window and sees so many people on their way home from church. She does not understand why they waste their time. She often thought if God is real like everyone says, then why doesn't He reveal Himself to her? "Where are you God?" she shouted out loud holding both hands up in the air, and turning around. "I want You to show Yourself right now," she said in a sarcastic manner believing that she will never see Him, nor will she ever hear from the powerful and invisible God. "That is what I thought, You do not exist," she said feeling stupid. She remembers hearing Maggie's grandma telling them to always give reverence to God, but she does not fully understand what that means.

She now feels foolish. She believed in God when she was young, but now she questions His existence because of the other things she heard over the years, those things that made her feel good about herself and lifestyle. Now she believes she is grown and because of it, she needs to question everything that Maggie grandmother told her, as well as the things that the church, members of her families, and other religious fanatics told her about the Bible and God. Her grandmother told her God is real, and because Grandma was so convincing, she believed she told her the truth. She knows better now, so she can't understand why so many people go to a building and worship something they never seen or heard. When she did it, she didn't know better. Now she considers herself to be wise beyond her years. She feels that she has total control over her destiny, she will make her own decisions, and no one can stop her. Not even God Almighty can stop her, and she truly believes this. She believes she is not hurting anyone by having a little fun before she evolves into another creature. "Isn't that part of living life to its fullness God?" she asked in a manner that said she was not expecting an answer.

Christians, to her, pretend to be happy. How could they be happy if they are not allowed to dance, sing songs, other than boring gospel songs, or go to the nightclub? And they say sinners are in bondage? Going to church is not the same as going to the club is something she always believed. They serve alcohol in clubs, but only bread and wine is served in the church. They don't even give you enough wine to drink to get a buzz. If they really want to feel good, they need to get a buzz, and in order to do that, they need to super size their glasses, and offer free wine refills during and after Communion. If they do that, then she just might pop in every now and then.

She tried reading the Bible a few times, and because she did not understand what she was reading, she gave up on it. "Why do so many people waste their time?" she asked trying to figure out why. "In order for me to go to church, Jesus will have to come down from Heaven and drive me there," she said. She believes the chances of that happening is zero. She decided to go back to bed so she can be well rested tomorrow morning.

Thomas enjoyed church service today. His pastor confirmed what he already knows, which is he should not party in the club. He does not want to have a relationship with the devil, and he realized that he worked so hard to keep his relationship with Christ. He thoroughly enjoys his relationship with God, and he cannot risk losing the Holy Spirit. He realized years ago that he couldn't survive without God, and that he knows God does not need him, but he surely needs God. He is so grateful to God. He knows it was God who saved him, and if it was not for God being on his side, he would still be trapped and in bondage. He wished his family would stop worshipping idols, but unfortunately, they think they are wise, and Christians are the fools. It is amazing how God will make the foolish things of this world to confound the wise. The Bible is so simple, but to them who are without understanding, and do not have the Holy Spirit, it is so difficult to understand. He realizes the main ingredient in gaining spiritual knowledge is the Holy Spirit. He is the One who teaches the children of God, and he feels so blessed to have God in his life.

He decided that he must tell them the truth, which is something that he should have done years ago. It is so hard to keep his relationship with God a secret from anyone, and every time he is around people, he wants to tell them about the goodness of God. It is getting more and more difficult to contain it because what's in him wants to come out, and it wants to come out all of the time. He wants to teach Eric about God, and to tell him about salvation, because one thing he knows for certain is if Eric dies right now, he will not go to Heaven. He knows this because Eric does not accept Jesus Christ as his personal savior. Eric and he were taught to worship themselves, which he knows is idolatry, and he prays that God uses him to convince Eric that Jesus is the only way, the truth, and the light. He knows that Jesus is constantly knocking on the door of Eric's heart, but Eric will not allow Him in. He needs to know how to approach the subject to him and his family. If he tells his family about God, will they disown him? He decided it was worth the risk.

The one thing he desires most of all is that his entire family becomes lovers of Christ. If he tells them about Christ and they accept, he will be the happiest man on earth. If they disown him, he will be sad, but he will also be relieved because it will no longer be a secret, and he would have done his part. He remembers reading in the Bible where it says that if you deny Jesus, He will also deny you in front of the Father. He feels that he is guilty of denying Jesus because he did not share Him with his family. He does not have an excuse because he no longer lives under their roof, and is not dependent upon them for anything. Besides, if he does not tell them about God, then he will feel guilty if one of them dies without him at least trying to convert them to Christianity. He feels he cannot handle the guilt any longer, and made a vow to God that he will never deny Him again. "I will tell them tonight," he said to God knowing that He will help him.

Thomas called his parents and asked them to allow him to take the family to their favorite restaurant, and their greed caused them to say yes. He called Eric, who hesitated at first, and then remembered that he did not have to pay for it, so he told Thomas yes, but he will leave his family at home. Thomas begged him to bring his wife and kids, and after five minutes of constant begging, Eric finally said okay. They will all meet at the restaurant at 7:00 pm.

Sophie had problems sleeping. She looked at the clock an hour ago, and discovered that she had slept for only four hours. She decided to get up. One of her partners did not show up. There were plenty of things that needed to be done around the apartment. She needs to wash dishes and tidy up the apartment. While she was sweeping the floor, she noticed one of the floorboards was slightly ajar, so she bent down, got on her knees, and pulled up the board. Below was a small metal box. She pulled it up, and sat it on the floor in front of her. She opened the box to see its contents trying to be as careful and cautious as she can for fear that something just might jump out of it, or something might be dead inside of it. When she finally got the box open, inside she found $350,000, a cross, and a loaded pistol. "Wow, the gods are good today!" she yelled, and then mellowed down because this has to be a secret and she does not want her neighbors to be suspicious. She immediately thought of ways to spend the money. She decided the first thing she is going to do is to put a down payment of a nicer apartment. She will buy very expensive furniture, and clothes. She can't wait until tomorrow! She wants to celebrate tonight, but first she has to take a shower.

Cory was still upset by what he heard today. He could not understand why his pastor was talking about him and Stephen like that. He wanted to know who he heard it from, and why didn't the pastor talk to him before preaching that sermon. He felt that he was attacked in front of many people, and he did not like it one bit. He decided that he would talk to him before Bible study, so he can clear the air.

He may have to move his plans forward by a couple of years. His plan was to take his time in hopes of choosing the right church, a church that has the amount and right people to supply all of his many greedy needs, and a church that will be glad to have him as their pastor. As soon as he finished that thought, he heard a voice telling him to take over the church that he is attending right now. "Good idea, but how?" he asked not knowing whom he was really talking to. The demon explained that he will have to talk to the other ministers and deacons to get them to see their pastor in a negative light. He can start by spreading rumors, by waiting until he hugs one of the sisters in church, and lying by telling everyone that they are having an affair. Wait until he hugs one of the brothers, and say he is gay, and then he gave him examples of other things that he could use to try to ruin his pastor's reputation.

At that very moment, the Holy Spirit told his pastor exactly what Cory was planning to do, and told him, "Don't worry, I will fight all of your battles. No weapons formed against you will prosper," and the pastor is glad that he has a listening ear and a willing heart to hear and obey God. At that moment, he turned Cory over to Satan.

By the time Maggie made it to the steps leading to her apartment, she decided not to have fellowship with devils again. She does not want to see them again, and knowing that they were also partying at the club made her decision more practical. She just can't get them out of her mind, and she will be glad when she can put that behind her. Her decision to become closer to God is a wise one. She remembered the pastor telling her that in order to fight demons, she has to tell them to flee in the name of Jesus. "Do I have a personal relationship with Jesus?" she asked herself. She was told to take the steps necessary to build a relationship with God, and she is going to start right now.

They were giving away Bibles at the church she attends, and because she does not have one, she gladly accepted one. Tonight, she will pray, and then read some verses in the Bible. She realizes the fact that only God can protect her from demons, so from now on, she will do whatever it takes to keep God in her life. "Jesus is so powerful, even His name can make Satan flee!" she said while dancing as if it was to a favorite tune. "I need to know everything there is to know about you Jesus. I need you Jesus!" she shouted to the top of her lungs and did not care who heard her. At that very moment, she felt a wonderful and loving sensation all over her body. It feels so good, and she knows Jesus heard her, and had come to where she is. She does not want to move for fear of the feeling going away, so she decided to stay longer, and after five minutes, she still cannot remove her hand from the doorknob. She remembers being told that Jesus will meet a person where they are, and she knows that it is true, and at this very moment, all is well with the world. It does not matter that she saw demons early this morning. What matters this very moment is the Spirit of Jesus Christ is with her. "God is with me!" she is now saying, "God is truly with me!" She cannot help it; she has to praise the Lord. It does not matter that people are nearby; all that matters right now is God is with her! She knows that this feeling is what she needed all along, but because of ignorance and youth, she did not know it until now, and no matter what, she has to hold on to God's unchanging hand. She now knows that He is more important to her than anyone or anything! Now she can relate to her Grandma. Her Grandma was right! Jesus is awesome!

Stephen has been home for hours, and he is still thanking God for deliverance. He feels free, so much so that he is determine to call Cory to tell him that he must change his ways immediately or he cannot be around him. He feels like a new creature in Christ, and he is thankful for the first time in a long time, he really feels great. It is as if a huge burden has been lifted from off of his shoulders. He has never felt this free before. For the first time in his life, he knows that he does not need Cory, nor does he have to have Cory in his life, and he feels that he can live without Cory. Oh what a feeling! He feels an overwhelming desire to call Cory right now to let him know that he will not be hanging with him anymore, because he has to keep his eyes on the prize, and his prize is Christ Jesus. He has to develop a relationship with Jesus, because over the years, he has left that which he once loved the most.

As he reflects on what he had became over the months, he realizes that anyone can fall for Satan's snares easily, because he did. He thought he was too smart for that, and the sad thing is that he did not know he was in bondage until God released him from bondage. He loves this feeling and does not ever want to break away from God again, so he decided that it is no time like the present to call his cousin.

"Hello Cory, we need to talk man," he said. "What's up Steve, I am watching the game, so hurry up and say what you have to say," Cory said as if he was annoyed that the phone had the audacity to ring. "Okay, I am not going out with you anymore, unless you change your ways," he said and prepared himself for whatever evil thing his beloved cousin has to say. "Change my ways!" Cory shouted and suddenly he became extremely angry. "Yes, you have to change your ways and start doing things that are right according to God's rules and not ours. Man, I am glad that I listened to the sermon today because I know that God was using Pastor Jones to talk to me. He told us about ourselves, well, what I really need to say is the Holy Spirit was talking to us. Did you get anything out of it?" Stephen asked hoping that there is at least a glimmer of hope that his cousin was touched by the sermon. "I felt he was talking about me, but I know that someone must have told him those things, and I finally got over being mad about it, but now since you called, and am mad again. I am not doing anything wrong, so if you don't want to hang with me, then just don't. I don't need you! Remember what you said about blood being thicker than water?" Cory asked Stephen with much venom in his words. "I belong to a bigger family now. I am a child of the most high and powerful God. Jesus is my everything, and He is more important to me than anyone and anything, besides, when you and I went up to announce our call into the ministry, we said we would follow Christ. I strayed, but now I am back on the right path. I must follow Him, and if that means that I will lose you, than so be it. I love you Cory, but I love God more, and I must stay free so I can honor and serve him with humility and love," Stephen said with so much love and kindness that could melt any iceberg. Cory did not fully understand what Stephen meant when he said he is free. He felt that slavery was over many years ago so all Americans are free now, but his pride will not allow him to ask for an explanation. "Whatever man!" Cory shouted and slammed down the phone. He was very angry and felt that Cory would come crawling back to him soon, because he has always done so in the past.

  Thomas arrived at the restaurant before his family members. He knows what his family likes, but decided not to order their food. He turned around and saw his parents walking into the restaurant as if they were in a hurry to eat. They scanned the restaurant as if they were on a scavenger hunt, and when they saw him, and they walked to the table where he was sitting and flopped down into the chairs. "Where is your girlfriend?" his Mom asked. "Hello Mom, she is working tonight," said Thomas, smiling at his parents. It is obvious that they are hungry and they are not embarrassed to tell him so. They quickly picked up the menus and called the waitress over to place their order, and as soon as they were about to order, Eric, Mary and the children arrived. "So, when are you going to marry her?" his dad asked him with hopes of getting the answer that he was expecting, such as next month. "In due time," said Thomas looking at both parents.

His parents want him to marry his girlfriend right away, because she is moving up in the group, and one day, she will become one of the most powerful witches that ever lived. Some believe that she will be greater than one of the most popular witches in Old Testament times, whose name was Jezebel. They wanted to tell others that they have someone important in their family, but they don't want Thomas to know that they were the ones who put them together until the right time, which is after they are married. She paid them lots of money to be with their son. They promised his girlfriend that they would help her, and after the marriage, they would agree to let her do whatever she wants to do to Thomas, but they made her promise them that they would not kill him. They knew that she was into beating and sacrificing people, and although they agreed with this type of practice, they still do not want it done to their son.

At a meeting before she was introduced to Thomas, she sacrificed her newborn baby to her god. The newborn was Eric's child, and their grandson. They felt so proud because everyone knew it. They will always remember that day because it seems that all of the demons came out to rejoice. The coven was packed, and they noticed that there were more spirits there than people. This was the first time that they saw spirits up close and personal, and for that reason, they know that there is more than one god because they saw them with their own eyes, and they heard them too.

"Okay, so what is the occasion?" said Eric. "I have something to tell all of you. I wanted to tell you years ago, but I didn't know how. I need to tell you before something happens to you, or me," he said looking at each of them. Eric and his parents believed they know the reason for the meeting, and that reason is he is about to tell the family he is gay, and they believe this because his girlfriend is beautiful and treats him very well, but Thomas keeps pushing back the wedding date, and the girls that he dated prior to her were also beautiful, and he refused to marry them. They feel that something is terribly wrong with their baby boy.

Thomas knew what they were thinking, but decided not to dispel their concern just yet. Thomas signaled for the waitress to come over, and all of them ordered what they wanted off of the menu. Of course, Eric, Mom and Dad ordered the most expensive items on the menu. Mary wants to order the least expensive item, which is a side order of fries, and Thomas told her to order what she wanted. She ordered fried fish and fries, and the children ordered the same.

The waitress arrived with the orders, and they began to eat. Thomas asked them to wait, because he wanted to bless the food. He asked that all of them hold hands, and they did, and at that moment he said, "Heavenly Father, please bless the food we are about to consume. Thank you for giving us the opportunity to get together as a family, and to enjoy each other's company. Please bless all those who prepared the food, and take out all of the impurities. In Jesus name I pray, amen." All of the adults stared at him in disbelief except Mary. She smiled at him. Each time before she and the kids eat, she does the same thing.

Everyone is hungry, so they started eating. Thomas decided it was time to tell them, and said, "The reason that I invited all of you to dinner is because I have to reveal to you my secret. No, I am not gay. And yes, one day I will marry a woman. Remember years ago, you asked me where I was going, and I told you I was hanging out with my friends? Well, that was the truth, but there was more to it. I was attending Christian church services, and learning about this wonderful God you did not want me to know. I found out that without believing in Jesus, I couldn't be saved. You see, it was Jesus who came down from his throne in Heaven to save all of us. It was Jesus who decided to become flesh, born of Mary and the Holy Spirit with no sex involved. The Holy Spirit is powerful like that; trust me, I know for myself. It was Jesus who grew up as Joseph's son, who was a carpenter and became the greatest prophet and teacher that will ever live. It was Jesus who was humiliated by humans, who was also loved and hated by his own people. It was Jesus who hung on the cross and died for all of us, but most importantly, He rose on the third day for us. It is his blood that saved us, but only if you accept and believe on Him. He is the only way that you can have eternal life. Can you imagine a life without suffering, without pain, without evil, and without hunger? Since the time I accepted Jesus, my life changed. The reason I did not tell you about Jesus then was because I knew you would throw me out." "Son, why did you allow those people to brainwash you like that?" his mother asked with a serious look on her face. "You are god, so why would you ever want to worship something that you can't see? If you come to the coven with me, I can introduce you to gods, they do exist because we meet with them all of the time. They told me that we are god, and that there is no such thing, as Jesus, and I believe them. Come to the coven with me, and I will prove to you that you are god," his father said hoping that he can influence his son to the point that he will snap out of his current state. "I did not have to see him, but I hear Him. I know He exists because when I talk about Him, I can feel the presence of the Holy Spirit. Ever since I accepted Christ Jesus, I have experienced joy, peace, happiness, and love. You talk to evil beings, and I talk to someone who is Holy. You cannot trust what you are hearing because they are evil spirits, so you need to be careful because they do not ever tell the truth, and their mission is to destroy you. You see Mom, Dad, Eric, and Mary, I love Jesus, and I will do anything to keep Him because it was He who delivered me from the bondage of sin.

I also saw the spirits that you are talking about Dad because they also dwell in your house. They are hideous and will always lie to you. They also told me that Jesus is not real, and I found them to be a liar, and I thank God that I did not believe them. Jesus revealed Himself to me through His Word and His people in the very beginning, now I have a personal relationship with Him, and since then, I have not been the same. He is more important to me than anyone and anything on earth. I knew the risks before I invited you to dinner, and if you never talk to me after tonight, and then it will have to be this way. I can no longer hide my love for God. He is in me, and I want him to use me. What's in me wants to come out all of the time. It was Jesus who stepped up out of that grave, and is now on the right hand side of the Father making intersession for all of God's children, and I am glad to be part of God's family. Jesus got up for all of us, and I do mean all of us. He died for all of us, and if you believe on Him, you can experience joy, peace, and things that you can only imagine, and He will always tell you the truth, and His love for us can not be compared to anyone or anything because it is greater," he explained hoping that his words will touch their heart, and they will allow the Holy Spirit to convict them, but each time he looked at most of them, he knows that there is no hope.

Eric stood up and told Mary and the kids it was time to leave, and Mary refused, and told the children to remain seated. After listening to what Thomas had to say to them, she finally had the courage to stand up to Eric. Thomas continued, and explained that Jesus will forgive all sins upon acceptance of Him, and each time you sin and ask for forgiveness, that sin will also be forgiven, and that was exactly what Mary needed to hear.

She and the children accepted Jesus right then and there. She grew up in the Church, and what she actually did was dedicated her life to Christ. She was so happy that she started to cry, and then she started praising God in the restaurant. She got up and gave Thomas a big hug, and asked him if he would take her to his church, or at least tell her where his church is located. He agreed to take her and the children with him to Bible study this week. Hearing about Jesus was not new to the children because they have Christian friends who shared their faith with them over a year ago, and when their dad is not home, their Mom would tell them Bible stories. What needed now is to give their hands to the preacher, and Mary and the children looked forwarded to it. She knows that Eric will try to convince her again to not go to church, but it is too late. She now knows that all of her sins are forgiven, and that now she is a new creature in Christ. All things are made new, and old things are passed away, and she will leave them in the past, and will not allow Eric or anyone else to use them against her starting right now. She has decided that nothing will stop her from becoming a good follower of Christ, absolutely nothing.

For the past few years, each time she looked at Eric, she believed she saw Satan. He and Satan have so much in common. Both of them try very hard to kill, steal and destroy. Satan has to leave her apartment immediately, and she will make it happen effective tonight. "I am more than a conqueror through Christ who strengthens me," she shouted with so much joy that most of the people were excited because she was excited.

Thomas was so happy because it felt so good to be used by God, and to witness Him in action. Mary and the kids are now saved, and he is so grateful for that, and even if Eric, Mom, and Dad refuse to believe, it was okay because he did what he is suppose to do, which is to tell them about the love of Christ, and how He died for their sins, and if they only believe on Him, that they will have everlasting life.

Mom and Dad ate in silence. They were not about to give up a good and free meal, but they lost their appetite. They looked at the other members of the family as if they would devour them at any moment because of the hate in their hearts. They were so full of hate and poison that it radiated throughout their entire beings, and at that moment, Thomas, Mary, and the kids felt sorry for them. If they only knew that the one and true God can change them into loving, kind, and gentle people, which would make them so happy. All they have to do is believe on Jesus, ask to be filled with the

Holy Spirit, and allow Him to use them, and they will be happy. Thomas decided he will pray for them, but if the Holy Spirit tells him not to, then he won't.

Mary was still bubbling over with joy, and still praising the Lord. All of a sudden, the entire restaurant was singing and praising God. It was so beautiful and amazing. What an awesome sight! Everyone from all walks of life and various ages praising God together.

Mom and Dad asked the waitress to bring them doggie bags, and when they arrived, they raked the remainder of their food into the containers, and ran towards the door as if something was running after them. Mom was running so fast that she could not maneuver fast enough to avoid hitting a bench. She hit the bench hard, and is now lying in the air, and landed flat on the floor. Her husband decided that he would just leave her there, as if he had to get out right now. To him, it was every man for himself, so he decided that he would not help her because it was not his fault that she hit the bench. As he was picking up speed, someone closed the glass door, and he ran head long into the door. It was painful, and the blood from his nose ran down his face, to his shirt. He managed to open the door, and stumble outside, leaving his wife behind.

Sophie could not decide on what she should do first. She was torn between eating at an expensive restaurant and going shopping at the mall. She could not remember what time the mall closes on Sunday, so she decided to go to the mall. She needed to get to the bus stop fast because it was due to arrive in 10 minutes.

She started picking up the pace, and as she turned the corner, she bumped into a man. Both of them started apologizing, and while they were straightening out their clothes, they recognize each other. "So, where are you going in such a hurry?" Eric asked her. "I was going to ask you the same thing," she said with a big smile on her face. Eric explained that he was going to go to his apartment and destroy everything his wife and kids own. He told her what Thomas had done, and how his wife responded. He was not happy about the entire situation. He was going to make her pay for her decision. He will destroy his children's things because he knew it would hurt her, and because she worked so hard at trying to get the children what they needed. He is happy that he did not do much for her and the children now. His heart is so full of hate for everyone in his family except his parents, and because of it, he wished that every one of them would die a horrible death.

He decided that he would move in with his parents, and ask them to help him to come up with a plan to get Thomas back on the right track, but for now, he plans to enjoy himself. "I am on my way to the mall, and from the sounds of things, you need a sympathetic ear right now," she said and was relieved to discover that he was not stinking. She reminded him about her beliefs in many gods, and he understood fully. He could not believe it. He finally met someone who understands him, and shares some of the same religious beliefs. He refuses to worship her, but believes each person should worship himself, the trees, the water, and whatever they want to. Right now, he needs someone to talk to, and she is it.

The bus arrived on time, and both of them boarded it. They sat down, and begin to talk about their families. Most of what they were saying is lies, but it did not matter because neither of them believed the other anyway. To them, this was pure enjoyment, or entertainment purposes, but she decided to keep what she found in her apartment a secret because she believes she knows Eric well, and she determined that he is totally untrustworthy. Besides, it's her money, and she does not have to share if she does not want to. But today, she will at least feed him, and then send him on his way.

The mall was crowded, but she noticed that some of the expensive stores have signs at the entrance stating that everything was on sale. She sees a dress in the window, and decided to enter the store so she can take a closer look. The dress costs $800, and with the 10% discount, she will pay $720 before taxes, which is a good deal, after considering the fact that the dress was made out of the finest materials. She decided to buy the dress and accessories from this particular store.

Eric could not believe his good fortune. This woman has money! He will have to somehow come up with a plan to keep her close until he can share some of her money, or at least find out where it is stored so he can steal it. But tonight, how is he going to get her to buy him something? He does not believe she will do it voluntarily because of her beliefs that it is the man who buys the woman something, and not the other way around. For now, he has to remain cool. He will carry her bags, and do whatever she asks. He will focus on what he wants the outcome to be, which is to help her spend her money and to find out how she got the money.

Her apartment is ragged, and he knows this to be fact because he was there this morning. So, where did the money come from because it was obvious to him that she did not have any earlier? If she had the money this morning, he believed her behavior would have been similar to what it is this very moment. She is behaving as if she is a little girl locked up in a candy store. Watching her makes him feel better, she is so happy, and it is contagious. At least, for now, he does not have to think about Mary and what she did to him. Hopefully she will allow him to stay with her for a while, a very long while.

Thomas was so happy. He shared his faith, and he was fortunate enough to see the Holy Spirit at work. That ground where the restaurant is on is now holy ground! So many different nationalities were worshipping the same God, on the same day, at the same time. He was accustomed to worshipping with those who share the same skin color and beliefs as he does, but this was great. He imagined that Heaven would be like this, where people from all nations will come together to worship Christ in Spirit and in truth. Everyone is still happy, and they began hugging and kissing strangers. "God thank you for showing up in this place!" he yelled and began smiling and laughing because the joy he has is so overwhelming. Unfortunately, it was now time to leave, and everyone started filing out slowly, and joyfully.

"How did you get here Mary?" Thomas asked. "We took the bus," she said and felt embarrassed because she does not own a car. He decided to take her and the children home. She was still bubbling over with joy, and he was glad because he has never seen her happy. She is absolutely beautiful and this is the first time he ever noticed it. She was too good for his brother, and it is too bad that Eric mistreated her since day one. It is amazing how someone can take a vibrant human being and turn her into a dreary old woman in a matter of five years. But now, she is turned once again, into a vibrant young woman because of God's grace and mercy.

She told Thomas that she would never allow herself to become what she once was. She now has Jesus, and she will do whatever it takes to keep him. Although she will have to totally take care of her children on her own, which is what she was doing since marriage, she will have the total responsibility of paying all of her debts, which makes her a little nervous, but relieved at the same time. She is at peace because she now has Jesus in the ship with her, and because of it, Eric has to move out. She will never be alone again, because she prayed that God will fill her with His Holy Spirit, and He showed up at the restaurant tonight. She hugged Thomas so tight that he could barely breathe. Once she released him, he told her that he was happy too. He decided to help her. He knows she is struggling, but at least she no longer have to take care of Eric.

While they were talking, he noticed an older woman coming towards him, and as she got closer, he knew it was his mother. "I curse you!" she yelled, and walked off, heading in the direction towards the bus stop that will take her home. He was glad to see that she is still okay. When he went to where she was earlier, she told him to leave her alone, and to go away. He wished they had accepted Jesus Christ, and because they refuse, they will not be saved. He prays that one day, their eyes will be open to the truth.

Thomas owns two houses and decided to give Mary the investment property he had recently purchased. The house needs some repair, and there is a crew working on it now. "Mary, I know you don't like to take handouts, so I want you to hear me out," he said. He explained to her that when someone gives her something, she must take it, otherwise, he will not be blessed, and neither will she. He went further and told her that he felt God was telling him to take care of her. Christians are required to take care of each other, and when one of us is suffering, and then all of us are suppose to suffer. If you need help, and if I don't help you, then I am not a good Christian or a good brother, don't you agree? "Mary, I have saved up so much money, and because I don't have kids, and for now, you and my nieces and nephews are my closest family, let me help you so you can get on with your Father's business. I can see God using you, and the sooner you become well; the sooner you can concentrate on God. I purchased a house a couple of weeks ago. I have to get it painted inside and out. The plumbing and wiring are done, and the roof will be shingled tomorrow. I am going to give you the house," he said with a big smile on his face. "Wow! I prayed and asked God for deliverance. I asked God to give me strength to leave Eric. I asked God to bless me financially, and I asked God to make a way out of no way. He just did, didn't He?" she said. Tears are now flowing down from both of their eyes, and once again, they feel the presence of God. He knows he did what was right and acceptable to God, and she knows that God had answered her prayers. Both of them decided that they would do whatever it takes to please God, no matter what it was. They love God more than anyone and anything, even more than themselves. She hugged him and gladly thanked him for the wonderful blessings.

Mary confided in him that she was given a notice from the landlord. She has to be out of the house in a week if she did not come up with the rent money. She told Eric and Eric told her that she has to come up with the money or he was going to beat her, and make her sell her body. It was very difficult for her to pay the rent and provide food for everyone in her apartment. She also told him that Eric constantly stole the money she made from tips. Thomas could only shake his head, disgusted at what his brother has become. He often wondered how a man could treat a woman so badly. How he and Eric could be so different? His parents were poor examples. He decided the difference is that he accepted Jesus, and his family did not. Jesus made the difference.

He knows that Jesus will make the difference in Mary's life as well. He knows she will be successful because she loved God before Eric came into her life. He is so happy because God used him to help her. Mary further explained that she does not have a dime to her name, but she will have money tomorrow because of tips. Because she is a kind and gentle waitress, she has always made at least $50.00 a day in tips. She does not want any money from Eric, although she knows that she could use it.

She is looking forward to her new home, and asked if he was sure that she could go to Bible study with him Wednesday. He joyfully said yes. He told her that when the house is ready, he will have a car for her, and at that moment, she started crying. So many blessings at one time are so overwhelming. She started praising God all over again in the parking lot. "Oh, God is so good, He is so good! I was lost and He set me free! Not only did He set me free, He showered me with so many blessing! Thank you so much God!" she shouted. "One last blessing, Mary. I will pay for your divorce. God does not want you to be unequally yoked with an unbeliever. Do you want it?" he asked hoping that she will say yes. "Yes!" she shouted. "I will call my lawyer first thing tomorrow morning, is that okay with you?" he said. "He's not working tonight?" she asked with a beautiful smile on her face.

The ride home was still full of praising and talking about the love of God, and His goodness. For the first time in her life, Mary was truly happy. She got out of the car, ran around to the other side, and gave her brother-in-law a hug and kiss. She decided that once the divorce is final, he will no longer be her brother-in-law, but he will become her brother. "Thomas, from now on, you are my brother," she said smiling at him. "I love you so much, and if you drift away after the divorce, it will break my heart," she said. He promised her that she and the children would always be family. He reminded her that his family now disowns him. She made him a promise that she will be with him, cheering him on, on his wedding day, if that is what he wants to do. He told her that he would probably be married in less than a month. He did not have time to tell the rest of the family.

"Thomas, do you know that your parents and Eric set you up with your fiancé?" Mary asked him. "No, he said. I introduced them to her," he said with a puzzled look on his face. "That is what they want you to believe. Your fiancé paid your mom well to be with you. Your fiancé is one of the leaders in their organization, so please be very careful. She is very dangerous. Keep your eyes and ears open at all times," she warned him. Thomas looked at her and felt that she was telling the truth, although he does not know why he was feeling it. "Is that the reason they are trying to convince me to marry her right now?" he asked Mary. "Yes, I am afraid so. She promised not to kill you, but she believes in human sacrifices. She believes it is the source of her power. She sacrifices to her gods and she believes they give her power. She and Eric had a child together a few years ago, and that baby boy was sacrificed to their gods. Eric still does not know that I know that the child was his. I overheard them talking about it. She appears to be beautiful but if you look closely, you will see the devil. Don't be fooled Thomas. Examine the fruit is what my mom would always say. I grew up in the church, and it was not until I strayed and married your brother that I broke fellowship with God. I still read my Bible, and have been doing it a lot lately. I still look at Christian programs on television because Eric is not there most of the time. I would have made it to church if Eric did not convince me that God did not want to have anything to do with me. God used you to tell me that I am forgiven. If you marry that girl, you will be just like I was before your sermon at the restaurant. I was trapped in an evil bottle and could not find my way out. My mind was under constant attacks from evil forces. She is the most evil person that I have ever met, and I put her in the same category as your bother. She is widely respected by those in their organization. I was there when she sacrificed her baby daughter, and I don't know if Eric was the child father. This happened a couple weeks before you came into her life," she explained. "Did you ever meet her relatives? Did you ever attend her church where she is supposed to be one of the leaders? Did you ever think to yourself why? One last question, did you ever discuss the Bible with her?" she asked. He answered no to all of her questions. He does not want to believe her because he loves his fiancé, but he will check for himself. He promised her that he would be very careful from now own hoping that she is mistaken or wrong.

Someone walked up the steps and asked Maggie was she okay. She told the lady that she was better than okay, and that she is blessed. The lady said that was great, opened the door, and went upstairs to her apartment. Maggie decided to do the same thing. She felt great! It was amazing to her because Jesus took the time to visit her on her steps. He really does meet you where you are. She wondered how anyone could deny Christ after feeling what she just felt. She knows the feeling was the power of God all over her. She wants to feel God's presence again. Now she understands why people said He is more precious than silver and gold. His free gift of salvation is the best thing since slice cheese and crackers.

    She opened the door and walked into her apartment. For the first time, she felt at peace. She is still bubbling over with joy, and the love she now feels is so great. Nothing matters now except God. She has never felt this way before, and she does not want this feeling to ever go away. She knows that she has to make a change because what she is doing is not pleasing to God. Her grandma is right; God is not in the club. This feeling is so much better than getting her groove on at the club. What she saw in the club was definitely not God. What she saw and felt in the club was hate, chaos, and evil. It is a sharp contrast to what she is feeling now. She prefers this feeling, and she made up in her mind that she has to know more about Jesus. She now knows God had delivered her from darkness. "Okay God, I will read the Bible. Please teach me about You," she prayed aloud. She took off of her shoes, picked up her Bible, sat down on the chair beside her bed, and started reading Matthew 1.

    Sophie spent over half of the money. She bought clothes, expensive prints, pictures, and enough furniture to fill a three-bedroom house. Her apartment will now look like a palace fit for the queen she felt she was, but she does not want the furniture delivered until she find another apartment. She decided to find another apartment tomorrow. She wants the furniture to be setup in a place that is more fitting to her mood. She can now buy some of the finer things in life, and she is going to enjoy this while it lasts. She has never been this happy. She will still have to work because she knows the money will not last forever. But for now, she will enjoy feeling rich.

    "So, Eric, what do you want to eat?" she asked and dared him to say something like lobster. "Steak and potatoes, and you for desert," he answered instead. "Okay, that sounds good, but I have a taste for something else," she said. She decided to take Eric to her favorite steak place. She told him they would walk there as soon as she puts up all of her clothes she purchased. She does not want to take them with her to the restaurant. When they went outside, they noticed the bus had just pulled up. They boarded and Sophie paid the fair for the both of them. They found an empty bench that was big enough to lay all of the clothes on. Both of their arms were tired. She asked the driver if he would drop them off in front of her apartment. He said yes after she gave him a $10 tip. They got off of the bus, and walked upstairs to her apartment.

She noticed that it was very quiet. Her apartment is next to Maggie's apartment. She concluded that Maggie was not home because she usually plays her music so loud that she and everyone else could hear it. Right now, it is quiet. She saw a faint light coming from underneath the door, and they thought that she might be on the phone or stepped out to get a bite to eat. She should have taken Maggie alone on the spending spree, but she did not want her to know about the money. She handed Eric the key, and asked him to open the door for her, and he did as she said, and handed the key back to her. She is careful about hanging the clothes in the closets. She does not want any of them to get wrinkles. She folded all of the underwear and put them in drawers. She waited until Eric left the room, and hid her jewelry. She did not trust him.

"Eric, are you okay?" she asked. "Yeah, I am almost finish washing my face," he yelled from behind the bathroom door. He felt a little faint. He was hungry. He should have eaten his food at the restaurant earlier. He has not had anything to eat all day, and now it was after 10:00 p.m. "Well, we better hurry. The restaurant closes at 10:30 sharp," she said and it was obviously to him that she would have left him there to starve if he did not leave right away. He opened the bathroom, and they left the apartment.

She decided to take him to the restaurant across the street, and when they got there she noticed it was almost empty. "I guess people don't come out Sunday night," she said and acted as if she was surprised that they didn't. "I guess not. Church service tires them out," he whispered and smiled at her. "Oh, I forgot. Your brother told you he was a Christian," she said forgetting what happened to him earlier.

She looked across the street and saw Maggie's silhouette. It looks as if she was in her rocking chair reading a book. "Wow, looks like Maggie had traded her music in and took up reading in its place. That must be a good book. Nothing comes between that girl and her music," she laughed and looked up and saw the waiter. The waiter came over to the table, and they both ordered the steak dinner. She noticed that Eric was not his usual self, and concluded that he has a problem with his brother and wife's Christian faith. She realized that he and his family practice paganism, which is the preferred religion of choice for her as well because of the freedom to do whatever and whenever. She believes people should be able to practice whatever religion they feel comfortable with, so to her, his brother's religion should not bother him. She decided to talk to him about it.

The waiter came over to the table with their food in his hand. He said, "The place will close in 10 minutes. Do you want to-go treys?" They said yes, and he took the food away and put it in carryout containers. She paid for the food, and gave the waiter a $20 tip. She asked Eric if he had a place to stay, and he said no, so she asked him if he wanted to spend the night at her apartment. He said yes, and she knew the reason was because he wanted to spend her money, but she has another reason for him to stay the night. She feels sorry for him, and because she grew up around Christians, she wants to help him understand them. Unfortunately, she does not understand them herself, but she thinks she does, besides, she knows more than he does about them. He opened the door to the apartment, and they both sat down at the table. She felt she could enlighten him while they eat their dinner.

Sophie explained to Eric that Christians are weird. "I know because I was raised in a Christian household. They believe what they are doing is right, and tries to justify everything they do by shoving the Bible down our throats. I tried reading the Bible, and I must confess to you, I don't understand it. To me, it is Greek. I do understand some of it, and the part I understand is the part I refuse to obey. I know my lifestyle is such that it breaks all of their rules. Because of it, I decided that I do not want to be a Christian anymore. They are not allowed to have any fun, and because I am a fun loving person, Christianity is not for me.

I like the religion you grew up with because I can do anything I want. Paganism allows people like us to be free Eric, and that is something that Thomas does not understand. It tells me that I am superior to man, and I like that too. It tells me that everything, absolutely everything is right. There is no wrong, and everything is right. Christians are stupid, Eric, so you are better off without your wife and brother. Why choose a religion that will not allow you to be you? It is not logical, is it? I used to believe in the Christian God, but now I know better. The Christian God wants all of the power Himself. Our religion tells us that we are gods, but if a person chooses to be a Christian or stay one, it should not have an effect on your beliefs," she explained hoping that he gets it.

He is having problems believing all of what he is hearing, but because she provided him with a free meal, he decided he better at least pretend he is agreeing with her. "I can do all things once I harness the power, which exists in nature. I plan to attend the next conference to find out exactly how to do this, but this is something you already know. My goal is to become a powerful leader in the pagan community, and I believe I can do this. Everyone will eventually bow down to me, including you," she said being very serious about what she is saying. He could not believe his ears. She is deceived. Why would he bow down to her if he were also a god? He admits that certain pagan religions recognize the woman as being superior to man, but he is a member of the group that says they are all equal. His mom was subservient to his dad, and his woman will be the same. He will never bow down to a woman, unless it is to get what he can get from her. But once he gets it, she is history. Most of what she said he agrees with. He does not know of any good Christians, and the reason for this is that he does not socialize in places where they are. He regrets that his brother has now turned into his enemy. He believes that a good Christian is a dead Christian. He can care less about his wife and children because Sophie is capable of taking care of him, but she is wild. He believes he can change that by beating her once he marries her. He likes the position that he finds himself in, and decided that he will take advantage of this. "She feels sorry for me, so let the games begin," he thought to himself, and feels that he has the ability to win at this game. He will listen to her, and try not to talk too much. He needs a place to stay, and she said he could spend the night, so he will try to extend his stay for as long as it takes to make her his slave, or at least until the money runs out. All he has to do is to make her believe that he has the power to make her a powerful witch, and she will be eating out of his hands in no time.

After she paused, he asked her if he could stay until he finds an apartment. He told her that he believes he is not welcomed at his wife apartment any longer. She said she will allow him to stay for a week, and after the week is up, he has to go even if he does not find shelter first. He knew she would not go back on her word unless he continues to play the victim to the point that it gets on her nerves. She just might see through it because she is just like him. She will allow him to stay at her place for a week, and not a minute more.

Cory waited a long time for his guest to arrive, and as soon as she walked through the door, he realized that she is the same woman that he met at the club, but she does not look quite the same. Something was different, and he cannot put his fingers on it. He invited her to sit down in the living room, and she accepted his invitation for a drink. He noticed that she was graceful, and decided that he wanted to know more about her. "So, are you originally from here?" he asked, and she said, "Yes, my father is one of the famous people that built most of the banks in this area." She came from wealth, and it was obvious to him. He finally figured out what was different. She was wearing a sweat suit with no makeup. She is a natural beauty, and he decided that he must take her to church with him to show her off to the losers who were once his so called brothers. "Will you go to church with me Wednesday night?" he asked with a grin on his face, and as if he could take a knife and fork and pretend that she was a piece of delicious steak. She looked at him and because of the grin; she knew that his motives were not honorable, which she found to be intriguing. "So, why do you want me to go to church with you? I want the truth," she asked and waited for his response. "I want to introduce you to everyone, and show them what beauty looks like," he lied with a straight face. Because he looked so serious, she decided that he must be telling her the truth, so she decided to go with him, but under one condition. "What condition?" he asked and waited for her response. "I want you to introduce me as your fiancé, and to make it a fact, I want you to ask me to marry you right now, or I will not go," she said while starring at him and looking for any signs that tell her that she needs to leave. To her surprise, Cory got on his knees and asked her to marry him, and she said yes. He felt chills running up and down his spine, and wondered if he had made a serious mistake.

Leonora Austin

Chapter Two

Monday

Mary woke up and was surprised that it was raining outside. Usually, she worries about getting the children to the bus stop in the rain, because she does not want them to catch a cold, but today she felt different. It was as if everything is made new. Sure, there still remain the same old problems with her finances, but not the same old troubles. No more Eric, and she thank God for it. Today is a day that she never saw before and a day that God allowed her to see. She knows that it is not the rain that causes the cold, but it seems that when people get wet, they are more susceptible to colds and other viruses. She cannot afford to take them to the doctor, but today, she welcomes the rain because she knows Dr. Jesus. The rain sounds so peaceful, and to her, it washes away all of the dirt and grime. It was as if Jesus was washing away everyone's sins. She wonders why she never saw this before. She knows that it is because she now has Christ back in her life. He made the difference. She will pray that God keep her children, and keep them and her in good health until that great getting up day, when Jesus returns for all of his saints.

She is still so very happy. She woke the children up, and decided to pray over them, while anointing them with oil. She does not want them to get hurt, and wants God to protect them from all harm, hurt and danger. She also prayed for herself and others, but this time, it is different. She realizes that there is something that she cannot see that is causing every creature to become more and more wicked, and it takes prayer and walking with God to stay away from evil. She prayed for this nation and our government, hoping that they take heeds to God, and do what is right regardless of what money or promises that are thrown their way. All of them are tempted, but most of them are unable to resist temptation. She only wishes that they would think before they act.

They have to hurry because the bus will arrive soon. She told her daughters to get into the shower together because it is late. They were told to rinse off, lather up, rinse off again, and get out of the shower. She told them to eat after they are dressed. They have less than forty-five minutes before the bus is scheduled to arrive. The children did as they were told, and did not complain. She thanks God for her obedient children. The bus arrived, and Mary watched the children board the bus. She is so happy because God allowed the rain to stop. As the bus pulled off, it began to drizzle. She just witnessed a miracle, and she thanked God for it.

The future seems to be so much brighter now. She thought about everything that occurred last night, as she got dressed for work. She wished she had better clothes to wear. Since the children were born, she has not bought herself any clothing or shoes. She made sure her daughters had what they need and she spent the rest on rent, utilities, and food. On many occasions, she was not able to buy food or pay rent because Eric stole her money.

The food she has in the house is not much. She cannot afford cereal and most of the breakfast food is too expensive to buy. It was not uncommon to have bologna and grits for breakfast and dinner. Sometimes, she and the other employees were allowed to take leftovers from work, and when this happens, it was a welcome treat. Although her life is hard, she knows God has something special for her, and as she walks to work in the rain, she dreamed of a better life.

After she moves into her new house, she plans to enroll in college. She always wanted to be a nurse because of the money she will make, but her passion is cooking. She loves seeing the expression on people faces, as they taste something she prepared for them with love. She loves cooking everything from vegetables to breads, and she knows with God's assistance, she can be anything. She wants to be a good example for her children, and because time is ticking away, she needs to start making changes immediately.

They have witnessed too many negative things, and she prays that what they have witnessed thus far will not influence their behavior in the future. They have seen their dad beat and curse at her, and each time it happened, she sat down and talked to them about it. It was very difficult to tell them that they should not accept it, when they were seeing their dad beat her to a pulp. She does not want them to think things are supposed to be like that, and that is one of the reasons why she wants them to attend all church services and learn what God says about how to treat their fellow man, and how a man is suppose to treat his wife. She does not want them to hate their dad, but they need to understand why he is the way he is, and what happens to a person when he refuses to accept Christ.

The children already know that their dad and his family dedicated themselves to the devil years ago. After the children were born, she was told to give them to the devil, and she refused. She would not allow the children to attend service after they witnessed their dad sacrificing an animal. He told the children about Satan, but refuses to allow them to get to know Jesus. She decided at that moment that she will teach them, and from then on, they had regular Bible study classes when their dad left the apartment. She was too afraid to leave their dad because she feared for her and the children's lives, and because he was able to convince her that she was not worthy. She knows that her family has so much to learn, and now since she is filled with the Holy Spirit, she is able to teach them better. There are so many things in the Bible she could not explain because she does not know. She looks forward to learning, and prays that God will reveal things to her.

Mary arrived at work five minutes early, and the owner was glad to see her because two of her four daughters called in sick, so they were short of help today. Mary and her boss will have to prepare for the lunchtime rush. Mary usually makes a about $30 in tips during lunch, so today she knows she will make more because of the shortage. Her job description varies, and to avoid paying her more money, the owner makes sure her primary duties is that of a waitress. If the owner takes the advice of the patrons, she would change the job description to cook, but she does not want to pay Mary more money. She can afford to, but she does not want to.

Today, she needs Mary to help her prepare the salads and prep for this afternoon's meal. She hopes that her daughters will learn everything they can from Mary so one day they can be as good as she is. She knows that Mary is the reason why so many people come to her restaurant. At one time, Mary was the head cook, and people from all over world came to eat her food. She is famous for her pastries, and she has not found anyone that is as good as she is.

Mary put up her purse and laid her umbrella under the cabinet, and put on her apron, reached behind her back to grab the apron stings, pulled them to the front and tied them. She asked her employer what she wanted her to do first and she was told to make the salads, and she is in charge of the meats. She also made it crystal clear that Mary is still a waitress by repeating it several times. As if she read Mary's mind, she told her that she would give her $50.00 extra today. She hopes Mary will teach her daughters by using them to help her season the meats, and prepare the salads so they will know her secrets.

Mary decided the first thing she will do is to season the meats quickly and put them in the oven. Their mother told the two oldest daughters that they are responsible for the vegetables, and by the time they got what they needed from the storage area; Mary had already washed and prepared the meats. They know enough not to ask Mary questions about what seasoning she used, so they decided to stand over her as she prepared the salads. There are two salads that the owner wants her to prepare. She washed and cut up the cucumbers and tomatoes and put them in a large container. She asked one of the girls to get five large onions for her and was told that she is not her mother and stood there for a moment, until the other daughter told her to do it anyway. Mary peeled, washed and sliced the onions and added them to the salad. She walked over to the cabinet and got down the sugar and vinegar and added appropriate amounts to the salad. She added water to it, and got a spoon and stirred the salad. She put plastic wrap over it and put it in the refrigerator. She walked towards the storage room and one of the girls asked her where she was going, and she told them that she needed corn to make the corn salad. They decided that they needed paper and pen to write down the ingredients, deciding not to rely on their memories for making the salads. One of the major problems is Mary does not measure, so they will have to guess and experiment until they get it right. When she came back with the ingredients, they were still trying to find something to write with. Mary opened up and drained the liquid from the canned corn. She walked to the refrigerator and got onions, peppers, and mayonnaise. They were still looking for something to write with. She chopped enough tomatoes when she made the cucumber salad to make sure she also had enough for the corn salad. She poured the corn in a large container, added the tomatoes, chopped and added the onions and peppers and then she opened the mayonnaise. After she added the right amount of mayonnaise, salt and pepper, she stirred up the ingredients and put plastic wrap on top of the container and started walking towards the refrigerator. As she was putting the container in the refrigerator, they found a pen and started writing down all of the ingredients they remembered. Unfortunately, they did not see her add some of the ingredients because they were busy looking for something to write with. Mary washed her hands and went to the dining area. "The meat will be ready just in time for the dinner crowd," she told the owner and kept walking. "What are my daughters doing?" she asked Mary, and was told that she does not know. "Did you teach them anything," she asked Mary, and was disappointed with Mary's expression. "Was I suppose to teach them?" she asked, and continued by saying, "I asked them to get something for me and I was told that I was not their mother, so I did almost everything else myself while they watched, so you will have to ask them if they learned anything." Their mother was obviously disappointed and decided that she will have to talk to the girls and tell them to be nice to Mary, so she can tell them all of her secrets.

Thomas woke up early and called his lawyer. He explained to him what he wanted done, and wanted to find out if it was possible. He answered all of Thomas' questions and told him that he will handle things for him. The lawyer said he will draw up the papers and will have them ready for signatures tomorrow. He said it is simple because Eric and Mary do not own any property, but the only problem is that Eric did not work, so he will have to find a job to help support his children. Thomas's concern is he might want the children, but the lawyer reassured him that he could not get them. Thomas knows his brother will not be happy if he knows he is helping his wife.

A week ago, he would not have gotten involved for fear of his family rejecting him, but now he does not need their approval to do what he feels that God is telling him to do. He truly loves God, and wants to please him at all times. He decided to call Mary and give her the good news.

Mary picked up the phone after the first ring, and was surprise when she heard Thomas' voice. He told her what his lawyer said, and she was so happy. She started jumping for joy. She thanked God and then thanked Thomas for everything he was doing for her and her children. She knows he does not have to help her, and she wants him to know she appreciates everything he is doing for her. He told her to thank God, and to give Him all of the credit, and she did as he asked.

She remembered that her family tried to do what they could, but they are not able to help her financially, and in the past, when they did, she regretted it. Unfortunately, she is the type of person who does not like asking anyone for help. She felt she got herself in this mess, and she has to get herself out of it with God's assistance. When she asked her family for help in the past, they would constantly bring up the fact that she should have picked a more suitable spouse than the loser she chose. It was so bad that she would work extra hours to pay them back each time she borrowed money from them. Often, she would pay them back, and not buy groceries that week. She knew God would help her and her children, and He did. She has not asked her family for help in over a year, and she does not plan to. God is a present help in a time of trouble!

She will go to the lawyer's office tomorrow afternoon to read the papers, and if she agrees with what she reads, she will sign them. Thomas told her he would pick her up at 3:00 p.m. She prays that Eric signs the papers. She knows that God does not want her to be unequally yoked with an unbeliever, so she trusts that He will make Eric sign the papers. She also knows Eric will refuse to find legal employment, but that does not concern her that much. Since the birth of their children, she has been their only source of income, shelter, food, clothing, etc. She feels good about being divorced, although some may think that she should stay in this. She knows that God wants her to be happy, and she also knows that if God had put them together, she would have been happy, but He didn't.

She counts her blessings, and thank God for the job she has. It is not the best job, but she is able to get some of the things she needs. For the first time in her life, things are looking up. God provided her with a house that is already paid for. He gave her a car that is paid for. She also knows that she must go to school and she hopes that God will bless her with her own business one day. The gifts from God make life at this restaurant more bearable. She does not have to be overly concerned about the things that she sees with regards to everyone trying to learn everything they can from her. Her fear was that as soon as they are comfortable, they would fire her. She is a hard worker and does what she is told, but she will be glad when she no longer has to work alongside snakes and vipers.

Thomas said he would support her while she is in school, and she believes him, but she wants to support herself. She knows that he will never make her feel that she must pay him back. Besides, he said God told him to do it. She knows he is telling the truth, and believe that God will give everything back to him, plus so much more. He is a good man, and he will make a good husband to the woman that God sets him up with. She prays that he discover the truth for himself about his fiancé. She loves her brother-in-law, and does not want to see him harmed in any way.

Maggie woke up early with praise still in her heart. She had a wonderful night with the Lord. There was no fear, nor thoughts of the evil one. She knew angels were watching over her while she slept last night because she felt their presence. She can't

The Fullness Thereof

wait to see Jesus face to face. She knows for a fact that Jesus is beautiful. How can He not be? After she got up, she talked to God for a long time. She wanted Him to know that she loved Him, and that she is willing to do everything He asks. She knows there is but a short time remaining before Christ returns.

She can see signs everyday, which confirms that fact. Most of the members in the apartment complex are openly gay and because it is widely accepted by many corporations, many of them believe they are special. One of the tenants sued his supervisor because he refused to allow him to wear a dress to work, and he won. Now, he is the owner of that business. There are so many businesses that are afraid of these people, and because there are so many of them, they are using them as their poster child to increase their clientele and profits. They are giving them many privileges for choosing that lifestyle. The homosexual couple that lives across from her, just returned from their honeymoon. They went to Missouri to be wed, and invited her to go with them. She and they are friends and she loves them dearly, but she does not accept their lifestyle. So far, Missouri is one of the states that allow people of the same sex to marry, and she believes if things continue as they are, many other states will follow suit, and Jesus will be here very soon. Even Sodom and Gomorrah was not this bad because they were two wicked cities, but the United States is becoming a very wicked country with many cities.

She believes America is quickly turning from her Christian roots to what she knows to be new age. She is familiar with new age because Sophie constantly talks about it. Her eyes are now open because sees things differently. She could not believe she was so blind. She believes that everyone has a right to their own beliefs, but if America is to remain a Christian nation, the laws should reflect it. She has friends who believe that everyone should have a right to get an abortion, but they say they believe it is wrong. To her, that is being double minded. If you are against abortions, then you should claim pro life and not pro choice. Say what you believe, and believe what you say. So many people are hypocrites, but they are not aware that they are. If someone wants to break the laws of the land, then that should not concern others is the popular belief. We are responsible to God and He is our judge and jury. She remembers acting the fool at her graduation party, believing herself to be wise. She was a big fool. "Today is a day that the Lord has made and I will rejoice in it. Old things are passed away, and all things are made new. Thank you Jesus!" she said aloud with her heart full of joy. She is so glad she prayed for forgiveness. She has so much to learn.

Sophie and Eric woke up about the same time. She was glad to have him there, but she knows her sympathy for him will only last for about 30 minutes. She hated the fact that he is good for nothing, and lazy. She only sympathized with him because his brother and wife turned to Christianity and she had flashbacks of being made to go to church. Church was good, but being reminded of the things she enjoys doing is not acceptable Christian behavior was awful. Every time she attended church service, it was as if the preacher was talking to her. She was told that the word of God is sharper than any two-edged sword, and she knows that it is the truth. Every time that woman opened her mouth, the words seem to cut her, which made her uncomfortable. It was so bad, that she could not wait to get out of there. Maggie's grandma explained the meaning to her, so she decided at that moment that she would not attend another church service. It was as if the God she refused to believe in was speaking directly to her. She does not want to hear Him because she will have to obey Him, especially if she once again acknowledges that He exists. She does not want to do that right now, so she had to find another religion that will allow her to do whatever she wants.

One of the reasons she chose New Age was because it has all of the non-Christian religions under its umbrella. She was surprised that Judaism is considered pagan, and she later found out that they do not believe Jesus Christ rose from the grave. She said to her, "Why should I believe if His chosen people do not believe on the name of the only Begotten Son." She asked Maggie's grandma and she took her to the Bible passage that explains the reason why. She was surprise that the Bible revealed the lie that was told and how the priest paid the guards off.

The only thing she likes about Eric is his looks. She knows he will eventually ask her about the money. She does not plan to tell him anything because he is too much like her, and besides, he is a bloodsucking leech. She can accurately anticipate what he is about to do because she thinks of what she will do. So far, it is working. She knows he is trying to stay with her until the money runs out. Right now, he needs a place to stay, however, he still have parents. She will talk to him tonight about that. She will not give him more than a couple of weeks to find a place, and they will not pretend they are married either. When it is time for one of her partners to come by, she will tell Eric to find another place to hang out. She decided not to allow him to interfere with what she is doing. She does not have a bleeding heart, and is not interested in developing one. She is a thinker, which some people may disagree with that, but she thinks he will try to use her.

She knows that she will have to work for the rest of her life because of the amount of money she spent yesterday. She should that thought before she bought most of the items. If she does marry a rich man, and he allows her to spend his money, he will be broke in less than a month. She believes she needs help because to her, she is a compulsive spender.

She woke Eric up, and told him that the first thing he must do is to go home and get dressed. He needs to find employment so he could afford to pay rent. She plans to move out of her apartment immediately, and will give her building superintendent her 30-day notice tomorrow morning. Her fear is that if she does not find an apartment quickly, the money will be gone, and she will be stuck living in this run done raggedy apartment. She plans to find another apartment within a week, and plans not to spend any more of the money she found. She plans to let Eric stay for the remainder of the month if he is a good boy. That is the least she can do, and it is her way of giving back to society. She accomplished her goal of doing something nice for someone once a year. If he wants to, he can sign a lease for her apartment. The apartments are one of the cheapest in the city because it is located in a very bad and depressed neighborhood.

She ran to the shower. She is running late, and does not have enough time to make coffee. She will try to buy some on her way to the deli if she has enough time. She took her money with her into the bathroom, and locked the door. She will not give him a key to the apartment until she moves out. She will talk to the landlord this evening about Eric. She knows it will not be a problem with him getting a vacant apartment because there are several vacant ones in the building. Her only concern is that Eric will not be able to afford the cheap rent.

Eric opened the bathroom door and sat down on the toilet. He wanted to make Sophie glad that she allowed him to stay by stating the fact that he is good looking and has a muscular body. He went on and on, and then he started boasting about not paying any rent at all. He made his wife take care of him and the children. "You are a sorry, good for nothing boy!" she shouted and it was as through venom spewed all over the room. If you let a fool talk long enough, she knows that he will eventually tell on himself. Sure she loves muscular and good-looking man, but what woman doesn't like looking at such magnificent creature, but Eric takes the cake. She knows too many men who should never call themselves men and Eric is one of them. "How can a man say he is a man if he is being taken care of by a woman?" she asked him and it is obvious to him that she finds him disgusting. She turned off the water, and told him to get out. He got up and closed the door behind him. She stepped out of the shower and got dressed. She continued talking after Eric left the bathroom, and Eric heard everything she said about him. He wished she would stop, but she continued saying awful things about him and men like him. After about 15 minutes, he heard something telling him that she was not talking about him. "She is talking about someone like your brother. You are a good-looking man, and all women want you," an imp told her, and as he was telling Eric lies, another imp was talking to Sophie and told her, "Why are you saying such things about him. He is not that bad. Haven't you been with worst? He will get a job and take care of you, but concentrate on how he will make you look good just by being with him. Come on, think about how your girlfriends will be envious of you because of this good-looking muscular man. Thank about it, come on, just think about it."

"Eric, why are you still here?" she asked after opening the bathroom door and still thinking about what the imp said to her. "I was waiting for you to get out of the shower. I want to bathe before I leave, if you don't mind," he said, trying to sound pleasant but knowing that she is very angry, but noticing something different. She knew he was waiting for her to leave so he could search for her money. She thought about how good-looking he is, but it was not worth him staying at her house searching for her money. "No, you need to go home, get in the shower, and then get dressed. Why would you take a shower and put on dirty underwear?" she asked him with her nose turned up to symbolize that he stinks. She remembered how he smelled when he spent the night wit her the previous night. At that moment, he knew he was defeated, and started mumbling something to the imp. He got dressed and walked out of the door. He plans to return this evening, just in time for dinner. He hopes she will be cooking him steaks and potatoes because the imp told him that he should not give up, and she will soon see him in a new light. She hid the money by putting it in its original location after she looked out of the window and saw him walking down the street. She had to move the table first, and after she put the floorboard back in place, she slid the table over it, which made it impossible for anyone to see it unless they remove the table and bend down. She made sure the floorboard looks as if it was never pulled up. She has to get to the deli quickly.

The Fullness Thereof

The wind felt so good to her skin as she ran towards the deli. She was so happy. For the first time since working at the deli, she looked forward to going to work. The money made the difference. She knew many real estate professionals who would often dine there for lunch. Her chances of finding an apartment or small house seemed great in her eyes. She wants to pay for her new place in cash, providing that she does not spend anymore of the money.

She still plans to keep all of her partners. She needs them to give her the extra spending money and to help her maintain her high maintenance lifestyle, which to her, is necessary. Sure, she could go to school, and in some years, she could become a professional and take care of herself financially, but why should she if she can allow others to take care of her. She decided she would prefer to reap the benefits of being a professional without suffering by spending their hard earned money.

She does not see any of them often, so she does not have to run the risk of one of them finding out about the others. She loves taking risks because it gives her a rush. If she loses one of them, oh well. She never had any problems finding replacements. Its amazing to her that there is so many women and men out there who do not mind taking care of their lovers. She is glad that she is smart enough to know it, and know how to take advantage of it. She knows the risks about getting a disease, but she cannot concentrate on that. Her challenge is to make sure each of them feel special. She would often walk the streets dreaming of a better life, and now she has it. "Boy, what luck," she thought and smiled to herself.

She is almost in front of the deli now, and as she looks to the sides of the building, she notices that there are many cars in the parking lot. She went inside and found it almost empty. "Why are there so many cars in the parking lot?" she asked one of her coworkers. She was told that the people are next door attending a conference. They hired the deli to prepare lunch for all of the participants. From the looks of the cars outside, the people were either wealthy or deep in debt because they are driving very expensive vehicles.

She put the hair net on, walked over to the sink, and washed her hands. It was now time to get busy preparing sandwiches and salads. She noticed Maggie was working in the back, and she wanted so badly to go back there and talked to her. She wanted to know what she was doing late last night. Did she have a man, and if so, why was she sitting alone in front of her window last night reading a book? She wanted to know the reason for the sudden change. Not only did she change her habits, by switching from music to reading books, but also even her appearance is different. She does not know exactly what changed, but she knows there is one. "What changed?" she looked at Maggie and tried to get her answer. She wanted to know if she actually saw something in the club last night, and if so, is that why she was reading last night, to do some research. Was that the reason she is acting differently? Maggie does not have an active imagination and she knows that to be fact. She is realistic, but maybe she is having a nervous breakdown or something. She will ask her questions later. She might need professional help, and she knows the right person that can help her friend.

Thomas arrived at his lawyer's office at 9:00 a.m. sharp. The lawyer had all of the paperwork prepared. He told him that this is a very simple divorce. The problem is getting Eric to pay child support. This will be a major task, and he felt that if God does not make him work, then he would not work. He knows Eric does not have a generous bone in his body and he will want to hurt Mary and the children to the point where they will never recover. He will not work and everyone knows that you cannot get blood from a turnip, especially a turnip like Eric, who is rotten to the core. "Eric is a real scumbag, and if I were not so greedy, I would do this for free," said the lawyer smiling at Thomas with warmth that would melt a large glacier. His goal is to build an empire and to rule the world; at least that is what he tells his friends. He decided to not charge Thomas anything. Thomas is someone whom he admires, and he knows that God's hand is on him. He believes he can actually see it. When Thomas is around, he feels great because of the anointing that is on him. He wants that anointing, and he knows exactly what he needs to do to get it because Thomas told him. He truly wants to be more like Thomas, and after this divorce, he decided that he would go to church and rededicate himself back to Christ. He will do it this Sunday, which is what he decided to do as he greeted his friend. This time, he felt something that felt like electrical power, but instead of hurting, it felt better than good, and after experiencing this, he wants it badly.

He feels that Mary should count her blessings any way she can. Getting rid of this scumbag is a wonderful blessing. He is doing his part by expediting this. The process will take a couple of weeks because of his contacts. He sent a couple of his buddies over to Eric's place to make sure he signs the papers, which is the reason why he decided that he will wait until Sunday to get closer to God. He knows Thomas is a good guy, and he has sent people his way, so if he is willing to help Mary, she must also be a good person too. "I am surprise you already have the paperwork ready. I called you a little over an hour ago," Thomas said surprised that this man is so efficient. He told him that he does not have to do much work because almost everything is automated and technology makes things so simple. To save time, he will take the papers to Mary so she can sign them. He knows she does not have transportation, and if he does it, she does not have to leave work. She told him earlier that a couple of the ladies called in sick, and they are short today, so she wants everyone to work hard and pitch in to take care of their customers. He does not believe her boss will allow her to leave. He hugged the lawyer and told him he will return with the paperwork later this morning.

The lawyer told him that he would take care of the other set of signatures. "How? Never mind. Please don't kill him. Man, I really got to get you to my church," Thomas said, knowing it would be a miracle, but still hopeful that one day he will accept his offer. "How were you planning to convince Eric to sign the divorce papers? He is already upset with you because you are a Christian. He is upset with you because his wife converted to Christianity after listening to you preaches the Gospel, which left him without someone to feed and clothe him. So, what do you want to do?" the lawyer asked feeling that he made a valid statement. "Okay, you got a point, but don't kill him," Thomas stated again. "Besides, a couple of my friends said he is walking in the direction of his wife's apartment right now. I told them to make sure he does not take what does not belong to him. While they are in the neighborhood, they may as well ask him to sign the papers, right? Don't you agree? It is convenient, don't you think?" he said looking at Thomas with a wide grin on his face. He went further and explained that the men have sisters that dated scum like his brother, but he will remind them not to kill him. "But if he resist, they may have to beat him a little. Just a little bit, to make sure he is fully aware that they mean business. Just kidding," the lawyer said while laughing, but Thomas knows that he is very serious. "Man, you are crazy. I will be back soon. I love you man," he said as he left the office shaking his head, with a smile on his face.

What he did not tell Thomas was that the men took their jobs seriously. They are self-proclaimed executioners, and pride themselves on how well they do their job. They want to rid the earth of no good people who have the nerve to call themselves men. The lawyer hired them because they are family, and they are good at what they like to do. They are the best in their field, and they have many satisfied customers to prove it.

Eric arrived at the apartment with the intent on destroying everything. He knew Mary would not be there because she had to work, and even if she were there, it would not matter. He knew she walked because he took her last dime last night prior to going to the restaurant. He hopes she suffers because of what she did to him. How dare she turn her back on him! She is now his number one enemy and is worthy of death, in his eyes. He depended on her and now he is forced to think of other ways to feed himself. Although he stayed with many women, he knew she would always be there in the event the other woman kicks him out of her house. He knows he is no longer welcomed at home, but the fact remains that he is still her husband, but he does not want to be in the same house with a Christian. His name is not on the lease, so he knows that she thinks she can have him arrested, but he has the law on his side because she is still his wife. He will never give her a divorce until he is ready. First, he has to find a suitable replacement. He wants someone who makes more money than Mary, who does not mind taking care of him, or someone who he can mold into the perfect sucker. Someone who will not constantly bring up the fact that he does not work. He needs to start hanging out in better neighborhoods so he can be around better class of women.

As soon as he finds a replacement for Mary, he plans to kill her and the children. The perfect time to do that is Halloween, where he can offer them as a sacrifice. He will plan the whole thing, and will tell the members of the coven that he has three people who will be sacrificed. That one event will cause him to become very powerful, which will make him and his family happy. "Sophie will really want me then. I will become a powerful warlock, and she will become my witch bride. We can live forever!" he thought as he continued walking.

As he was walking up the stairs, he noticed two big gentlemen standing on the sidewalk. He knows that he is muscular, but these guys are bigger and taller than he is, but he looks better than them. They rushed ahead of him and opened the door for him, and followed him up the stairs. He greeted them but they did not say anything. When he got to his door, he took out the key, put it in the lock and turned it. When the door opened, one of the men pushed him inside of the apartment. He went flying into the chair, and landed on the floor in front of the television. He bumped his head against the coffee table, and felt the blood gushing from his head. He is in so much pain, and wants to pass out. He looked up, and saw the men standing over him with a look that says, "I dare you to move an inch, and if you do, I will kill you immediately." They stepped back allowing him room to get up, and he tried to, slip, and bump his head against the television, and now, blood is flowing from both openings.

Thomas knows very little about his lawyer, but the one thing he knows is that he is heavily connected in the city. The man knows all of the heavy hitters in government, so he is able to get things done quickly. He is very honest about telling him whether or not what his clients are doing is legal. He never saw this side of him before. This is a fun loving side, and he was glad to see him this way. He hopes he is kidding when he said he sent his friends over to convince Eric to sign the paperwork. If he did, I hope they do not use mob tactics. He would rather pay Eric to sign the papers than to have him hurt. He knows Eric will sign for money, especially if he knows that Mary is moving out of the apartment. He does not have to know where she is moving. If she disappears, and he is unable to locate her for more than a day, he will sign because he cannot pay the rent, but because he knows his brother well, defaulting on the rent will not be a problem for him. According to Mary, the lease is up this week, and she thought about signing a month-to-month lease after she comes up with the rent. She wanted to move to a neighborhood where her children would be safe. Right now, the neighborhood is drug infested, and because of it, her children cannot play outside for fear of stray bullets killing them.

As he pulled into the parking lot, he noticed the restaurant was unusually busy. As a matter of fact, he has never seen it this busy before, although he only ate here a few times. This was a good idea. He knows she would not have been able to leave to sign the papers. He got out of the car, and walked into the restaurant. He saw Mary waiting on a table and decided to wait until she completes the order before he goes over to talk to her. She was happy to see her brother-in-law. She asked him to come to the office, and he did. He handed her the papers and because she trusts him, she signed them without first reading them. She knew Thomas had already read them, and she heard a small still voice telling her to sign them, and everything will be okay. "It's going to be okay Thomas! God said it is going to be okay," she said through tears of joy. "It is true that the joy of the Lord is my strength," she said looking up at him after she signed the papers. He agreed with her, and all of a sudden he felt full. He knows, without doubt that it is true. Without God, he would not have made it. He has been in so many situations, and he knows God delivered him from all of them. He hugged her, and they left the office. She thanked him again, and told him she loves him. He asked her if she needed money, and she told him no, so far today, she has made over $200 in tips. This is the first time the breakfast crew has been this large. She believes God has intervened on her behalf. God knows she needed the extra money, and she does not mind working for it. She worked hard today, but she was not tired. The restaurant was still extremely crowded with a long line of people waiting to be seated. In a couple of hours, the lunch crew will arrive. If things continue at this pace, she will make over $1000 in tips if the restaurant remains open. The restaurant usually close after lunch is over, and reopens at 5:00 p.m.

Eric was furious! He quickly stood up to face his attackers. One of the men quickly told him that if he wants to live, he better not do what he thinks he is about to do. The other man pulled out the papers from out of one of the pockets in his jacket, set them on the table and told Eric to sign them. Eric wanted to know what he was about to sign. He found the men intimidating, but he knew enough to know that he would rather die than to be forever tied to the mob. He does not know any good mobsters and considers all of them to be cold-blooded killers. He asked them what this was all about, and they stared him down for over ten minutes, then they told him to sign the divorce papers. He believes he knows what they will do to him if he refuses to do as they say. He asked if he can read them first, and they said yes. "Sure, we will allow you to read them, take you time and read every word." They told him to sit in the middle of the couch, and both of them sat next to him with pistols pointed at his temple. They handed him the first sheet and Eric read it, then one of the men handed him the pen. He wanted to know if his wife had something to do with this. They told him no, but they informed him that they just adopted his wife, and they are now her big brothers. They explained to him that their biological sister had a girly man just like him. They explained in graphic detail what they did to that man, and after hearing it, Eric signed the paper, and signed the rest of them without first reading them. They told him to get his stuff, and to never enter this apartment again. Eric knew her family did not like him, but taking steps like this was not necessary. He would have given her a divorce one day, although he also planned to kill her and the children during a sacrifice ceremony. He now feels it is not worth his life to cause her problems. There are other fishes in the sea, and he has one on the line right now. "Oh, one more thing Eric, you will find a job to support your children financially. If you do not, we will start removing body parts, starting with your foot. Do I make myself clear?" one of the men said giving Eric one of his most popular death stares. "Crystal," said Eric, believing every word the men were saying. He wants this nightmare to end right now. The sooner the better, and because he realize that he prefers living, he will try to take the sooner route. After the men told him their names, he became very fearful. The men are well known in the community. They enjoy torturing their victims. They are worst than he is, and that is something for them to be proud of, but it is also something that is scary. He is also a cold-blooded killer but these guys made him look like a little girl. They are guns for hire and they thoroughly enjoy what they do. They wrote a best seller, *How to Thoroughly Torture People Right in Front of the Police Station*. Now, he was given a more important reason to get a job. He plans to ask his dad for a job right away.

    Sophie finally got the opportunity to talk to Maggie. "What is wrong with you?" she asked while looking at her so she will not miss the answer. "Good morning to you too. How are you doing?" she said returning the look. "I am doing great, so what is wrong with you?" she repeated and cocked her head to the side. "What are you talking about?" Maggie said and sounded as if she was tired of a charade. Sophie explained that when she went to the apartment last night, she noticed that Maggie was not playing her music, and she saw her reading something by the window. "What's wrong with that? I needed to think and to slow down. I wanted peace, and that is what I got," she said believing that she really does not have to explain herself. Sophie was still suspicious, for she knew Maggie was not telling her everything. "So, did you have company?" she asked and cocked her head to the other side, as if she was auditioning for a silly movie. "No! I told you I needed to think," she said and Sophie believed her. "So, are we going to the club tonight?" she asked looking serious this time. "No, I just divorced the club scene effective last night. I have to grow up girl. I have too many responsibilities now, so the club is out," she said looking as serious as she could, but wanting all of the questions to stop. "Responsibilities? Girl please! You don't have children! You better party while you can. I am going tonight with or without you. You have been acting weird since leaving the club Sunday morning. Are you having a nervous breakdown or something?" she asked and stared, as if she had the ability to tell whether she was telling the truth or lying. "I have never been better. Let's drop the subject. I don't have to explain myself to you or anyone else. I am not going to the club, and that is final, so don't ask me again Sophie," she said looking at her as if to say she meant every word of it. Sophie said she would not waste her time again. They agreed to remain friends, but Sophie refuses to give up on her yet. She will take Eric with her tonight, and she knows that she will not have to beg him. If it were not for Eric, she would beg Maggie to go with her because she does not want to go to the club alone.

Maggie wanted to tell her about Jesus, but did not know how to do it yet. If she talked about God inside the Deli, someone may hear her conversation, report her to management, and she will get fired on the spot. It is sad that she cannot share her faith with others at work, but they can share their faith with others without fear of being fired. The Deli has a policy against sharing the Christian faith because they say it does not embrace the real world. Their clientele are people from varied backgrounds. Sophie shares her faith with others on a regular basis, and it is accepted because they believe that everything and everyone is god. All of the employees are female, and hearing that paganism embraces the feminism makes most of them happy. She knows that there is only one true God, but it is a shame she cannot say it at work. Everyone who appears to embrace paganism at her work is the ones who frown on Christianity. It is a shame, and it makes her feel so sad. Her friends are obsessed with the occult. The challenge for her is to introduce her friends to Jesus by her actions. They are deceived into believing a lie, and if they do not believe on Jesus, they will not have eternal life. She knows that it will not be easy because people run away from Jesus freaks, and she is proud to say that she is one of them. She always believed, but she thought she had enough time to experience everything this world has to offer before committing herself to Christian living. She felt she had time to repeat years from now, but after seeing what she saw, she knows that she does not have time to play around anymore. She is so glad that she repented and decided to live a life that is pleasing to God. Life without Christ is no life at all. He is the only one that can give someone like her peace and joy. She hopes her friends discover this well known fact before it is too late. Too bad they could not see what she saw. If only they see them, they will change their minds just like she did. At least, that is what she hopes will happen.

She knows people embrace the occult because not only do they acknowledge the feminine rather than the masculine, but they also call evil good. Women are so tired of being treated as if they are second-class citizens, especially in the church, so paganism is attractive because it makes women the head rather than the helpmeet. Remember, it is the witch that rules the coven. Her emotions make her more dangerous than any man can ever imagine, although she does know many men who are just as emotional as women. She had to admit it; she was also attracted to paganism because of that fact. She knows that the Bible is the truth, and she has to accept the fact that women are not viewed as highly as men in society or in the church. "That darn Eve. Why did she have to mess things up for us? Could she have been a dumb blond? Probably not since the Garden of Eve is located in Africa. Well, she was still dumb, and now all women have to suffer because of her deception and Adam's unwillingness to give up the one he loved. God would have given him another spouse. What part of no did Adam and Eve not understood? However, I still love Jesus, and I am going to live the life He wants me to live," she thought wondering how God is going to use her. She is also grateful that men are held more accountable for their actions than their wives, so being a woman is not bad at all. She also realize that because of prejudice against women, God will have to change lots of hearts in order for women to be all that He will have them to be. If it was left up to some women, and the boys they raise, women will never do anything important other than giving birth, be wives, slaves, secretaries, or other things that they believe women should do or be.

If only others could have seen what she saw in the club. If they only knew they were entertaining evil spirits, then she believes some of them will change their minds about going to the clubs. She would rather spend eternity in heaven, than in hell. The club scene reminded her of Halloween. Monsters were coming out of the walls and were dancing with everyone in the place. People were turning into demons, and there were more demons than people. It was truly a time where evil was celebrated. She wonders if people would do what they do if they saw the spiritual world. She wonders if everyone knew what he or she was celebrating when they go trick-a-treating. She understands why her parents did not allow them to celebrate that wicked holiday. Sophie loves it because she worships evil, and all those who she feels will give her more power. She prays that Sophie does not turn into a devil in her presence. She knows that he is in her, but she does not want to see it.

"Can I ask you one more question Maggie?" she asked hopping that Maggie will say yes. Maggie looked at her, and nods her head to say yes. "What did you see or thought you saw in the club?" she asked wanting her to telling the truth regardless if it does not sound as if it is. "Remember the stories you told me about your religion. Remember you said the spirit world exists in everything and in everyone. You said there is no such thing as good and evil, but you are wrong. What I saw in the club were evil spirit beings. It was as if Halloween came to life, and all of the evil spirits came out to celebrate," she explained hoping that Sophie understands. "Wow, so they are real. Did you try to talk to one of them?" Sophie asked being serious. "No!" she shouted and looked at her as if to say she does not believe she would want to talk to such beings. "I wish I had seen them. I would try to talk to them. I want to become one of them. They are not evil Maggie. I was taught that they are wonderful and powerful beings, and they can help us to attain greatness. Witches consult them all of the time, and I want to become a powerful witch one day," she explained with so much excitement that it became scary. "My Bible said they are evil, and I know it is true because I saw them. You know the story about Satan being kicked out of Heaven because he wanted to overthrow God. Well, God kicked him and one third of the angels out of heaven. They are now ruling down here on earth, and there are so many of them. There are too many of them. The Holy Spirit, who is also God, is the One who prevents evil from taking completely over, and I thank Him for doing that often. Once the Holy Spirit leaves, God will allow the devil to have total control of you and the rest of you pagans if Jesus comes back to this earth right now," Maggie explained. "Girl, you are confused. You need to come to a meeting with me," she said. Sophie did not believe anything Maggie said. She does not believe in one God, and Maggie knows it. She considers herself to be wise, and to her, Maggie sound foolish. Others had tried to convince her that the Bible was factual, but she still does not believe it. She often talks to Satan, but decided not to share that information with Maggie. She knows more than Maggie thinks, and that information will scare her. The Deli was filling up with people so they had to end their conversation.

Maggie went into the back of the Deli and talked to God. She does not know how to help her friend, and after over ten minutes of praying, she felt God was telling her to separate from Sophie. She will do it, although she does not have any other close friends. She remembered her grandma talking to her about choosing her friends wisely, but she did not understand that statement until now. She now knows she needs to know more about Jesus. She has to get more of the word on the inside so she can use it when she needs to, is what her grandma told her and others. She now understands what that means too. If she had not seen demons the other night, she would not have met Jesus. "Wow, do I find myself thanking the devil for making me run to Jesus? No, God forbid. Thank you God for showing me spiritual things. Now, I will serve you the rest of my life, but you will have to help me. In Jesus' name I pray, amen," she prayed silently. She felt better now. She walked out of the kitchen and saw Sophie turned into a devil. She turned back into Sophie a moment later. She will definitely separate from Sophie immediately.

Eric left the apartment with a garbage bag full of his clothes. He was not allowed to take the television and microwave. If those two bullies were not there, he would have destroyed them or sold them to the highest bidder. He was trying to come up with a plan to steal them, but how would he carry the heavy items? He decided to go to his dad's garage because it was the closest location to where he is now located. The two strong men followed him for a couple of miles, and he felt very uncomfortable. When they finally turned down a side street, he became more relaxed and grateful that he was no longer being watched. He finally arrived in his old neighborhood, and was happy to see that his dad was alone. He did not want to beg for a job while others were in his office. That would be degrading, even for him. Then he thought about the things that he just experienced, and he realized begging for a job in front of a couple of people is less degrading than being thrown into a table or chair.

"Hello Dad, how are you this wonderful morning?" Eric said trying not to look directly at his dad. He combed his hair in a way that hid some of the wounds, but it made him look silly. Eric's dad was not in a good mood, so he did not answer Eric. "What's wrong with you?" he eventually said, and walked closer so he could see the eyes of his dad. "You don't know? You were there at the restaurant last night, were you not?" his dad asked while returning his son's stare. He saw the wounds and decided not to say anything for fear of Eric needing money so he could see medical attention. Eric explained that he suffered more than he did. He is now homeless because of last night. His dad sit down to hear what Eric had to say. Eric explained further that he was made to sign divorce papers, and was told that if he does not find a job, they would kill him. He told his dad the name of the men who made the threats, and because his dad knows them well, he knows the men mean business, and their threats are to be taken literally. "So, you need a job? I have been trying to convince you to work here since you were a boy. One day, this business will be yours. I refuse to give it to Thomas now because he turned out to be a major disappointment. How could he betray me and the rest of the family? How could he turn his back on his mother? I will never lift my hands to help him, although unlike you, he has never asked me for help," he said and Eric heard the bitterness in his voice.

Eric realized at an early age that Thomas and he were different. Thomas was always interested in learning about new things, and he was not. Thomas did not possess the desire to hang out with the crew, and do things that would make an average mother weep, but he possessed that and more. The crew met every night around 6:00 p.m. to come up with a plan to rob from others and split the wares among themselves. Thomas went once, and he was not invited again because he constantly told them that what they were doing was wrong, he was a "goody-two-shoe" and because of it, he was a thorn in all of their sides. He really did not fit in this neighborhood, but his father thought he was perfect because he is intelligent and good with his hands.

When Thomas was thirteen, his dad was sick and it was Thomas who ran the shop for six months. During those six months, the shop made so much money. After Thomas had computerized the shop, there was still so much money left to take care of the family for years. His dad was amazed, and often wondered where he had the knowledge, because he was fully aware that he did not teach it to him. The one thing he did not like was that Thomas gave the employee raises, and as soon as he got well enough to take over, he lowered the raises immediately. That was the first and last time the shop was organized and clean. Some of the employees quit after he abolished their raises, and unfortunately, he never made that amount of money again. He wanted Thomas to continue to work for him, but Thomas was not interested after his dad refused to consider his suggestions.

Because Thomas turned from his religious upbringing, he has to rely on Eric to take care of the shop after he retires. He had hoped to live the good life before he dies, and the more he thought of Thomas' betrayal, the more he hated him. He wants to enjoy what this world has to offer. He wanted to travel around the world, and if Thomas took over the shop, he knows it is possible. He has to teach Eric everything he knows, and now Eric was willing to learn, which makes him happy, but he would have preferred to teach Thomas instead, but in reality, Thomas would have to teach him.

Eric has death hanging over his head and his dad decided to use it to his advantage. His dad was glad to hear that his only son has a very good reason to work hard now. "So, when do you want to start? I suggest you say immediately. Those boys will check up on you regularly," he laughs, and then started laughing harder, chocking every now and then. Eric did not find any humor in his dad's statement, and looked at his dad is if he was heartless. Eric is now forced to work very hard because he wants to live and his dad plans to make it work in his favor. He may have to invite the two men over every now and then to make sure Eric stays focus. He also wants to make sure Eric stays in his place. He knows his son will do anything to get what he wants, and if that means killing him, he knows his son will do it for a dollar.

Eric wants to drop his clothes off to the apartment first, but he does not have a key to get in. He believes he can pick the lock, but someone might see him. He decided

The Fullness Thereof

that it was too risky. He wanted to stay with her, at least until every penny of her money is spent. He can envision her new lavishly furnished place, with him kicking back in an easy chair. He must come up with a plan to get her money, all of it. He will latch on to her as if he is a leech, and suck her dry. Sometimes his greed even scares himself. This world system has taught him well, and nothing is beneath him when it comes to making or stealing money. He plans to work for his dad, and when his dad dies, which he hopes is soon, he will consider selling the business. If he keeps it open, he will use it as a front to sell drugs and people. If there is a dollar to be made, he does not believe anything should be off limits, not even selling children. The only problem is he has to make sure he does not get caught.

Because Mary has protection, he will not bother her again. If something happens to her, he knows those two goons will come after him, even if he had nothing to do with it. He hopes the worst for her, his daughters, and for those who are protecting her.

The family has disowned Thomas, so he will not get a dime in the event his parent's unfortunate die. When or if Eric inherits the business, his mom will have to fend for herself because he plans to take everything from her. The house is paid for, and he is sure his dad will leave her money, but the business will be his. If his mom was smart, she better start making plans for her future. He is aware that it is not normal for a son to not have compassion for his parents, but Eric believes his greed does not allow him to have compassion, not for them or his children. "Okay, Dad, what do you want me to do first?" Eric asked.

After Thomas left the restaurant, he drove to the lawyer's office and handed him the papers. He did not want to know anything about how he planned to get Eric to sign the papers. He promised him that he would not kill him, and he believed him. The lawyer told him that his men are on their way with the signed papers. When they arrive, he will send the paperwork to the county clerk. The divorce will be finalized in two weeks. "Wow, you are the man!" Thomas told the lawyer. Thomas gave him the address to Mary's new resident. "Why don't you come to Bible study with me Wednesday night, I can pick you up at 7:00 p.m." he said looking at him and praying that he says yes. "You are not going to give up, are you? I will go with you eventually, I promise. I will let you know when, okay?" the lawyer said and continued to tell him that he will be in Church first thing Sunday morning to be himself back to God. Thomas smiled and hugged his friend, and because of the spiritual battle that is going on around all of us, Thomas knows that he will have to constantly pray for his friend. He loves him as if he was his biological brother. He hugged the lawyer and thanked him for everything. He smiled and closed the door behind him.

Thomas thanked and talked to God all the way to work. He is so grateful that God used him. He knows he will forever be His servant, and by being His servant, he is expected to serve others, even when he does not want to. Helping Mary was a true test of his dedication to God. He gave her money, gave her a new vehicle, and gave her a house that will be in better shape than the apartment that he is staying in. His plan was to move into that house, but he knows when God tells you to do something, he must do it without question. Besides, how can he say no to the all-powerful God? How can anyone say no to our Creator? For some strange reason, he felt good giving those things away. He loves Mary. Since he met Jesus, he loves everyone, including those mean people he works with. God never told him it was going to be easy. Once you put your hand in Jesus' hand, you are persecuted for no reason other than the world does not like seeing good in you. Every time something unjust happens to him, he quotes scripture and focus on Jesus. In the past, when things happened, he grew worse and worse each moment, because he kept thinking about the miserable situation he found himself in. It was not until he learned to focus on God when he discovered that he is able to walk out of his state of depression or misery. God is the key to everything, and he is so glad that he learned that fact. A most important fact, he was glad to discover, and he thanks God for it.

He will have to continue to take care of Mary until she gets on her feet. He is so glad that she turned back to God. She searched for so long, and after God used him to tell her what she needed to know, she immediately said yes to Jesus. He loves it! As he is thinking about this, he is able to imagine Jesus knowing on the door of her heart, and unlike the rest of the adults in his family, she was the only one who opened up the door and allowed a beautiful, wonderful, and all power Jesus to come in a sup with her, and she with Him. Seeing the Holy Spirit at work is awesome! He is so glad God allowed him to witness such an awesome event. He is looking forward to picking up his family Wednesday night to take them to study God's word. He wants to know more about what he needs to do to please God.

It is now 5:00 p.m. and Mary is so tired. She made over $1000 in tips, and she is happy. She has to hurry to pick up the children from sister's house. Her sister has to work tonight, and she wants her to watch her niece and nephew tonight. She wants to rest, but a promise is a promise. She has to make sure the children go to bed early.

Once she gets home, she will have to pay bills. She is so glad that God made a way out of no way, and because of it, she will pay a loan off. She remembers when Eric forced her to take out the loan she he could purchase a gift for his mother and buy himself a suit. She did not want the loan, but did it because it will allow her to pay her monthly rent. Because of terrible financial times, she fell behind. Her $100 balance quickly triples to $300. She will pay them today! "Thank you Lord for being so good to me!" she said through tears of joy.

Her family was so glad that she turned back to God. It is amazing that a person could grow up in the Church, learn about God, and then turn away from everything they had learned. They know it is possible because they saw it with their own eyes. They told her that they noticed she was aging, and now because Eric is no longer a part of her life, her appearance is becoming younger. Mary has a new look and walk since Jesus is now a part of her life, and the look and walk are spiritual. She did not change that much physically except she is smiling and laughing more. Even her continence is brighter, and she knows it is because of Jesus. Eventually, she knows she will return to her youthful appearance as she continues to walk with God. She is filled with the Holy Spirit and it shows throughout her entire being. Because they see God in her, they want to help her and they are willing for her to help them. She is grateful that her sister's house is within walking distance from her job.

Cory is still upset. He said in his heart that he will do whatever it takes to take his cousin down. He will not allow anyone to treat him that way. He is a preacher, and he should be treated well by everyone. He hopes to rule the world one day, and he hoped that his cousin would always remain by his side. He feels that he does not need God's permission to do anything because God gives all of us freedom to choose, and his choice is not to choose Him. He knows that God is all-powerful, but that power does not extend to him, in other words, God will not bother him. He believes in God, but he does not believe He is who He says He is in the Bible. He does not ever remembering God ever punishing him, and maybe that is the reason that he does not believe God will do it now. He decided that he would move forward with his plan to become the biggest and baddest pastor in the world. "Even more powerful than this so-called Jesus himself," he said to himself and truly believing it.

He takes offense to the fact that some may think of him as a false prophet. He believes that if he preaches from the Bible, at least a small portion from the Bible, although he is not called, then he should simply be called a preacher, just like anyone else. Yes, he called himself, but he also believes that he is doing God a favor by telling others about him. He does not have any regrets. He just wants to get paid.

Mary arrived at her sister's house and found her sister waiting for her with a smile on her face. She ran to meet Mary and gave her a big hug and kiss. Mary told her about her unusual day, and the amount of money she made in tips. Her sister reminded her that God would meet her needs in ways that are not normal to us. Sometimes He does not hand you things, but give you the opportunity to work for them.

Her sister knows this because she was once in a similar situation that Mary was in. She was addicted to men, and in some ways, she knows that she still is in bondage. She has not recovered, but she is better than what she used to be. She once believed that any man would do. But now, she thinks she found the right man, a man who will love her and her children. She stopped going to clubs a few years ago in hopes of finding a church going man. She prayed and asked God to straighten out her life, and God brought her out. She was doing so well. Because she was making it without a man, she moved up at work after finishing school, she bought a very nice home, and she lost weight and is looking good. She is happy that God also brought her big sister out too, and she knows that He is going to bless her. It was nice to have her sister again.

"Girl, you are really looking good!" her sister said to her with a big smile on her face and continued smiling and said, "After your divorce, you can date and get another husband." "I am not interested in getting another man right now Sis. God is perfectly capable of taking care of all of my needs, and right now, I need to heal." "I need to listen to God. I need to find out what He wants me to do. If God wants me to marry again, He will find a husband for me," Mary said. Her sister believes her, and she also agrees with her but she believes there is nothing like having a man around. Sure, she flourished when God delivered her from an abusive relationship, but now she found a man. While Mary talked, she remembered that she did not pray for God to put a man in her life. The man she is now with just popped into her life one day, and now she believes that he consumes most of her spare time. She hopes that she does not end up in the same shape she found herself in before. She wonders if it is too late to pray. To pray that God makes this man love Him, because she knows for sure that he does not want anything to do with God. She decided not to talk to Mary about this yet. She will choose the right time to introduce him to her family.

The children gathered their books and clothing, and Mary's sister dropped them off at the apartment. On the way there, she stopped and allowed Mary to run into the loan office to pay her bill. Mary offered her fare for dropping her off, which she gladly took because she gave her last dollar to the man that is now in her life. She lied and told Mary that she had to loan money to one of her friends.

When Mary walked into the apartment, she discovered that someone had left a note on the kitchen counter. She read it and discovered that Eric had signed the divorce papers and he will not interfere in her or the children's lives except to give her money to take care of them. Beside the note was Eric's key to the apartment. Eric took his clothes and left everything else. The person who wrote the note must have scared Eric to death, because she could not imagine Eric doing this on his own accord. Eric does not have one compassionate bone in his body, and it is not beneath him to try to make her and the kids suffer. He would have rather torch her and the children's belongings than to let her have them. She told the children to sit down at the table and finish their homework. Her sister gave them a snack, so they were not hungry but she knew it was a matter of time before the food dissolves in their stomach.

She decided to walk to the store to buy groceries. Because there are four children, she decided to take her cart to put the groceries in. She had enough money to buy lots of groceries but she also has other bills that are behind, including the rent. Since she accepted Christ, she put ten percent of her tips aside so she could pay tithes on Sunday. She is grateful to God! This is a new start for her, a brand new start.

When she arrived at the store, she discovered that the items she needed were on sale. "Another blessing from God," she thought and thanks Him for being a good Father. She purchased more items than she could fit into her cart. She asked the store clerk if he would call a taxi for her, and he said he would. She has never purchased this much food before. It was enough to last until the house is ready and have so much left over to take to the new house. She started praising God in line. She did not care what the others thought, this was something that was between her and God, and others were welcomed to join in if they wished. When the taxi arrived, she and he loaded the bags into the truck of the car, and some on the back seat. When they took the groceries up to the apartment, she noticed the children were asleep. They completed their homework and left it on the table for her to review. She put up the groceries, checked their homework, and then began to cook dinner before waking the children up. She wanted them to sleep throughout the night.

Sophie was so glad. It was time to go home. She plans to get some rest, and then go to the club. She knows the exact outfit she wants to put on tonight. She wants to party all night long and she is willing to spend as much money as necessary on her favorite mixed drinks, although she will leave the other money in her secret location. She plans to have a good time tonight, and as a matter of fact; she wants it to be the best time she has ever had.

She will not ask Maggie to go with her again. She believes the girl has lost her mind, and she does not want to deal with her issues because it will cause her not to have a good time. She believes Maggie looks at too much television and now she is seeing things that may or may not be there. What an imagination, or if she is seeing things, she wish she could see them also. She grabbed her purse and yelled good-bye. She walked to the curb and hailed a cab. It is amazing how things fall in place when she is ready to live it up.

She arrived at her apartment the same time Eric did. She noticed he was carrying a large garbage bag. "I hope he found a job! I know he does not plan to shack up with me," Sophie said to herself. She will not allow him to take advantage of her kindness. "Eric, what's in the bag?" she asked. "Clothes. It has been a tough day, but I do have a job, just in case you were wondering," he said and chose not to smile. "Do you know that woman hired people to make sure that I do not take items other than my clothes? They also made me sign divorce papers," he said showing her the wounds on her head. As soon as he said it, he thought about the divorce papers and the advantages of being a single and good-looking man.

Mary may have done him a favor after all. After he met Sophie, he remembered the fact that she had a problem with him being married. Since he signed the papers, she should know that the divorce would be final soon. He will soon be a free man, and he is available to marry her or should he say, her money. He can visualize turning her into his slave. She noticed that Eric had a smile on his face. "So, what are you thinking? You said your day was not pleasant, but you are now smiling. Why?" she asked and looking at him as if she had the ability to look at his soul. He lied and said he thought about how he missed her. She smiled. She does not know if she should believe it, but it still made her feel good. Deep down inside, she knows she wants someone to love her. "Were your dad glad to see you? I want you to tell me all about your day," she said smiling at him as the demon reminds her that Eric is a good-looking man. They walked upstairs, unlock the door and entered the apartment.

She was glad to be home. Eric laid the bag of clothes on the bed. He has enough clothes in the bag for a week. She wonders why he did not put them in a suitcase, and why he did not stay with his family. He walked into the living room, sat on the chair, and started telling Sophie everything. He studied her while he was recalling the events, and guessed that she was feeling sorry for him. He was fascinated because he did not feel that she possessed that type of feeling. To him, she is as hard as nails and he believes she is the ultimate challenge. She will do anything to get what she wants, and he knows he can only go as far as she will allow. If he goes beyond a certain point with her, she will have no problem throwing him out. If she makes him leave, he will move in with his parents. He always makes sure he has a ram in the bush. He will have to put up with their horrible attitudes, but at least he will have a soft bed to lay his head. He knows they will make him pay rent and buy groceries. After he finished, she told him they were going to the club tonight. She wanted to get some rest, and suggested he do the same.

She made it clear to him that he will not be left at her apartment alone. If she has to leave, he has to leave also. She told him that he must go soon, and she will remind him each and every day. She made it perfectly clear that he will not move into her new place. She will allow him to visit her every now and then but he will not become a permanent fixture in her place. He got the message, but he refuse to give up just yet. "How did I read this woman wrong? She did not feel sorry for me?" he thought to himself. "How can I be so wrong?"

She ate at the deli and she hopes he ate something before he came to her apartment, but if he did not, it's too bad. He is a grown man and she is not going to take care of him. She will treat him to the club tonight because she does not want to go alone. "Do you have any money?" she asked him, and she knows the answer but she wants him to say it. He told her he had some money, but not much of it. She was not surprised. "I will pay for your entry into the club tonight and will buy you a couple of drinks. There will be women and men there tonight, so I suggest you search for another sucker to support you," she said. "I don't do men," he said. "If I were you, I would be a little more open-minded. Why should you care about the sex of the person who is willing to sponsor you? Just because a person develops a relationship with someone of the same sex, it does not mean that they are one hundred percent gay. They could be curious or on the down low," she said. "You don't believe what you just said do you? If you are having a relationship with someone of the same sex, you are gay or homosexual. Don't believe the hype, it will only confuse you," he said. "Don't get Christian on me, you and I both know that nothing is off limits, absolutely nothing. Isn't that what your religion says? The Christians are hypocritical fools, and the rest of us are wise," she said. He decided to drop it. To him, she is stupid. What he said was not Christian knowledge. He was stating the facts. Some things are beneath him and what she is suggesting is definitely one of them.

They have been talking for hours, so they both decided to go to bed for a few hours. They plan to party until the wee hours of the morning. They have to go to sleep because they still have to function at work tomorrow morning.

Maggie just finished reading a chapter in the Bible and did not fully understand it. She was surprise that after she prayed for understanding, the meaning of what she read is now being revealed to her. She knows enough to know it is the Holy Spirit who is talking to her. This is the first time in her life that she is not lonely. It is amazing that you can be alone, but you are not alone. You can be by yourself and not be lonely. The presence of God is real. She refuses to be without the Spirit of God again. He is a wonderful companion, and she understands what it means when people say Jesus is all you need. She knows she still has so much to learn, but what a wonderful start. For the first time in her life, she does not need another human to interpret everything she reads. God is telling her what it means! She felt the Holy Spirit was telling her to go to bed. It is now thirty minutes before midnight. She decided to thank God and obey the Spirit of God.

Chapter Three

Tuesday

Cory woke up in a cold sweat. He had a horrible nightmare, and now that he is awake, it is still troubling him. He walked past a man who was crying out to someone about warning his four brothers so they do not come to the place where they are currently at, and as he looked around, he saw people in flames. People were burning, but not burning because they were not burning, but they were in fire. Then something chained him in the pit of hell. There were fire all around him, and people, including him, were screaming because of the torment. He and others were having a conversation with Satan, and every now and then, he would laugh at them. He explained to them how he deceived them into believing all of his lies. He members the devil telling him that he was a fool and that he was one of his best servants, and because he was so good, he got his just reward. Then the devil started laughing so loud that it shook hell. At that moment, Cory woke up. "Is hell real?" he asked himself and for the first time in his life, he was terrified. "Am I going to hell?" he asked himself, and then he heard a voice saying, "Oh no, my most precious and prized servant. You should surely not go to hell because I plan to use you for my purpose. You will be in the same place I will be at, and it is surely not hell. You continue to do what I tell you to do. This is what I want you to do, I want you to destroy your cousin and your pastor," the devil told him.

Maggie is now feeling a powerful electrifying sensation throughout her body. This is new to her, and she does not know what it is. Then all of a sudden, she was going through a dark tunnel and into a place that she did not recognize. She is now on the most beautiful grass she has ever seen and there were no weeds. She looked up and saw trees that she has never seen before. They were perfect, and as a matter of fact everything was perfect, it was as if she was in the Garden of Eden before sin entered into the world. Everything around her was beautiful and nothing was out of place.

She was so happy. She stood up and started walking and then all of a sudden, she was walking down the street. She was no longer in the Garden. She remembers seeing someone working on making a sidewalk after concrete was poured. She walked around it. She entered a house and started talking to the occupants. Everyone went to another room. The older lady was loading the clothes into the washing machine and ironing clothes. There were three children sitting on the couch. She recognized one of the children. Something was going on, and everyone started searching for a hiding place. It was as if it was the end of the world. She found a hiding place for the occupants but the old woman did not want to hide. She wanted to stay in the open. Either she has an agreement with evil beings, or she was not afraid of them or it. She recognized the old woman and believes she knows what was going on. The children were innocent, but the girl she recognized also was exposed to the occult. She felt she was there to save her from herself, and to hide her from evil. This girl is trying her best to find Jesus but does not know where to start her search. She experimented with the occult because she wanted to fit in with her associates. Now since she has children of her own, and is having a hard time trying to raise them, she is trying to seek Jesus and ask Him to help her raise her children. She needs guidance and she believes she is there to show her the way. After she hid them, she moved on to another house. As soon as she entered the house, she had to hide the occupants again. It appeared that they were after her so she had to find another place to hide to prevent them from going after others. After she left that house, she looked up and saw demons destroying every household, one by one. She continued to find hiding places for people and moved on to other houses. She finally arrived at a home that was already destroyed by the demons. There were people there and for some reason, they felt safe. They believed that because they destroyed all of the occupants, they will not return again. She realized that they had destroyed almost every home on earth. She woke up and prayed to God. She needs to know what this vision means. It was very disturbing, so much so, that she began to cry. She now feels at peace and tried to understand how something that is so perfect can be destroyed so quickly. She wonders if the place God took her to was the Garden of Eden. She walked out of it, and everything except the garden was full of sin because of Adam. She knows the devil will not stop at nothing in his quest to destroy every home on this planet. Our only defense is Jesus. Jesus is the only safe place. If a person does not accept Him, and everyone is raptured, there is no safe place to stay. After the rapture, Satan will not stop until Jesus returns again to destroy this wicked earth. She fell asleep again.

It is now three o'clock in the morning and the club is still crowded. Sophie knows she needs to leave but she does not want to. She is having so much fun. She is drunk and is barely able to stand up without assistance. What she does not see was the demons. There are ten of them sitting at her table and were constantly whispering in her and other people's ears. One of them told her to curse God and she did. Another demon told her to get up and slap the bartender. She got up and staggered to the bar. Because the club was crowded, she was not able to slap the bartender but she was able to give him a good tongue-lashing while leaning on the person who is in her way. He could not understand a word she was saying to him. There were only four of them in the club that were completely sober. It was beginning to be too rowdy, so the supervisor decided it was time to close the club.

It was as though everyone has lost their minds. They noticed that people was doing weird things. There is an older couple stripping in the middle of the dance floor. They are cursing and barking at each other and everyone else in the club. This is wild! Eric has never seen anything like this before. It is as if everyone has lost their minds! There were couples making out on and under tables as if they were in private rooms. Now, there are a few people taking out their guns and other weapons. It is becoming too dangerous for him. He loves to have a good time, but this is ridiculous.

Mary got up early to cook breakfast for her and the children. She also wanted quiet time. This was the first time she did not have to worry about Eric coming though the door. This was the first time in a long time that her money is where she left it. She was grateful that she was able to catch up on all of her bills, bought groceries, and still have money left. This is a first, and she knew it was God who did it. He performed another miracle. She decided to make pancakes and fry up some bacon. She stayed up late last night to read scripture from her Bible, and to clean her apartment. She feels well rested now and looks forward to going to work. The odors coming from the kitchen woke the children up and they ran to the kitchen. She made them turn around and go into the bathroom to take a wash off and told them to get dressed for school. She told her nephew to go first and told her daughters and niece to make their bed. When all of them finished, the food was on the table waiting for them. The children were so happy. This was the first time that her children thoroughly enjoyed their breakfast. They ate sausage, grits, eggs and bacon. It was nice to have something different to eat. They thanked their mother and her niece and nephew thanked her after they ate all of their breakfast. After they finished, they ran off to the bathroom to wash their hands and brush their teeth. It was time for the bus to arrive, and they made it to the bus stop just in time. Mary washed the dishes, tidy up the place and headed for work. She was still grateful and decided she will never go back to what she used to be. She welcomes the change and is looking forward to getting closer to God. She knows it will not be easy, but it is still better than being with Eric or anyone that will bring her down. She knows she deserves better, and she thinks God for the change. For the first time in years, things are looking up. She was moving backwards for so long, and for a period of time, she stood still, but now, she is moving forward once again.

Eric woke up and discovered he was lying in a pool of blood. The blood was coming from his head and the left side of his body. He is in pain. He looked around the club and saw others that were also injured. Sophie was leaning against the bar drinking a shot of whisky. She also had blood on her clothes but she looks weird. Her eyes do not look normal to him. The medics were tending to the people who had injuries that were considered more serious than his. He could not believe it. "What happened?" he yelled and looked around to see if he can find an answer. No one answered. Sophie staggered towards him, and when she reached him, she fell to the floor as if she was a blob of jelly. She was too drunk to sit down next to him, so she slouches over and lay down. She was too drunk to move, and when she did, all of her movement looks distorted. "You are drunk," he said looking at her with disgust written all over him. He managed to stand up, and pull her up too. He walked past several dead bodies. He wanted to get out of there as fast as he could. When he stepped outside, he saw many spectators. He needed a ride to Sophie's apartment right now. He needs to figure out what happen. Everything happened so fast. He knows Sophie is too drunk to remember. He grabbed her purse from off of her shoulder and started going through it looking for money. He did not have enough to take a cab. He found a little over a $100 and put some of it in his pocket. He knows she would not remember it. Besides, she just went though a traumatic experience that she would not remember. She is drunk. There were several cabs so he decided to take the first one. He got in the car, and the man told him to be careful. He did not want blood in his cab, and if there is blood, he will have to charge him extra for cleaning it up. Eric told him to take him home, and gave him Sophie's address. He found her key in the purse. He wished he had time to make an extra copy of it for himself.

He finally arrived at the apartment. He paid the cabbie and carried Sophie and her purse up to the apartment. As soon as he got inside, he dropped her on her bed and went to the bathroom to clean him up. Sophie's wounds were not as serious as his, but they were still wounds just the same. A bullet glazed her left temple, so he knows she will live. When he examined himself, he noticed the bullet also glazed his temple, but one went through his side. He was glad that it did not hit any organs or at least he hopes it did not hit any of his organs. He hurts but he knows he will also live. Being in the wrong place at the wrong time cost him dearly. He will have to explain this to his dad in a few hours. For now, he has to get some rest so he lay down next to Sophie in the bed after he took pain medication.

Thomas woke up early and thanked God for allowing him to see another day. He was grateful for another opportunity to store up more treasure in Heaven. He understands what it means to be Christ-like, and he must admit, it feels good. He no longer carries the burden of wondering what his family would do if they found out that he is a Christian. Unfortunately, they did as he expected. They hardened their hearts and disowned him. He was glad that Mary did not. God used him to bring Mary back into the family of God, and his nieces into the family. It was a wonderful experience, and seeing the entire restaurant coming together on one accord was great. As he meditates on the last couple of days, he wondered what Heaven would be like. He knows it is more wonderful than what the Bible describes. The Bible describes, but some things have to be seen because words are not able to capture its true essence. Being in the presence of Jesus is worth all of the hell he has to experience down here. He knows that Jesus will always protect him down here because it is a promise He made to all of God's children. God cannot lie, so He must keep His promises.

God took care of him all of his life. It's amazing to him that he practiced Christianity under his parent's nose. They did not have a clue, although he did not behave in a manner in which they behaved. He would disappear for hours and they thought he was at the club. They would have been upset if they knew he was attending church and revival services. "Isn't it ironic Holy Spirit?" he asked. "Godly parents would not want their child in the club, but his parents hoped he was going to the club rather than church," he said shaking his head back and forth.

He loves spending time in the Word before going to work. It helped him to concentrate on the Kingdom of God and reminds him that he must be an example for those who are lost in this place where they call home. He learned that this world is not his home. His citizenship resides in Heaven. He can endure all things that come up against him because he knows it is the Lord who strengthens him, but he is required to focus and not concentrate on the problem.

He finished studying some of the verses in the Bible and decided to cook breakfast before taking his shower. He usually takes a shower first, get dressed, and then cook breakfast. He has to get started right now, or he will be late for work. He also decided that he would not call his fiancé right now. He is bothered by what Mary said, and some of the things that he remembered. He cannot think about her right now, he has to hurry.

He has a big presentation to present to his senior management staff today. This is not an ordinary presentation, but one, which will make or break him and his staff. This presentation can cost him and others their careers if not done properly. He has to explain why they need his department. They are looking for a reason to keep his department and a reason not to contract their service out. There are so many others who want his department because they believe they can make it better by telling lies. They believe if he can make so much for the company by being honest, he can make so much more if he lies every now and then. Thomas refuses to lie to his investors. He already prayed and got his answer from God, so he will do exactly what the Holy Spirit tells him to do during the presentation. It can only go according to God's plan. He is prepared for whatever happens.

He arrived thirty minutes early, and has just enough time to setup the conference room. He added the finishing touches to the slides yesterday. He wanted the information to be as current as possible. He feels that his department is the reason why the corporation is doing well. His department was the only department that showed a profit for five consecutive years. He does not believe another company can do better. The problem they are having is that he is honest in all of his dealing, and he refuses to lie to their clients, which he believes it is the reason why business is increasing.

God revealed to Thomas their plan. What they propose is that Thomas steps down from his position and allow his assistant to take the lead for a year. The assistant is his number two men, and does not mind lying to clients. Because Thomas is his boss, he was not allowed to lie to their clients nor potential clients, which is what the

The Fullness Thereof

assistant made the managers aware of. He knows this man wants to be boss, and will do anything to achieve his goal because he told everyone that Thomas taught him everything he knows. Although it is a lie, he will let the board make the decision by presenting the facts. He will not destroy anyone's character by telling the board about something other than what value the department added to this corporation since he became leader.

He finished just in time and all of the employees and board members are beginning to come into the conference room. By the look on most of the employees' faces, he can tell that some of them have already decided to support the assistant. His secretary smiled at him, and then went over and hugged him. She held onto his neck and pulled him down closer to tell him to allow God to have His way during this unjust meeting. Maybe he needs to allow this guy to take the lead, and if he does, the corporation will lose money and business. He agreed with her, and told her that he will allow God to have His way. Everyone is now seated, so he decided to greet everyone and proceeded with his presentation.

During the presentation he noticed the board members nodding their heads in agreement. His department is a major player in the corporation, and is the only department that generated the target revenue. Not only did they make the target, they were well above it. He explained that each year, the number of clients they support more than doubled, and everything was done with the clients knowing everything. He explained that he dealt honestly and because of it, they trust him with their friends and family money. At the end of the presentation, some of his employees stood up and gave him a standing ovation. The board members and the rest of the employees remained seated with their arms folded across their chest. It was okay because he told the truth, and he knows that he did the right thing.

The assistant got up and talked to the board members. He explained that he can do better, and nothing was beneath him. He explained that he has the support of most of the employees and the board. At that point, Thomas looked at each of the board members, and when they looked by, they cast their eyes down. He knew that the assistant was telling the truth. These were the very men and women who said that they had his back. He is glad that he put his trust in God rather than man. The board then voted, and decided to give the assistant a chance. Thomas remained quiet.

They decided to keep Thomas and move him into another position in the company with the same salary. His secretary asked if she can be transferred with

Thomas and was told yes. They decided to create another department, which is similar to this department. Thomas will have to get clients. He is okay with it because He asked God to have His way, so he accepted everything that God allowed. It is amazing that the corporation will support evil rather than good. Then he remembered someone saying "Isn't the world strange? How they would rather do things that they know are wrong, and making others think it is the right thing to do. Things are becoming more evil every minute, so nothing should surprise us?" He has to agree. It did not totally surprise him but he had to admit that he is disappointed in them. He thought he had the support of most of his employees, but he found out today that only five of the thirty employees support him, and four of the five will not do it in pubic. He was glad that he would keep his salary. He was also grateful that he made investments and chose to pay everything off. He thanked God and sat down. The board members wanted everyone to hear each member of the board explain their individual decision. Each of them said the same thing, which was they believe the assistant has what it takes to make more money, so it would be wise to allow him to move the department forward. Each of the said they appreciate all of the accomplishments Thomas made in the past, and they thanked him.

Because the decision was effective immediately, Thomas had to pack up his things in his office and move them into a vacant nearby office. His secretary had to do the same thing. It did not take him very long, but he wanted to make sure the office was clean. He found the cleaning supplies and took his time to clean the vacated offices. His ex-assistant was pleased and told him that he will be glad to help him and to let him know that he is available for the asking. He told Thomas that they are now on the same level, and because he got closer and looked him in the eye, Thomas knew exactly what his intent was. Thomas responded by congratulating him and shaking his hand. He decided not to say anything else and released his hand. He turned around and left the office and took the cleaning supplies to his new office to clean it.

The new office was smaller but the view was nicer. He knows he has work to do and he will need the Holy Spirit to help him. He will continue to be honest in all of his dealings, and will require his employees to behave in the same way as he does. After he cleans the office, he plans to call human resources to start the hiring process. He was told that this department would be smaller, but just as important. He has authorization to hire 15 employees immediately, and it helps to know that he could still use most of the clients from the other departments because of the additional investments they were interested in. His former clients were looking for other places to grow their money and he now has a solution for them. He decided to get the ball rolling by asking his secretary to call them now. He wanted to talk to all of them at the same time. To his amazement, his secretary called all of them immediately, and all of the former clients were excited and wanted to talk to him in less than an hour. This will be the largest videoconference he has ever conducted. He is grateful that he is very familiar with their financial portfolio.

He went to the conference room to set up the videoconference with his secretary by his side. She has been a faithful employee to him and has been that mother figure that he badly needed. He knows she truly loves him and would often call him her son.

The videoconference went extremely well. He explained that he has to hire employees and told them about the department being new. He explained the fund to them and all of them were excited. They hated the fact that he will not manage their other accounts and thanked him for growing their money and being so honest. They know that this way of doing business was extremely rare. They thought he would fail initially, but was glad that he did so well at making them wealthier. They promised to follow him wherever he goes because he is their golden child. One of the clients told him that he reminds him of the stories they heard about Jesus. How he turned water into wine, and how Thomas turned their few dollars into millions, and Thomas told them that it is similar because it was Jesus who performed the miracle for them, and all of them laughed and thanked God. One of the clients said because he is a Christian, he knows God used him to make him rich so he could send all of his seed to college. He has not met some of them, but they fully trust him. His secretary told them that they do not need to fax their information; she will use the information that is already in their files. She was glad that she has not finished moving her items out of her office yet. She started copying all of the files immediately after the conference was over.

Everyone felt good about what they heard, and Thomas ended the conference by asking permission to pray, and they all agreed. After praying, he joyfully went back to his office and started cleaning it.

In a few hours, it will be as if he was always in this office. He decided to clean his secretary's office too. She was still in the copier room making a copy of each client's file. His former assistant and the rest of his former employees took the rest of the day off to celebrate their victory in overthrowing their "goody two shoes boss." It's a shame because they are the highest paid workers in the company because he took care of them. He was glad they left because he does not believe they would have allowed his secretary to make copies of the files although they are members of the same corporation. His former assistant is very selfish and would have preferred that his secretary create all of the files from scratch. He also did not want him to know that he will be using the same clients. God worked everything out, just like He said He would.

He wanted everything moved today, but he does not want his secretary to work late. She finally finished creating the folders and she put them in their new file cabinet. She returned the original files to their proper location. It pleased her to see that Thomas had moved all of her belongings and emptied out her desk drawers. She told him that she thinks he is an amazing young man. He almost finished putting all of her things away when she walked into the office. She hugged and kissed him, and told him that she never had a boss like him. It was because of him, she decided to go to Church a few years ago. She decided earlier today that she would do what is right at all cost. She realized that what she did today was risky, but she did it, and still have a job. He is her example and she decided that the clients were right. Thomas is a godly man. She will follow God, no matter what, and as what she witnessed today, she knows that God will take care of those who refuse to do wrong or side with wrong.

Eric woke up in pain; in fact it was excruciating pain. He was not sure if he was glad to be alive. He needs medical attention immediately, for he fears that if he does not get antibiotics in his system right away, he may get an infection that will kill him. He decided to call his dad. He is not feeling well and he is afraid of dying. His dad picked up on the first ring.

"Dad, do I have health insurance?" he asked and his dad heard the desperation in his voice. His dad said yes, and wanted to know the reason for his question. Eric explained that someone at the club shot him early this morning. He did not get into the ambulance because he did not know if he has insurance. Because he has to pay child support, he does not want to risk missing a payment for obvious reasons. The consequences were too great. He told his dad that he would go to the hospital first, and then come to work. He told him where the injuries were, and explained that he was in pain. His dad gave him all of the information he needed to receive care. He told him not to worry about anything. He wanted to know if Eric wanted him to come to the hospital and Eric told him no. If he has to be hospitalized, he promised to call and let his dad know.

After he hung up, he walked over to the bed to check on Sophie. She was waking up, and is a little confused. He knelt down by the bed because it was painful to sit down. He asked her if she remembered anything. She remembered very little because she was very drunk. She does not remember much of anything so Eric told her what he remembered. She rubbed her hand over her wound, and she realized that Eric was telling the truth about being shot in the club. She asked for her purse and he gave it to her. She opened it and found money. She closed it and lay back down. She decided that she would call in sick today. Her head is hurting, and she does not believe she could function at work very well.

Eric decided to walk to the hospital because if he called a cab, he would have to sit down. It took him over an hour to walk to the hospital, but he made it. If he were not wounded, it would have taken less than fifteen minutes. He had to stop and rest along the way. He walked through the emergency room doors, and walked up to the receptionist. She asked him to fill out the required paperwork and as soon as he completed it, she hand it to the nurse. The nurse took his vitals and took him to see one of the doctors. The doctor heard about the shooting because others arrived in the very same condition as Eric was in.

The doctor started asking Eric questions with regards to what went on at the club and Eric answered him to the best of his knowledge. The doctor explained that he used to go to the club, but soon realized that it was not a safe place to be. He asked him if he has children and Eric told him that he has two daughters.

He let the doctor know that he rules his house and if he wants to party, then he will party and no one can do anything about it. To make a good impression on the doctor, he told him what he should do to his wife to make her more submissive. The doctor asked him what planet he came from. He considers his wife to be a queen and a gift from God. He would not dare lay a hand on her, and will not allow anyone to lay a hand on his daughter. The doctor told him that if his daughters marry a low life like him, he would gladly serve time for murder.

After the doctor examined and treated his wounds, he told Eric to go to the pharmacy to pickup his prescription immediately before he kills him himself. Some of the other staff members heard Eric bragging and came over to introduce themselves to him. These guys told him what they wanted to do to him, and how they plan to carry it out. Eric decided that he had enough and felt a strong urge to get away from these people. The doctor yelled and told him to take all of the antibiotics to ensure that there is no infection as Eric was running out of the Emergency Room towards the pharmacy.

Eric thought about the club, and wonders how they can kill without cause. He hopes those doctors were not serious about killing him and making it look like an accident. Unfortunately, he forgot about killing people and animals just because he was bored and needed something to do. He forgot about the innocent people he killed, those who came back without having the right amount of money. He forgot about his recent killing of a man who could not pay for drugs. Eric felt he is the only one justified in his killings.

He refuses to stop going to the club, but he will make sure he carries a piece the next time. The club is a wonderful place to find beautiful and lonely women who are willing to take care of men. If Sophie kicks him out, or does not allow him to move in with her, he has to find another woman who he can easily charm into becoming his slave. Preferably a nice looking woman, with money, and a nice place to live. There are so many suckers to choose from, which makes him grateful that he looks good. A man that is not attractive will need money to attract women. It is so easy to find a stupid woman, but it takes more to find a smart one. He wants someone who would prefer that a man lie to them rather than tell her the truth, which makes them easy prey for a predator, such as himself.

He is still sore, so he decided to walk to his dad's business. He will tell his dad that he will not be able to lift heavy items because of his injuries. He is not concern that his dad will fire him. He wants him to run the business one day, so he believes he has the advantage. He believes he has the ability to make this business big one day. He does not fully know how yet, but he knows he will not involve any mobster type people. One day, he will not depend on women for his survival. He thought of Mary when he had that thought. He will continue to use them because to him, all women are dumb. Every now and then he runs into one who will not give him the time of day, and will not allow any man to use them. He is not talking about those women.

His dad was outside when he walked onto the property. He looks very concerned and ran to meet his son. He wanted to know everything the doctor said, and Eric told him everything. He told Eric to go to the house and lay down for a few hours. He will wait until he heals, but he wants him here every business day. Eric agreed and felt the pain return. He went into the house, greeted his mom, took a couple of pain pills and the antibiotics, and went to bed.

The Fullness Thereof

Mary arrived at work thirty minutes early. As soon as she walked through the door, her supervisor asked her to clock in and help her in the kitchen. She believes it will be a day just like yesterday. She told her that there were various conferences going on in the area. Mary put on her apron, washed her hands, and went to work preparing the breakfast meal. It blows her mind when she thinks of the amount of bread this business buys daily. The bread she bakes tastes so much better than the bread she purchases. She believes if she goes into business for herself, she can sell her bread without any problems. She can wake up very early in the morning, and be finished before noon. She can also close on Sundays and some holidays. She can also spend more time with her children. She is no stranger to hard work. As a matter of fact, she discovered that hard work keeps her from dwelling on negative things. She hopes to one day open up a neighborhood bakery. Maybe God will allow her dream to come true.

As soon as she finished with the eggs, she noticed the dining area was filling up. She took off her apron, washed her hands, and pick up a pad so she could take orders. It looks as if it is going to be another busy day. She was grateful that most of the customers are friendly. If she makes as much as she made yesterday, she could start buying nice things for the house. She wants to also save most of the money. She is tired of being broke all of the time, and she thanks God that she does not have to worry about Eric stealing her money. It was very difficult to feed the kids when he was around. She often wonders how a husband and father can behave like he does. It does not bother Eric when his friends tell him that he should be a shame of himself. They talked to him and told him that he should be the breadwinner, but he refuses to work. "Why should I work?" he often said believing that she was the fool, and not he. She has to work fast because more customers are coming in through the front door.

Sophie woke up feeling awful. Her head has never felt this bad before. She was accustomed to having hangovers, but a hangover and a head wound at the same time is something that is undesirable. She believes the only remedy for this is to die or pass out. It hurts to lift her head. She needs the strongest medication, and she needs it now. If only she had a pistol, she would end her life right now in order to get rid of this pain. She opened her eyes and believed she saw something. It was so pale and ugly that it frightened her. She closed her eyes and opened it again and she did not see it. She believes it is because of her wound and told herself that she is seeing things. Now, she is hearing things too. One of them is telling her to jump out of the window. She is beginning to hear many voices, and they all are talking at the same time. They are talking very fast, and she is not able to understand what all of them are saying, however, she is able to understand a few of the words. The voices are telling her to kill herself! She can barely lift her head up from the pillow, but she managed to walk to the bathroom to try to get away, believing if she goes in there, they would leave her alone. When she entered the bathroom, and closed the door behind her, and heard a voice telling her to fill up the tub with hot water and jump in it. She started yelling and told it to shut up. Another voice told her to fill up the sink with water and wash her face by submerging her head under the water and keeping it there. She put her hands over her ears. She ran to the bed and fell down, but she continued hearing voices. She doesn't know what to do to get them to stop talking. She wants them to stop right now. Why won't they stop? She started crying, and while she was crying, the pain increased significantly. She finally passed out but the demons continued talking to her as she slept, and because of it, they were influencing her dream because she is now having a nightmare.

Stephen stayed up most of the night talking to God, and he is so glad that he did. He wanted to know more about what God is planning to do with regards to his ministry. God revealed some of it to him, and he is so grateful for the fact that God would even talk to him. Every time he thought of it throughout today, he felt joy that an awesome God would even talk to one of his creatures. God revealed to him that he will be used in a mighty way, and that he will reach so many people. He plans to use him in the television ministry, so Stephen knows without a shadow of doubt, that he must be developed. He plans to talk to his pastor about attending seminary because he realized that he is about to go into something that will cause him to be tested beyond measure. Something that can cause him to send a babe in the wrong direction if he truly does not know what he is talking about, so in order to help those who God will send his way, he must gain much knowledge. He must do this right away because he feels that God will perform it in a very short time.

He does not know how God is going to do this, or which doors God will open for him, but he can't help himself by becoming joyful at the thought of being used by God. He plans to work hard, realizing that everyone that is added because of what he says will cause him to get an extra star in his crown. All of Heaven rejoice over one person being saved, and he plans to cause Heaven to rejoice often, with the help of the Holy Spirit.

The only problem is that he does not feel that he is the best one to do this. Cory has the ability to woo the crowd, and Joseph has the ability to do anything, but he is a sinner saved by grace, and does not feel that he measures up, but God told him that all he has to do is to depend on and trust in Him. He has to put all of his trust in God, and allow Him to lead and direct his every step, and he knows that in order for him to be a success, God has to do it all through him.

He cannot believe that a few days ago, his thoughts were not on God, but after that awesome Spirit-filled sermon, all he could think about is God. He fell on his knees and cried out to God, thinking him for giving him another chance to work for Him, and for His grace and mercy. He is so glad that God is not man, because if He were, he would have been dead for his disobedience. He thanked God for restoring him back to where he was before he fell for Satan's tricks. He knows that Cory will never understand, but he will try to explain it to him anyway. He will continue to love and pray for his cousin realizing that Cory is one of the most dangerous false prophets that were ever born. He knows what his cousin is capable of, so he must warn his pastor.

He dialed his pastor number, and was surprised when his pastor answered the phone. "Hello, this is Watkins," said his pastor. "Hello Pastor Watkins, this is Stephen. First, I want to thank you for talking to me after church, I really appreciate it. I need to talk to you about Cory, if I may." "Stephen, you do not need to tell me anything about Cory because I already know. God talks to me about the flock that He put me in charge of, and he told me what to do with regards to him, but I appreciate your concern," said Pastor Watkins, and they said their goodbyes and hung up the phone. Stephen felt relieved.

As soon as Thomas walked through the door of his apartment, he went into his room and knelt beside his bed. He wanted to talk to God, and to thank Him for all that He has done for him today, yesterday, tomorrow, and the days after that. He talked to God throughout the day, but there was something special about getting on his knees and humbling himself before his almighty God. He was so amazed at how God worked everything out, and He did it so quickly. He was so thankful that he did not interfere with what God was doing, because if he had done so, he knew he would have messed everything up. He was willing to let the chips fall where they may, and they did. He knew that whatever happens, God was in control. He knew that God would make the impossible possible. God is the Alpha and Omega, the beginning and the end, and he wanted to let Him know that He is his all and all, forever and ever. He is so glad that he learned to put all of his trust in the Lord years ago. As he was praying to God, he began to feel something he has never felt before. He was feeling this wonderful sensation all over his body. It was a wonderful tingling type of sensation, something that is not easily explained. He noticed that his fingers were beginning to go numb as his conversation progressed with God. He started praising God more because he knew He was listening to him. He then began to talk to God about his childhood, and asked Him questions, and to his amazement, God started answering him. Thomas was so caught up in the Spirit, that he found himself not wanting his conversation with God to end. God told him that He is available all day, every day and night, every day of the week. He was so happy to hear this, and he wants to remember this, especially when things are not going well. He realized that God was there all along, He saw everything that has happened to him, and all he had to do was talk to the only One that was there from the beginning of time. God was waiting for him to talk to Him, but he did not know it. He was so overjoyed, before he knew it, many hours have passed, and he thanked God for everything again. This was the best experience he has ever had. As he climbed into bed, he continued to talk to God. His conversation continued while he slept.

 Mary's day was similar to yesterdays, except she made more money in tips. She was tired but she is very happy. As she walked down the street towards her sister's house, she noticed that all of the kids were outside. Usually they were in the house doing their homework or eating a snack. As she neared the house, they saw her and ran to meet her. She hugged and kissed each of them. She asked if they finished their homework, and they told her no Ma'am. She asked why, and one of them told her that they were told to go outside and play. Mary told her she couldn't believe her aunt told her that. She told her that it was not her aunt, but the man in the uniform who told all of them to go outside, and to not to come back in the house until he calls them. The children told her that they did not eat a snack either. This was not like her sister. She can't image her sister allowing any man to tell the children to go outside without first doing their homework or eating. They have been out of school for a couple of hours now, and she knows they are hungry. There must be a good explanation for this, but she could not think of one right now, except she is being forced to do something against her will.

 She walked up the stairs, to the door and turned the doorknob. The door was locked. She decided that it must be an accident. What if one of the children had to use the bathroom? An ugly thought popped in her head, and she thought to herself that her sister better not be doing what she thought she was doing. How can someone put a man before their children? Although she married the devil himself, she still did not put him before her children because he was a bad man. Her sister is not married to this man, so why should she put someone over her children, unless she is born stupid. And as soon as she thought that thought, she remembered her sister's past. She will put a man in front of her children. She hoped that she learned her lesson, but she guessed she did not.

She walked to the back door and it was open, and she did not see anything unusual. At that moment, she realized that she was not prepared if her sister were being robbed or raped at gunpoint. She is glad that she told the children to continue playing outside. She walked into the kitchen and saw snacks on the table. She heard music, and it sound like it was coming from the bedroom. She walked into the living room and noticed a pair of men shoes on the floor beside the couch, but still, there was no sign of a struggle. She walked towards the bedroom, and as soon as she was about to put on hand on the doorknob, the door suddenly opened and her sister came out of the room and closed the door behind her. She cursed Mary out and told her that if the front door was locked, she should not have come in through the back. She told her that she would not have done that to her. She did not give Mary a chance to say anything, not even to apologize. She told Mary to get her children things and get out of her house at that very moment. She said that what she does in her house was nobody business except her own.

Mary picked up her daughters' book bags and asked if she would like for her to take her children over to her house as well. She had to raise her voice to talk over her sister. She told Mary yes through clinched teeth, and it was obvious that she was furious. Mary grabbed all of the book bags and opened the front door and walked out. She then turned back and said, "I wanted to call you, but I did not know what type of situation you were in. I felt the element of surprise was best because both of us could overpower any man. I did not want to think that you would do this with your and my children outside. You did not even have the decency to give them water or let them use the bathroom before allowing a man to make them go outside so both of you can sleep together. I am sorry for disturbing you, so good-by." She closed the door behind her and walked down the steps. She did not bother to ask for clothing because the clothes the kids had on yesterday was still at the apartment. She will have to wash them tonight. She decided that she would have to pray for her sister because she has lost her mind once again. She also decided that she would not allow her kids to go over to her house tomorrow, or anytime soon. She will enroll them in the after school care tomorrow morning.

She feels sorry for her niece and nephew. She will call her mom tonight and ask her to watch over her sister's children. She will tell her mom what she witnessed and will give her only the facts. She does not know what is going on, so she will keep her opinions to herself. She does not know who the man is, and this is the first time her niece and nephew saw the gentlemen. They said their mother never did this before, although she talked on the phone for hours. They also saw her leave at night, and return early in the morning on numerous occasions. Mary was not aware of this. She was too busy with her own problems and if she had witnessed it, she probably would not have noticed it. She was sinking fast in quicksand, and needed help. God pulled her up out of the mess that she found herself in, and she knows he will have to do the same thing for her sister. She is going down the wrong road, and her sister should know better because she went down that road before, but this time it was different.

When she got outside, the children wanted to know what was going on. She told them that she does not know much, and that she wanted to take them home so they can eat and do their homework. She felt she told the truth because she does not know exactly what was going on with her sister, only God knows for sure. She and the children rushed to the bus stop as the bus was coming up the hill. They made it to the bus stop just in time to board. Mary was tired and concerned about her sister, but there is nothing she can do other than pray. All she wanted to do tonight was rest and read her Bible, but instead, she has to take care of two additional children.

She was grateful that God worked it out that she made so much money in tips yesterday and today. She is not going to buy any more groceries because she did that yesterday. She will have to wash clothes so her niece and nephew will have clean clothes to wear tomorrow. The laundry room is located on the first floor, which makes her a little nervous. There is so much crime in this neighborhood, but all she has to do is watch and pray. While the children do their homework, she plans to go downstairs to wash and dry clothes, and study her Bible. She wants to wash all of the dirty clothes, so she will make them take a bath first and put on their nightclothes, which consists of her t-shirts. She cooked so much food yesterday so she has plenty of leftovers. She will heat them up while she sorts clothes. Instead of giving the children snacks, she will feed them dinner. She wants to go to bed early tonight because she is very tired, and she believes tomorrow will also be another busy day.

It took over twenty minutes to get home, but she noticed the laundry room was empty and she was glad. She only hopes it stays that way. She and the children walked up the steps to the apartment and as soon as she opened the door, the phone began to ring. She picked it up and talked to her sister. Her sister apologized for her behavior, and said she should not have reacted that way, but Mary left her no choice. She explained to Mary that she has not had a boyfriend in months and she really like this man, and that he is going out of town tomorrow and she wanted to spend time with him. Mary continued to listen while her sister tried to justify her actions. She said she met him a couple of weeks ago and found him to be a nice looking man. She likes the fact that he treats her so well, and she hopes that he gets to know her children and treat them like his own. She said he will move into her house this weekend, and that she knows the family will have a problem with it but, as she stated earlier, she is an adult. She continued and said that she has always done what she thought was right, and only made a few mistakes, and this was her time to do what she wants regardless of what she and her mom think. She wants to make her own mistakes now, and if she falls, she hopes that they are there for her. She feels that this is a chance to be happy, and he makes her happy. She said he is willing to help her take care of her children, so she wants him to move in so she could have a family of her own. She still had not given Mary a chance to say a word.

She asked Mary not to tell the rest of the family, and finally, Mary was given the opportunity to tell her that she must tell their Mom tonight, and if she does not, she will tell her what she saw, no more and no less. She continued and told her that she can do whatever she wants to do, but she will not sit back and do nothing, especially if she thinks the children are suffering. She reminded her that she is married to someone who looked like a knight in shining armor in the beginning, and it did not take long for him to show his true self. Mary warned her by asking her to not allow this man to move in until she can at least get his social security number so she can do a background check on this guy. She advised her to remain friends and give their relationship time to grow. She told her to ask his family and friends questions, and to find out that his ex-girlfriends were and to talk to them. She told her to do this for her children's sake.

Her sister told her she would do it, but Mary knew she was lying. Mary told her that he could molest, rape and kill the children, and by moving this unknown man in, she was putting two innocent and helpless children in danger because of her lust. She knew that her sister did not want to hear this, but she did not care any longer. To ensure she will call her Mom, Mary told her to hold on and called her mom, then Mary conference in her sister. "Okay Sis, I got Mom on the phone," Mary said and waited patiently for her Mom and her sister to talk.

Mary allowed her sister to tell Mom what she told her. It surprised her that Mom did not have much to say, but she told her daughters to be careful. She told them that they know the difference between right and wrong and that one day, they will have to stand before Jesus to explain things. She told them that they alone are responsible for their actions, and if they make the wrong choices, it could have a major impact on their children. She told Mary that she was glad that she is turning things around and is allowing herself to be led by the Holy Spirit. She told her other daughter that she knows there are very tempting things in the world but she must resist them, because the Bible said to be friends with this world is to be an enemy of God.

She then explained that she did so many things that she was not proud of, and one of the biggest mistakes she made was to allow a man to move into her house who she was not married to. She said he was handsome and because she wanted a man so badly, she allowed him to do whatever he wanted in order to keep him. She told her daughters about all the things that she went through, and all of the things that she allowed. She went further to tell them that they once had two other sisters and she heard her daughters sigh. The man that she allowed to move in raped and killed her two precious daughters. Mary and her sister were shocked because they did not know this, and they always thought their mom was a perfect Christian. She told them about the other failed relationships and repeated failures regarding men, even after her daughters were killed, and what happened when she was strung out on drugs and hit rock bottom. Her family refused to help her and wrote her off as being without hope because they thought she would cause them to suffer by constantly stealing from them to support her habit. They allowed her and her babies to sleep on the street rather than sleep under the roof of their doghouse. Her parents did not want to have anything to do with her children after the first two died. She explained that she went from shelter to shelter and when there was no room, how she and they slept under bridges or anything that provided some sort of shelter against the elements.

Then one day, she asked a stranger for help and she took her to her church. That was the first time she heard about Jesus. She admitted that she went to church but she did not listen to what was being preached because she did not understand what they were talking about, and then all of a sudden, she asked for help and she got spiritual help. She accepted Jesus and although she needed financial help, she found out that she had all of the help she needed over a period of time. Jesus was the only one she could rely on and because of it; she was listening to what He had to say every time she attended church service.

God made a way for her to work as a maid and for a few years, she lived in an apartment over the garage of this particular family house. She went on welfare because the wages was low but they provided rent-free living for her and them. And at that moment, the daughters realized that they were the babies that were rejected by their family members. She went to school and the professors allowed her to bring them with her to class, and it was at this moment that Mary's sister interrupted her mom and asked about their biological dad. She told them that because of the experience with their older sisters, she did not want them to be around any men. She eventually married her youngest daughter's dad, and the last time she heard, she said Mary's dad was doing well, and that he tried to find her. She then began to cry because she realized that Mary did not have the opportunity to know her dad, and as she reflects on her past, she knew that he was a good man. She wiped the tears from her eyes, and continued telling her story to her daughters.

During that time, people helped people so she did not have to rely on one particular man for help because the entire community helped each other. Some of the people in class bought their older children with them, and they helped with the younger ones. Most of the time, she provided sandwiches or whatever she made before class. That was how they supported each other during that time.

"God touched all of our hearts. After two years, I became a registered nurse. I went to work after I got off and got home just after midnight. I dropped the both of you off at one of my friend's house so their daughters could take care of you while I was away at work, and that was the way we did it back in those days. I did not have any savings so I had to keep my job as a maid until I could find a place I could afford. I paid the girls to take care of you, so it took me an additional year to save up enough money to move into an apartment," she said with a smile on her face because she was allowed to look back to discover how far God has brought her. Then through tears, she said, "If I had not accepted Jesus many years ago, I don't know what would have happened to me or the both of you. So, please keep close to God. You don't want to go though what I went through. The key is to put God first, and unfortunately Martha, you are putting that man first."

After Mom finished, Mary saw her mom in a totally different light. She did not have a clue as to what her mom was like as a child or adult. She was glad that the family eventually embraced their daughter after many years, but her sister said she still wants to give this a try, which surprised Mary. Her mom and Mary vowed to never turn their backs on her, but they will not uphold her in her wrongdoing. They told her that they would always pray for her and the children. Mary told her that her nieces would not go to her house after school starting tomorrow, and she will enroll them in the after school care program tomorrow morning. She continued and told her that she promise to pickup her nephew and niece every now and then. Her sister understood and told her that she loves them. Mom and Mary told her that they love her too, and they hung up the phones.

After their conversation ended, Mary told the children to take their baths. She told the girls to go into the bathroom with their nightclothes. They did as they were told. They jumped in the shower and Mary picked up their dirty clothes. After they finished, she told her nephew to take his nightclothes in the bathroom with him, take off his dirty clothes, crack the door of the bathroom open and throw them out. She separated the clothes while the food was heating up on the stove. After the food was sufficiently heated, she fixed the children a plate of food, and told them to sit down and eat. After eating, she told them to finish their homework. They did most of it while she was on the phone. She told them not to let anyone in the house, and that she was going to go downstairs to do the laundry. She locked the door behind her and took the dirty clothes and her Bible to the laundry room.

On her way there, she reflected on what her mother said. She was not aware of her mother's past. She has childhood memories but thought they were false. She remembers when she married her dad, but she always thought he was her biological father, now she knows the truth. She loves her dad, and he never made her feel less important than her sister. He showered her and Martha with lots of love.

She now understands why her mom behaves the way she does. A little knowledge makes it all make sense. How she made sure they went to church and how she constantly told them to stay close to God no matter what. She often told her to take

The Fullness Thereof

her grandchildren to church, Sunday school and Bible study so they will grow up knowing the difference between right and wrong. Now she knows why her mom was so persistent about doing the right thing. She was glad her mom told her about her past because now, she knows that her mom understands the struggles that she went through with Eric. She was very grateful that she could relate to it because she also reached out to Jesus and accepted His free gift of salvation. She plans to talk openly to her children about the goodness of God, and the importance of having a relationship with Him rather than trying to find love in other places. She often said, "No one can ever love you as much as God loves you." She knows that this world, in which she lives, is so wicked, and if it were not for the Holy Spirit, life on this planet would consume everyone. This planet would be one hundred percent wicked if it was not for the Holy Spirit. Mary will pray for her sister as often as she thinks of her. She is looking forward to reading her Bible and was still glad that the laundry room was still empty because when it is quiet, she can hear God so much easier.

Cory woke up late and found the bed empty. He propped himself up to look at the clock and was surprised to find out that he slept for a very long time, and for some reason, he does not remember much. It was after 7:00 p.m. It is a good thing that he does not have a real job because he is pretty sure he would be fired right about now. He turned on the lights and reached for the glass that he was drinking from, and saw some type of power-type substance around part of the rim. He tried to think of what it could be, and then all of a sudden, he remembers that woman that he invited in got up and said she was going to pour him some juice. "Boy, was that juice powerful," he said a little above a whisper. He is beginning to feel weak, but he needs to use the bathroom badly. He finally made it to the bathroom, and after he finished, he noticed that there is blood in his urine. He flushed the stool and went over to the bed and sat down He does not know what to do, so he reached for the phone, and as he put it to his ear, he noticed that it was silent. He began to panic, and as he stood up again, he had to sit down right away. He is too weak, so he was forced to lie down.

Sophie woke up and noticed the house was dark and scary. She can see movement. They were moving fast, and were quickly multiplying. She remembers what Maggie said about the demons she saw in the club, and now she is afraid. She felt for a familiar body next to hers and became concerned because she did not feel one. She wondered where Eric was. Her head was still hurting, but at least she is no longer hearing the voices. She only wished that she did not see anything. She cut on the light and reached for the phone, and called Eric's parents house, his mom told her that Eric was there, and he was sound asleep. She does not want him to get up and leave because of his injuries. She understood and felt a little guilty because she wanted him there to take care of her. She did not realize that Eric was severely wounded until now. She thought he had a flesh wound just like hers, and it was not until now that she discovered that he was shot twice. After their conversation ended, she got up and made herself a sandwich. She still feels off balance and was careful not to walk very fast for fear of falling and being unable to get up. She walked back to the bed with her sandwich and began to eat it slowly. She is glad that she no longer sees things.

She grabbed the remote control and turned on the television hoping to find out what happened because she still does not know. The nightclub experience is still a blur to her. She wished she could remember. She knows that it was a weird night, and she thinks she remembers hearing someone tell her to do things. She watched the news hoping to find out what went on at the club. After the news went off, she turned the television off and decided to go back to sleep because she missed most of the news. All of a sudden, she started hearing loud voices telling her to kill herself. They told her to go into the kitchen, grab a knife, and to stab herself in the heart.

Cory had to get to the other phone because he felt his life slipping away more rapidly now. He knows that if he does not get help soon, he will not see tomorrow morning, at least that is what he is feeling right now. He inched his way towards the end of the bed, and then fell off of it. He crawled slowly to the living room, which seemed to have taken hours, and when he got to the phone, he pulled it down. He was glad to hear a dial tone, and then he dialed 911. The lady answered, and he was able to whisper, "Help me please," just before he passed out.

Mary loaded the clothes into the washing machines, sat in the chair and prayed. She prayed that God would reveal His truths to her as she reads the Bible once again. She wants to know the truth so she can do better. She wants to be a godly example to her daughters and everyone that is around her. Like so many others, she realizes that she does not know anything about God, because the more she learns, the more she realizes that she needs to learn. She understands some things but she realizes that it is not enough to make a difference in her life, which is what she believes. She loves God with all of her heart, mind, soul and strength. She wants Him to watch over and care for her and her entire family all of the time. She vowed to keep her children in Sunday school, church, and Bible study so they can learn about Him. She knows that Jesus used scripture to fight the devil, and when Jesus returns after the rapture, He will use scripture to destroy His enemies. She and her family must learn scripture before it is everlasting too late. She is looking forward to Jesus' second return. She wants to be raptured and wish that it could be right now until she thought about her sister. "What if Jesus comes and she is in the club? Will she be raptured?" she thought. She is tired, so she finished her prayer and opened the Bible and began reading the book of Romans. As she began to read, she felt the presence of the Holy Spirit. He was teaching her scripture! She remembers a scripture, which says, "You have not because you ask not, and when you ask you ask amiss." She asked God for help and she is receiving it right now. Eternal life and life in Christ is great!

Sophie's head felt as if it was going to explode. She went into the kitchen and picked up the knife as she continued to hear voices telling her to stab herself, repeating those words as if the record is scratched and the recording continues to go to that very same spot. She does not want to do it, but the voices are so persistent. She screamed and told them no, and as she was screaming, she noticed that she is hearing more voices as if the entire apartment is filled with people. Some of them are saying "stab yourself in the heart," some are saying "stab yourself in the eye," and others are telling her to stab other parts of her anatomy. She was making so much noise that it woke Maggie and her other neighbors up. Sophie was obedient to the evil spirits and began to stab herself in her arms and legs. The voices continued, and got louder and louder, as if someone was turning up the volume on her radio. As the voices became stronger, she stabbed herself believing she was having fun by competing for a major acting role in a horror movie, as if she was not aware that the blood that was coming from her body was real. From the looks of things, if she were nominated for an academy award, she would surely win, but in reality, she was losing her life force and if help does not arrive right away, she would be among the dead in less than ten minutes. She thought she heard a knock at the door, and because she was so weak, she was not able to answer it.

"Sophie, are you alright?" yelled Maggie while knocking on her door. The other neighbors were also in the hallway. Maggie turned the doorknob and the door opened. She could not believe it! There were so many demons in that apartment! They were packed as if they were sardines in a can. The neighbors and the building superintendent rushed in to try to stop her from killing herself. As Maggie was standing in the hallway looking at all of the demons, she noticed that they were getting into some of the residents and they began to look weird and say things that they should not say.

All of a sudden, an older lady grabbed her hand and told her to walk with her into the apartment. She told Maggie that the Lord wants her to cast out the demons. She told her not to be afraid because she has help, and for some strange reason, Maggie was not afraid. She entered the apartment with the holy lady, and they began to pray to God the Father. Both of them had their arms extended out before them telling the demons to go back to the pit of hell in the name of Jesus. The apartment began to become more chaotic than before, and Maggie and the lady continued to pray to the Father in the name of Jesus, and then all of a sudden, the demons disappeared. Maggie and the lady embraced. She was exhausted and she felt strange. The lady told Maggie that it is normal. Once the Holy Spirit fills you to this magnitude, it takes a little while to become normal again.

They walked over to Sophie and began to pray over her. She told Maggie that it is now time to heal Sophie, and if they do not pray for her, she will die right now. In the background, they heard sirens and they knew the paramedics were on their way. Her wounds were extremely severe and she noticed that she lost so much blood. It was as if all of her blood was on the floor. The lady reached into her pocket and pulled out her bottle of oil. She told Maggie to anoint Sophie with the oil and pray over her. Because Sophie was passed out, they became her intercessors and anointed themselves before they prayed for her.

Maggie saw the Lord healing Sophie. She believed that the Lord would heal her, but to witness it is something else. She saw her arteries mend back together. She saw blood flowing through her veins again. Why God chose to use her, she does not know, but to be used in this way is awesome, and as a matter of fact, to be used by God is a total blessing.

She knew the healing power of God because he healed her grandmother of cancer. Her grandmother was given two weeks to live, and once God healed her, He told her to go back to the doctor. Her doctor ran test after test and found nothing. That was ten years ago, and her grandma is in perfect health. It was her faith that made her grandma whole. Maggie knows that if Sophie were awake, she would not have had the faith that is required to be healed, because she is an unbeliever. She believes God has plans for Sophie because He chose to heal her, and she thanked God for giving her another chance. She heard the paramedics coming into the room.

The paramedics asked who was in charge, and the superintendent said he was. He was not able to answer all of the questions and told them that no one will. He told them that he should ask Maggie questions since it is her friend that is on the floor. He admitted that all of them arrived at the same time, and he entered the apartment first, but it was Maggie who opened the door.

They told him that the wounds were very serious. She severed an artery, and as they examined one of the wounds more closely, they shook their heads in disbelief. It looks as if someone went in and repaired the artery! The wound was so deep that it sliced to the bone but the artery is intact. The superintendent said there was blood shooting out from the wound before and that Maggie prayed over her. The paramedics asked to talk to her and the superintendent pointed at Maggie.

They wanted to know what happened, and Maggie told them that another lady was by her side when she prayed for Sophie. Everyone in the room told her that she was there alone. Apparently, no one, other than Maggie, saw the lady. Maggie told them that she couldn't change her story because she told them what happened. One of the paramedics believed her and told everyone in the room that the same thing happened to him about a year ago, and that he knows that it was an angel. He told them that sometimes God would send angels to come to our aid. The ones who believed shook their heads to acknowledge that fact and Maggie was amazed. She actually talked to a real angel? She started praising God where she stood. She continued to praise Him as she left Sophie's apartment and walked into hers. She closed the door behind her.

The paramedics loaded Sophie into the back of the ambulance, and to Maggie, she looked like a living corpse, something like the living dead to her. It was a miracle, and most of them had witnessed the power of God bringing someone that they had believed was clinically dead back to life again. Sophie should have been dead because of her deep wounds, and from the look of things, that was what she was trying hard to achieve. They drove as fast as they could to the hospital. The unbelievers in the room decided to go to church as soon as possible because of what they saw and heard. They witnessed a true miracle, and after the paramedic told them about Jesus, they believed instantly.

Maggie decided that she better call Sophie's parents to let them know what she saw. She called and Sophie's mother answered the phone. She told her that Sophie is on her way to the hospital. She told her that she does not know what happened but

Sophie was stabbing herself. Her mother started crying and fell to her knees. She told Sophie's dad and he rolled out of bed and joined his wife in praying for their daughter. They thanked Maggie and hung up the phone. The phone ring and when Maggie picked it up, she knew it was Sophie's mother. "I have one question Maggie, what did you see when you opened my daughter's door?" she asked knowing that her daughter was part of the occult, and believing that Sophie was the type of person who sought the dark things of this world. Maggie was hesitant, and with a little encouragement, told her about the demons. She told her about the angel, whom she thought was an older lady, telling her to go into the room with her to cast out demons and to pray for Sophie. She told her about the artery and what the paramedics discovered after they examined the wound. She tried not to leave anything out. Sophie's mom explained that after she prayed, she had a desire to ask because she felt that something else had happened, and she knew it was spiritual.

She told her that she was aware of Sophie's new religious beliefs and how she warned her about the consequences of worshipping idols. She told her about demons and the devil, about them controlling and talking to her. She hate that Sophie did not listen to her. She was happy to hear that Maggie was drawing closer to the Lord, and only wished that her daughter did the same. She will not give up on her and hope that she will see the light after this event. She told Maggie that she is proud of her. She also told her that if after this, Sophie continues to do what she is doing that she may have to back off because she should not let anything or anyone get in the way of her fellowship with the Lord. She told her to please continue to pray for her daughter until the Lord tells her to stop, but she must not continue the close friendship unless her daughter change. She told her to love her from afar if she has to. She told her that it was difficult for her to do it because she is her child, and continued by saying that she continued to pray for her and knows that if she had not prayed, Sophie would have been dead. She hopes one day that Sophie will turn back to God. She refuse to give up on her but she will not have fellowship with devils because the Bible said light should not have fellowship with darkness, even if it is her daughter. Sophie knows better and chose the dark anyway because she wants to experience the dark side. Maggie understood and told her that she talked to Sophie earlier today and told her that she could not go to the club with her anymore. Sophie's mom was glad to hear it, but she was still a little sad that her daughter is almost died. She was grateful to God that He spared her life just one more time. She will not give up on her daughter and told

The Fullness Thereof

Sophie that she and her husband will go down to the hospital to be with their daughter right now. She thanked her again and hung up the phone.

Maggie walked across the hall and locked Sophie's apartment. She does not have time to clean things up, and she believes it will help if Sophie saw the blood. It is a miracle that she has any blood left in her body. As a matter of fact, she knows that God gave her more blood. She hopes she will change and realize that she believes a lie. She has to get some sleep because it is almost midnight. She decided that she would give Sophie her key back as soon as she is out of the hospital.

Mary was so glad that she found the apartment peaceful after she returned from the laundry room. She ironed and put away the clothes. The children were already in bed, and she decided that she must do the same. The apartment is clean and all of the clothes are laid out for her and the children to put on tomorrow morning. She is looking forward to another prosperous day of work tomorrow. In a few more days, she will move into her apartment. She was surprise when Thomas called earlier today and said it will be ready earlier than expected, and she could possibly move in Friday morning. She thanked God then and is thanking God right now for His mercy and His grace. She is so grateful! She went to bed with praise on her mind.

Cory was conscience enough to hear the knock at the door, but he could not move. After a few minutes, the paramedics entered his apartment. He was glad to barely see them, and he was also grateful for this type of home evasion. He does not know if he will ever be the same, but for now he is glad that help has arrived. He would pray, but he does not believe he knows how. Sure, he faked it in the past, but now, this is the real thing and he truly does not know how to reach out to God. Until now, he never had a reason to reach out to God, and for some strange reason, he is not sure if he believes there is a one true God. He does not believe that the Bible is the authority on anything, and it is a shame that he still does not believe it now. He has enough money in the bank to cover his hospital expenses, and enough to last for years to come. If he runs short, he can go to his family members. But, it is a shame that his money cannot fix the sickness that is plaguing his body right now. He remembers his dad telling him that even illnesses will pass, and the only thing he needs to do it last. He does not know if his dad believes it God. He does not believe he does, and he remembers a family member said, "It's a shame that the preachers in our family is going to hell." He believes she, his aunt, was the only Christian in his immediate family. He has not talked to her in years, but he remembers her now.

The paramedics are now leaning over him trying to get him to breath into something that looked like a balloon. He cannot move! He is beginning to panic now, and he does not know what do. He heard one of the men tell him to calm down, but he does not know how. "I am going to die," he tried telling them, but unfortunately, they are not able to hear him, and his mouth is not moving. They finally got him onto the stretcher, and are now carrying him to the ambulance. He has never been this scared in his life. He is alone now.

It took only 10 minutes to reach the hospital, and they hurried to get Cory out of the ambulance and to the waiting doctor to be seen. Because he has on pajamas, he did not have any identification on him, but one of the paramedics saw his wallet, and took out his driver and ministry licenses and brought it with him. He took the license because he recognized the name on the person who signed it. Cory's pastor is his brother.

While the staff was trying to work on Cory, the brother called the pastor and let him know what was going on with his sheep. The paramedic was told that he was on his way, so he went back to check on Cory. Cory found himself floating above his body, and as he looked down, he saw a deformed ugly body. He had become a dead hideous creature, and he was not happy, then all of a sudden, creatures were coming towards him. As they got closer, he recognized the tall one and believed he was the angel of death, and now he is moving closer to him, and each second, he heard him say his name. Each time he said, "Cory! You are going to hell," he felt terrors going throughout his body.

Chapter Four

Wednesday

Cory woke up and knew he had just had a nightmare, and after he realized that he was still among the living, and that he does not see blood nor feel any discomfort, he is grateful to God for the first time in his life. He thought about his cousin and fellow brothers of the gospel, and just for a brief moment, he wished he could call them to get a word of encouragement and some advice. The dream disturbed him; so much so, that he believes that it will come true. He does not know what to make of it, but he knew that he is in danger of dying. He does not know what to do, nor does he know whom to call to try to get an interpretation of the dream, although it was very plain. He does remember reading that only God interprets dream, and because he is the last person on earth that will hear from God, he knows that he will have to talk to someone else to get help. He is afraid to go to his pastor because he will have to tell him that God does not talk to him, and if he does, it is possible that he will never get the opportunity to preach again in his church.

The only person he feels he can trust right now is Joseph. Joseph, to him, has a connection with God, and his cousin Stephen does not, simply because he has been hanging out at the club, and doing those things that are not right according to the Bible. He realizes that it is early, but he has to talk to someone, or he just might go crazy.

He dialed Joseph's number and he answered the phone on the third ring. "Hello," said Joseph. "Hello Joe, this is Cory," he said. There were a long silence, and Cory continued and said, "I am sorry for all of the things I said, so will you please forgive me," Cory said. "Yes, Cory, I will forgive you, so how may I help you?" Joseph said hoping to get this conversation over with. Joseph knows Cory well enough to know that he does not call him to chitchat. He concluded that Cory wants something from him. Cory said, "I had a dream, a bad dream, and if I do not tell someone about it, or talk about it, I think I just might blow my head off." "Tell me your dream," said Joseph realizing that only God interprets dreams. He immediately started praying to God for him to talk through him to Cory.

"There was a house that someone was interested in, so this person decided to buy it because it was the house that she grew up in. She went around the house, and behind the house was a huge lot with a big dog. It looked like a great dame. Well, this great dame's territory was huge, it was as far as the eye can see, and it ended at the fence where the lady and the children were standing. As the lady was looking, she saw the great dame carrying two people, who looked like children, and unfortunately, it seems like one of the children was I. I and someone else were dead. We had puncture wounds on our body, and the great dame carried us to a different location. I believe he carried us up from the pit. The pit was bigger than any swimming pool that I have ever seen, and I know that the other person and I could not climb out of it because there were no stairs. The dog deposited us on the ground, and this lady walked up to the great dame and told him to climb up onto the hammock. He did, and she put the two bodies on top of it, as if she was proud of his kill. No one rescued us. She eventually took us away. I saw another women talking to her grandchildren, and the other children about the dangers of opening the gate, and going into the backyard where the dog was, and as she was talking, two girls slipped behind the gate. She saw them and talked them into coming from behind the gate. I know that they will do it again as soon as she leaves. I am afraid that the dog is the devil, and the woman is his helper," Cory said. "Was I turned over to Satan?" he asked and hopes Joseph let him know that he was okay. "I don't believe you were turned over to Satan, it seems as though you went in the back yard on your own accord. Do you remember being among the group of children?" Joseph asked. "I don't know, but I have a feeling that I was," he said trying to remember his first nightmare. "Sometimes the world attracts us, and we will often leave the arch of safety and venture into dangerous territory, which is what the two back yards represent. What were the children doing in the other backyard," Joseph asked. "They were playing and having fun, so much so, that the lady had to call for her grandchildren more than once. After she got their attention, she warned them about the other backyard," Cory explained. "The backyard where the children were playing was safe, but God gives us choices. You and the other person had a choice, and you chose to go to the other side. You, I and the other children of God are no match for Satan. Even if you do not see him in the other backyard does not mean that he is not there. You already know that he is there. When we profess Jesus, we become children of God with freewill. Some of us continue to grow spiritually, and some of us decide to go back to the other backyard, which represents the world in which we live, where we die spiritually and sometimes physically. Obviously the other person went with you. As ministers of the gospel, we have to be careful about our walk because we do not want anyone to follow us to hell. You saw a pit on the other side, and the only pit I know of is the one that was made for the devil and his angels. You said the dog brought you and the other child up from the pit, but you and he were already dead. You have to ask yourself a question, which is are you spiritually dead?" Joseph asked and did not expect an answer from Cory.

Cory thought for a moment, and decided to confess. I was not called into the ministry. I love to preach about prosperity because I desire to become rich. I realize that Jesus said to preach Him, and about His crucifixion. I do not because I want people to believe that it is okay to give me money so they can be rich. I realize that I am suppose to give them something to make their life better, but I always felt that my dad did a good job at making people feel good about making his and our life better by making sure we could live at a level where a man of God should live, which is high on the hog, so to speak. I know that it is wrong, but I never saw my dad suffer any consequences for his actions, and I believe it is because of his lifestyle why I am the way I am. I know I was supposed to believe in a holy and righteous God, but it took the last dream for me to believe. I don't know if I have what it takes to change! I want to change, but I also want what this world has to offer. I must admit that I am spiritually dead, as the Bible defines it. I was never spiritually alive. Sure, I heard about Jesus. What should I do?" Cory asked Joseph.

Joseph advised Cory to talk to their pastor. He knew that Cory was not called, but now he also know that Cory is going to die. Cory said he had a second dream, but God revealed the meaning of the second dream to Joseph after he finished telling him about the first dream. He does not know of anyone that Cory has led to Christ. Cory does not preach Jesus at all because he does not believe in Jesus. He preaches tithing and taking care of the priests. He is aware that Cory does not spend time in the word, but spend as much time as possible in the world. He hopes the other person is not Stephen. He talked to Stephen the other day, and Stephen decided that he would develop a relationship with God. He was so happy. He prays that Stephen is not the other person, and at that moment, he heard a voice telling him that humans have freewill, and that all must make their own choices. His heart sunk, because he knows that Cory is responsible for taking someone into the world to be destroyed by Satan.

Mary got up early and looked forward to Bible study this evening. This will be the first time she attended Bible study in years. She cannot believe she allowed a sorry, good for nothing man to stop her from seeking God. She used to enjoy church, and all of that changed when she hooked up with him. She cannot blame him because God gave her a brain and Eric did not point a gun to her head. It is so sad that so many women allow men to influence their behavior. She is so glad that she is in the right frame of mind. "Never again!" she whispered.

She is very excited, and wants to know everything there is to know about God! She wants to know about these new feelings that she is now experiencing. She wants to fully understand what she reads in the Bible. She wants to know how to hear God, and how to be sure if it is God who is talking. She had to admit that she does not understand some of what she is reading, so she needs lots of help. She believes the preacher will make it plain for her and she hopes that he is patient, and is able to answer all of her many questions.

She got the children up and told them to take a wash off, make the beds, get dressed and come to the kitchen so they can eat breakfast. The children did as they were told. The girls went to the bathroom first, then after they finished, they yelled for their cousin to take his turn. They were excited when they arrived at the table. There were three different kinds of meats. Mary cooked enough so she can have leftovers for tomorrow morning. She tries to be prepared just in case she gets up late. The children ate and went to the bathroom to brush their teeth. Mary told them to hurry because the bus is coming. They grabbed their bags and ran downstairs minutes before the bus arrived. Mary decided that they could not continue to get to the bus stop just in time to step on the bus. They need to arrive prior to the bus getting there. If they miss the bus, she will have to get them to school the best way she can. She cannot afford to be late for work because she needs this job.

Cory called his pastor and told him about the first dream and nothing else. His pastor immediately prayed for and with Cory. After Cory ended his story, his pastor said to him, "It is appointed once for man to die, and then comes the judgment." He asked Cory if he understood the verse, and Cory lied and said he did. His pastor explained that one day all of us will die, and that only God knows when and where, and one day, all of us will stand before the King of Kings, and Lord of Lords to answer His questions about all of the things we did in the body. He asked Cory if he is prepared to do this, and Cory said he was not sure. He asked him if he talked to anyone about Jesus Christ, and Cory said no because he did not have time. He asked him if he visited the widows and orphans, and Cory said no because that is something that the deacons should do. He asked him about the amount of time he spends talking to God, and Cory could not lie and said he does not talk to God at all. "Okay, if you do not talk to God at all, then how do you know that God has called you?" asked his pastor, and Cory lied and told him that he knows for a fact that God called him into the ministry. "Okay, then how do you come up with your sermons if God is not talking to you?" asked his pastor. "Well, you got me there. I don't know, I just do, but I cannot explain it." His pastor told him that what Joseph had told him was the truth. He advised Cory to get it right with God immediately. He told him to be sure to come to Bible study tonight, and Cory lied and said he will be there. He explained to Cory that if he does not believe in Jesus through faith, he would end up in hell. He asked Cory does he need to explain, and Cory said no.

Cory does not plan to go back to that church. He feels embarrassed that his pastor knows so much. He believes that they do not know what they were talking about, but he does acknowledge those moments ago, he did believe them.

After Mary washed, dried and put the dishes away, she decided that she has time to tidy up the apartment. She was glad that she cleaned up last night, so it should take less than 10 minutes to straighten up. She loves coming home to a clean place. The day looks like it is going to be a nice one, as far as the weather goes, so she decided to walk to work. She noticed that so many people decided to walk this morning also.

Less than a block away from her apartment, she noticed a couple sitting on the sidewalk next to a restaurant with a small child. The child was crying and complaining that she was hungry, and the more the couple tried to quiet her, the more she cried and complained. Mary reached into her purse to give the couple money and then decided that she better not do it. She remembers watching a show on television, which featured guests that scam people for a living. She decided that these people might be trying to do the same thing to poor generous people such as herself. It was not working for them because no one gave them anything, unless she is the first bleeding heart that noticed them. Everyone walked past them as if they do not exist. But, the child was not faking, so she decided that she would buy them breakfast instead of giving them money.

When she approached the family, there was something in the woman's eyes that caused her to have pity on them. She saw desperation and humiliation. She asked if she could buy them breakfast and they accepted. It was obvious that the couple was embarrassed. This was not something that they were accustomed to doing. They entered a diner and sat down at the nearest vacant table. The diner was not crowded, so there were many tables to choose from. The waitress came over to take the order. The couple tried to pick the least expensive item on the menu. They said they wanted a side order of eggs only, and they will share it between the three of them. Mary told them to get anything they wanted, and they thanked her again but said they did not want to be a burden on anyone. Mary placed the order for them, and told the waitress that she wanted two of the biggest selling breakfast meals and a child meal. She gave the waitress the money plus a sizable tip. Tears began running down the couple's faces. The man told her that she was the first person to help them. The both of them admitted that they never asked anyone for assistance before. They had been sitting out there since last night, and no one stopped. He went on and explained how they got in this situation.

They were a newly married young couple that decided to move here from a small town in Connecticut. They were excited when they got a call from a potential employer to move to Atlanta. They were attracted to big city life, and seeing something other than the country. The husband accepted the job offer, and they moved a year ago and were living the good life. They wanted to live life to its fullness and after they paid their bills, they spent every dime they had on parties and drugs.

It was obvious that they never told their story to anyone because they were sobbing. They have been homeless for over a month now, and none of their friends would take them in. When they had money, so many people would come over to have a good time, but when they told their friends that they were on the verge of bankruptcy, their friends stopped coming by. When they started asking for a loan, they were given excuses, and most of them changed their telephone numbers.

They started talking about the things they missed back home. They grew up on a farm and the only thing they did, according to them, was to work and go to church. They said they believed they did not have a life, so when the opportunity presented itself to move to a big city, they jumped on it. They wanted to live the good life more than anything in this world.

Good life to them was one that did not restrict them. They wanted the right to party, to get drunk, and to get high if they chose to do so. They wanted to experiment with all forms of immorality because they wanted to make a complete change, and television makes it seems like it is the only way to live. If the Bible said don't do it, they wanted to experience it, then they wanted to go back home, step into the church, and say, "See, the world is prosperous, and there is nothing wrong with living life in a way you want to live it." They really thought their lifestyle was fulfilling, but when they reflect on it, they know they were not happy. They were in bondage because they could not wait for the next party, they could not wait for the next high, and they could not wait for their next sexual partner.

They came close to selling their only child, and if things did not turn out the way they did, their baby girl would have been sold to the highest bidder. The baby was getting in the way of their freedom. Her parents did not want to be parents anymore because maintaining their free lifestyle was taking priority more and more as the days went on. The both of them admitted that they would often fake doing drugs in the beginning, because they had to function the next day, and because they wanted to be well liked, they continued to buy it. They wanted everyone in their circle to believe that they can fit in, although they were not raised in a big city. They wanted to fit in at all costs.

When they arrived in Atlanta, they did not have any bills. When they lived on the farm, their little house with a couple of acres of land was paid for. His parents gave it to them as a wedding gift. They regret selling it. They used some of the money as a down payment on their lavish uptown apartment. Now, they are deep in credit card debt. Their cars and furniture were repossessed long ago. As they were talking, Mary thinks she hears the solution, so she asks, "When was the last time you talked to your family back home?" They said it has been months since they heard from them. Mary told them that they need to contact their family, and they said they were too embarrassed to do that. She asked them why, and they said they did not want them to know that they had become failures. They wanted to make it big and then rub their noses in it. They said they grew up being preached to about how to live, and what they should and should not do.

They were tired of hearing how they should live. How they should treat people. How they should handle their money and things, and how they should live as a married couple. They were brought up hearing and reading Bible stories. Now that they are grown, they met on night while they were teenagers and discussed what it would be like to live a life that they read about in their books that their parents were not aware of. They wanted to experience how it feels to not do things according to the way that they were taught. They wanted to live life to its fullness, which to them was a complete and fun life. This was their opportunity to experience different things, rather than doing the same old boring things.

They wanted to prove to everyone that they had been lied to, and the truth is, their family is right. There are ways that seem right to us, but the end thereof is always death. He said, "Look at us now; we cannot afford to buy our daughter a sip of milk. This is the first decent meal we have eaten in months. Before today, we had to eat out of trashcans. Usually, we hide in empty buildings and wait until nightfall to venture out for food. I could not take it any longer. You see, I am a proud man, and were taught if a man doesn't work, he should not eat. I tried finding employment. Last night I was forced to acknowledge that I need help, so I prayed for the first time since I accepted that job. I was going to a big city, so I thought I did not need God. I was going to make it on my own. I saw so many unjust people prosper, and my family and me tried to do what is right and acceptable to God and did not own as much as my mean neighbors. I decided that I wanted to have what they have, so I made up my mind not to talk to God again," he explained and then looked down and started weeping. "I am sorry Father,' he said to God.

Mary understood because she thought the same thing. How could mean people prosper and those who try to do well always are doing without? She knows that the devil will give you things to fool you into believing that you are blessed. She explained to him that people like that are getting things down here, but the goal is to store up treasure in Heaven and it is when saints get to the other side, that they will enjoy the very good life. She told him that he can have the good life down here, but they must do it according to the way God wants it done. She told them about what has happened to her this week, and they were grateful that she shared her testimony with them. Mary excused herself, and told them she will return, but first she needs to call her boss. Mary called the diner and told her boss that she will be there soon. She was not late yet, but she needed to call just in case.

She grabbed the phone book and called the bus station. The next bus to leave to take them to their hometown in Connecticut will depart in twenty minutes. She needs to get a cab, and as she ended her conversation with the attendant who will process the tickets for two adults and indicate that a child will be with them, she noticed a cabby finishing up his meal. She now knows that God is definitely involved in this. She asked the waitress for to-go containers and she was given one. She went over to the cabby and asked him if he was available, and he said he was. He will wait outside for them. She went over to the family and raked their food into the container and told them to follow her. They obeyed and did not question her. After they walked outside, they got into the cab with her. When they saw the bus station, they knew what was going on. Mary told them what the Holy Spirit told her. They felt she was telling the truth because this was what he prayed for. They went inside and Mary gave the attendant the money and thanked him. She hugged the couple and they got on the bus. "Oh no, I need to give them some money!" she said. The bus driver told her that she could board the bus. She walked down the isle to the family and gave them $200. They thanked her for everything. She told them that they were welcome and to thank God. They did. She got off of the bus and thanked the driver. The doors closed behind her. She waved to them as the bus rolled away. She got back into the cab and asked the driver to take her to the diner.

When she arrived at the diner, she paid the cab driver and noticed that it does not appear to be busy at all. It looks as if it was going to be a quiet day. She went inside and started telling her supervisor about what had recently happened, and then all of a sudden people started coming into the diner. She could not believe it. Her supervisor looked at her with an expression that says, "Are you responsible for this?" She understood and told her she does not know what is going on, but it is profitable. It was time to rush to feed their hungry customers.

The owner was overjoyed, but there was a problem, she wanted to keep all of the money. It was okay for her daughters to make money, but she saw the customers giving Mary money all day yesterday. She cannot understand why because her daughters are young and beautiful. Mary is an excellent cook, and she takes care of the people that sit in her section, but she still do not understand why so many people would rather leave if they cannot sit in her area and be waited on by her. She knows that in the past, if it were not for Mary, she would have been forced to shut down. She also notices that more of the people that are coming into the restaurant were not coming when Mary was the head cook, so pretty soon, she may not need her service. She wishes she and her daughters could cook as well as Mary. She will just have to find out her secrets, but right now, it will have to wait. There is so much money to be made right now.

Eric woke up to the smell of sausage, eggs, and hash brown potatoes. He eased out of the bed, and stumbled into the kitchen. There, he saw his mom placing the items on the table. She turned around, walked over to her son, and gave him a hug. She wanted him to tell her how he got the injuries so she decided to fix some of his favorite breakfast items. She knows he has not had hash browns since he left home, at least not the way she cooks them. She believes he was caught with someone's wife, but she needed to hear it from him. Her husband refused to tell her anything, and tells her that he does not know anything. She told her son to sit down at the table. He did, and she fixed him a plate of food. He started making noises as if to say he was enjoying his food.

She asked him about his injuries, and he decided to tell her the truth. She believed him because she saw the news, but she did not know that he was there that night. She thought he only went to clubs on the weekend. "Why did you go to the club on a week night? You are a working man Eric," she said looking at him with disapproval written all over her face. He told her about Sophie wanting him to go with her. He also told her about Mary sending men to threaten his life. For the first time in his life, Eric was honest with his mother. He told her that this is a first for him, and she knew it was true. Eric told her that he was staying with Sophie, and after he finishes eating, he needs to check on her. He said he would call her to make sure that everything is okay.

He told her about the money that she appeared to get over night. He wanted that money, and wants to stay with her until every dime of it is spent. He told her about Sophie's shopping spree. His mother listened to him and asked if he plans to buy her something with that money as soon as he gets his hands on it. He told her he would think about it. After he ate, he got up and called Sophie.

After no one picked up after the tenth ring, he concluded that she was at work. He decided that it was time to get dressed, and go next door to work. He thanked his mother for breakfast and kissed her on her cheek. She was still dreaming about the money, and started forming ideas on how she was going to get it from her son.

When Eric walked into the office, his dad was on the phone with a customer. His dad was explaining that the job was going to be costly because of the damage to various electrical components in the car. Eric was impressed and decided that he got most of his criminal ways from his dear old dad. It was amazing that his dad can tell a convincing lie so easily. He did not require practice at all. It was flowing from inside of him. He knew that his dad was considered by many to be one hundred percent evil, and he was witnessing it right now. It was told to him that what is inside a man will soon come out, and he was amazed that the saying was true. He wonders if others view him in the same way. He had to admit, he is not as devious as his dad, and his dad convinced him that he still has some learning to do.

He looked at that car and knows that it only needs a tune-up. As a matter of fact, only the spark plugs need to be replaced. His dad was able to convince an old widow, who is on a small fixed income, to pay over $3000 for bogus repairs. He now knows that his dad does not have a conscience. He had no problems ripping off the poor, as well as the rich. It is all about turning a profit. He knows that he is in the right business.

When his dad dies, he will still continue to perform automotive work, but he will add the drug business to it. He will be rich in no time at all. He will experience the good life soon, the only problem is, his dad needs to go ahead and die. His dad's performance already made him aware that he will not get anything over on him. He has to first learn everything there is to know about the automotive repair business. He does not want any mechanics to rip him off. "Okay dad, what are you going to teach me today?" he said. It no longer matters that he is sore. Learning the business has become more important than his injuries right now.

Sophie woke up and did not know where she was. She tried to sit up and could not. She turned her head to the side and noticed that she was tied to the bed. As she surveyed everything, she noticed that she had bandages on every part of her body. She was not able to see much of her lower body, but her upper body looked bad. She remembers hearing voices, but she does not remember much else. She knows that she is not crazy, but she needs to know how she could be sure of it. She noticed that she was hooked up to monitors. At last, a nurse came in and asked her how she felt. Sophie started cursing the nurse out and demanded that she removes the restraints. Then she realized that she needed this woman, and then apologized. She asked the nurse to release her, and the nurse told her that she could not because they have her on suicide watch. She told the nurse that she will not try to commit suicide, and the nurse told her that there were many witnesses stating that she tried to kill herself earlier. All of a sudden, some of the memories came back. She started crying as she remembers the voices she heard. She remembered wanting the voices to stop and all of them were telling her to stab herself. She wanted them to stop, and when they didn't, she remembers stabbing herself and hoping that they would leave her alone, and when they did not, she pretended that she was someone else. She remembers that after awhile, it seems as though she no longer had control. She does not remember anything after that, but knows that there was blood shooting out of her arm, but she continued stabbing herself after seeing it. The nurse listened to her, exit the room, and told the doctor what Sophie told her.

A couple of hours later, the doctor returned with the police. The police asked her questions and Sophie answered them. After they finished, she asked if they believed her. The officers did not say anything, and exit the room. Then the hospital psychiatrist came in and asked questions. Sophie knew what was going on and decided to lie. She knew if she continues to tell the truth, they would send her off to the loony bin. She was not crazy! After everyone left her room, she decided it was time to get out. She has to come up with a plan to get released.

Maggie got up late but made it on time for work. Ten minutes later, they asked her if she knows where Sophie was and she told them that she was hospitalized late last night. She did not want to give them any details, but told them where the ambulance took her. Her supervisor said she would call to find out about her, but then after thinking about it, she realized that they would not give her any information because she was not a family member.

Maggie was torn between going to see her and leaving her alone. She hates going to hospitals. It gives her the creeps. She feels that she should visit her friend although she knows that Sophie is possessed by demons because she saw them. All of them! She does not know enough about the Bible yet to stop them from jumping in her. She does not want them to jump in her like they were jumping in and out of people in Sophie's apartment. She doesn't know if she has what it takes to not become possessed, but she hears a voice that is urging her to visit her friend.

The gentle and quiet voice is telling her to not be afraid, that He will do the talking for her but she has to trust Him, and she decided to obey. She was taught that the Holy Spirit talks to us all of the time, so she knows that it is Him because of the way she feels. She knows enough to know that He cannot lie, and there are so many testimonies of God doing the impossible, which is what she had just witnessed. If she were to tell her friends, they would all vote to have her locked up in a mental institution.

She decided to call the hospital to inquire about visiting hours. She can go now or she could wait and go during her lunch hour. The voice is telling her to go now, so she decided to ask her supervisor if it was okay to personally check on Sophie and to bring back a report of how she was doing, and her supervisor said yes with conditions. She is to come back within an hour with her status, and if she is not willing to do that, then she will not allow her to go. She needed to know if she should hire a replacement or a temporary employee to fill in for Sophie.

She knew that the Holy Spirit was at work because He touched the heart of her supervisor. Her supervisor's normal response would not have been compassionate. She would have told her no, and would have gone further to state that if she went to the hospital during business hours, she may as well ask for her last paycheck. With great confidence, and a glad heart, she called a cab and waited outside until it arrived.

Finally the cab arrived and took her to the hospital. She was silent during the ride, and as soon as she paid her fair, she opened the door, jumped out so fast that as soon as the driver turned around and opened his mouth to ask a question, Maggie had made it to the front desk. He decided not to get out of the cab and ask her if she wanted him to wait. He decided to leave, and just maybe, he would get the opportunity to take her home.

She noticed that everyone appeared to be extremely busy. There was a long line of people waiting for their turn to receive care, and what she was seeing made her realized just how blessed she really is. A lady behind the desk motioned for her to come over to her. She did, and the lady told her where she could find Sophie without asking her any questions.

Maggie walked down the long corridor to Sophie's room, and as she entered the room, it broke her heart to see Sophie tied to the bed. Sophie turned her head and looked at her as she moved forward towards her. "I didn't think you would ever come and see me," she said as the tears came rolling down her face. "Me either, you know I hate hospitals," said Maggie smiling at Sophie. She was telling the truth. She has always hated hospitals, but when she went, they do remind her of how blessed she truly is. She remembered walking through the sliding glass doors, and when she looked to her right, she saw someone on a gurney that had multiple gunshot wounds. Beside him was someone who she believes is the person's wife, who was pregnant and also has two children she has to take care of. She cannot imagine how the young woman feels. She is there with her husband who might not make it, and might be forced to raise those beautiful children on her own. When she went to the counter, the nurses were saying how the man is there at least 4 times a year for gunshot wounds. He is a member of a gang, and his wife is trying to save him by pleading with him to turn his life over to Christ. She is trying to do the best she can, but unfortunately, she is trying to save someone who does not want to be saved. She is allowing her so-called man to bring her down. They said last year, she was forced out of nursing school because the police raided their home, and drugs were found. She is blessed because she refuses to lower her standards by dating a man who was not traveling forward. She thanks Grandma for teaching her about the nature of man.

There was a period of time when she was fooled into looking at a man's appearance rather than his character. She fell in love with a senior who did not want to have anything to do with her until he needed something. She thought that she was in love with him, so each time he came, she gave him what he wanted. Once he got what he wanted, he would not speak to her. Her Grandma had to talk to her, and convince her that she does not deserve to have scum in her life. Her Grandma told her what to do, and she did it. She stopped running behind that boy, and when both of them were seniors, and she was fully developed, he wanted her to date him. By that time, she was no longer foolish. She was able to look deep, and she did not like what she saw. She saw a user with very low self-esteem. She saw a boy who needed woman to take care of him. She saw a boy who had a burning desire to be important, which was the reason why he refused to speak to her when others were present. He said he only wanted to associate with the beautiful people, and she was not a member. Now, because she is shapely and beautiful, he wants to be with her. She has grown, and he remained the same. Each time she enters through the doors of the hospital, she remembers something painful that caused her to grow into this strong woman she is today. She thanks God for the growth, pain, and suffering that she went though in order for her to be what she is today. She knows that she is just beginning, but she also knows that she has come a very long way.

"I want out Maggie. I hate this place! I remember hearing voices and I remember cutting myself, but I don't remember anything else. The voices would not stop, so I thought if I cut my arm, they would leave me alone, then they got louder and louder," she said through tears. "Yeah, I know. I saw them," said Maggie not wanting to remember that moment. "You did?" Sophie asked looking at her. "Remember I told you about those things I saw in the club?" Maggie asked and Sophie said, "Yeah, I remember."

"They are demons Sophie. They are trying to destroy you because the devil does not love anyone. His entire mission is to destroy you and the rest of us. He will deceive many, and unfortunately, those he deceives may not make it into the Kingdom of Heaven. He does not want you to meet Jesus. He does not want you to know what it is to finally have peace and joy. He does not want you to be happy. He wants you to be miserable and because you go to the club and are doing things that the Bible say you should not do, you think you are happy and free. You are not, and the sad fact is that you will never find happiness and freedom without being a Jesus freak," Maggie explained looking at Sophie and hoping that she finally gets it.

"Why must I become like those weird people who do not appear to have any type of fun?" said Sophie looking serious. "Are you still having fun?" Maggie asked, and Sophie did not answer. Maggie went on and said, "The only way anyone can have happiness is by doing the will of God. I once thought that doing things God's way was bondage, but its not. Girl, I feel so free. I am free because I am doing things the right way, and of course, I still make mistakes, but I know that I have a Lord and Savior who will forgive me when I pray to the Father God in Jesus' name. I don't have to worry about going to hell now because I accepted Jesus. I believe that He lived, He died, He was buried, and on the third day, He rose from the grave with all power. It is because of my belief in Him that I will not go to hell when I die, even if I backslide by going back into the world. To me, the world is a huge prison for the lost. While you are doing things in a way that is not pleasing to God, or should I say, the way we want to do them, we are in bondage to the devil. That is why you have no protection against those evil beings. They are able to control your every move, and if you do not believe on Jesus Christ, they will talk you into destroying yourself, and you will gladly do it, just like you did last night." Sophie knows she is telling the truth. She started crying and asking for help. Maggie has never seen Sophie cry out for help before.

"Let me tell you about a man named Jesus," Maggie said. As Sophie listened, something on the inside was telling her to believe, and she decided to listen more intently. This voice caused her to become so calm that she did not want Him to stop talking. She found the Holy Spirit to be very pleasing to her senses. She started sobbing and told Maggie that she believed everything she said about Jesus. She said she heard it as a child, but thought they were made up stories that someone created to keep her in line. She told her that she noticed the change in her, and because she knew she loved the club more than anything, that something about her beliefs were real, and she just wanted her to know that small piece of information. She told Maggie that she believed, so Maggie asked her to tell her what she believed, and Sophie said, "I believed in Jesus, that He died, was buried, and rose on the third day!" Maggie told her that she is now saved. She explained to her the importance of going to Sunday school, Bible study, and church. "As a matter of fact, you need to be there every time the doors of the church is open so you can get a word from God," Maggie said. "As you know, Satan is real and very evil, unlike that religion you were in," she said and continued talking by saying," You noticed that I said were. You cannot be in the occult and also be a Christian. The Bible says you will love the one and hate the other. You can only be loyal to one at a time. Are you going to be able to divorce new age?' Sophie said she would.

Maggie told her that the doctor is on his way, and she will be discharged in ten minutes. Sophie wanted to ask her how does she know, and all of a sudden she saw something in Maggie that was so wonderful, something that she is unable to explain by mere words and a feeling of truth and warmth let her know that it was the truth. Ten minutes later, the doctor came in and removed the restraints from Sophie's arms and legs. She was told that she is okay and is released from the hospital, and that made her happy. She put on her nightclothes and Maggie removed her deli jacket and told her to put it on to cover up most of her flesh, and because the outfit she has on is sheer. They walked out of the hospital and got into a waiting taxi. On the way to the apartment, Maggie grabbed Sophie's hands and they prayed to God out loud, but not loud enough for the taxicab driver to understand each word. As they were praying, the demon that was in Sophie came out of her body, turned and faced the both of them and said he will be back soon, and when he returns, he will bring seven others with him. The other demons did the same thing, and it surprised Sophie because for the first time, she saw how hideous they look. Maggie told all of them to flee in the name of Jesus, and because they had no choice, they did.

Maggie explained to Sophie what had just happened. She told her that she is no longer possessed by demons and as long as she does things God's way, and become spiritually strong, she does not have to be concerned about being possessed again. She told her that she must study the Bible daily and she must pray continually, which are not her words, but are from the Word of God. She explained why it is so important to be strong in the Lord, and to be filled with the Holy Spirit. She paused and gave Sophie the opportunity to say something, and when she did not, she continued to explain godly things to Sophie as they got out of the cab. She paid the driver, and walked up to her apartment. She told her that if she decides to go back into the world that each demon will come back and he will bring seven demons with him to dwell in her body, and she can show her where it says it in the Bible. She asked her to imagine being possessed by eight demons and all of them are telling her to kill herself. Sophie understood immediately as she remembered the voices. She told her that it is better for her to not have known God than to turn her back on God after becoming saved because once she is possessed again, her later state will be worse than the original state because instead of just the eight demons that were in her, they will return and each of them will bring seven with them, so her later state will consist of fifty-six demons.

She told her about the story she read in 2 Peter, about the dog turning towards his vomit. She explained to her that the dog vomits, which represents sin being purged from the body, and as soon as she accepts Christ, all of the sins are forgiven and are never brought up again by God because God purge all of it from her, then He throws all of her sins as far as the east is from the west. At that moment, she is out of the world, and is now a member of God's holy family. She is clean and holy because God is holy and righteous. The dog turned back to his vomit, which represents consuming sin once again, so now you are defiled and are no longer clean because you decided to live it sin, and you are not filled once again with sin, which is filthy and nasty. Vomit is horrible. There is nothing good about vomit and there is nothing good about sin. Sophie understood and promised God that she will never go back into the world, and as soon as she got all of those words out, Maggie warned her that she needed help from God to stay out of the world, and one way is to ask the Father to be filled with the Holy Spirit, and allow the Spirit of God to lead and guide her. She said she would go to Bible study with her tonight. She wants to get dressed and go to work first. Maggie told her that she will wait for her, and they will go to work together, then Sophie walked slowly up to her apartment.

Thomas woke up still praising and talking to God. He could not believe the night he had, it was amazing because God revealed so much to him. He knew that he has to remain close to God, but he still does not feel that he is as close as he would like to be.

God took him to a place where everyone appeared to be dead. Instead of dry bones like the vision God showed Ezekiel, these bones had flesh and was submerged under water. They were men and women, and they were extremely white, and fully clothed. He and a group of people that he did not known were running from something and he knew the something was evil, but for some strange reason, he was not as afraid as the others. He did not know why but he appeared to be the stronger one. They ended up in a place that was beautiful, and it reminded him of the ruins in Rome with beautiful columns that were very impressive. There was a pool made of the same stone in the center of the column that was rectangular. There were walkways above the pool, which was the same width as sidewalks. As they walked towards the columns on the walkways above the water, they noticed that there were many dead bodies below the water. The dead bodies were not normal, and they looked like they were prepared for war, and if awakened, they would emerge and kill everyone around them. He and the others felt if they made too much noise, the bodies just might wake up, and that is something that most people did not want. They look like vampires that he often saw while watching television. They finally made it to the columns where there was a place where we could sit down. Another man sat one of the children on the block, and the child slipped and fell into the water. No one went into the water to rescue the child, so Thomas dived in and got the child. He sat the child back on the block. Everyone was afraid to go into the water for obvious reasons, but Thomas jumped in and saved the girl anyway. Thank God that he did not wake any of the bodies up.

All of a sudden, they heard a familiar sound and everyone started running across the walkways to find a safe place to hide. Thomas does not know what they were running from but he had an overwhelming feeling it was evil. As they were running, the child that fell in the water was not able to keep up with the rest of us, so Thomas went back to get her. He had to carry her on his hip while the others continued to run from whatever they were running away from.

He woke up and realized that the child was a relative. He does not know what the dream means yet, but he knows enough to know that only God can interpret dreams. He remembers a man in his neighborhood that claimed to be an interpreter of dreams. This man would throw bones and interpret what the bones were telling him. He believes a person like that is dangerous to himself and others. He will have to wait until God gives him the interpretation, which he knows will be one hundred percent right. He has an hour and a half left to get to work so he must hurry. He has to arrive on time. He decided to take a shower, get dressed and then make himself a small breakfast, if he has time.

As Thomas was driving to work, the dream began to bother him. He wanted to know the meaning. Was the child in danger? Obviously she was. Were the dead looking people in the pool were demons? What were they running from? What was worse than demons? Was it the devil himself? Was it a warning that he needs to stick really close to God, and what about his young relative? He knows that saints that are to say true saints have power over the devil and his demons, but there were so many. He knows he has to be patient with the knowledge that God will reveal the meaning to him when He is ready. He knows that God does not give us everything at once because if He gives us so much information, our feeble minds cannot handle it. God does not think the same way as humans do. God is God, and that is a fact. He is grateful that God spent the night with him. It did not take him long to get to work. Thinking about God made the time go by quickly.

As he pulled into the parking lot, he noticed that he no longer has a dedicated parking space. His space was given to another. He decided that he is not going to let that bother him. He is grateful that he did not let success go to his head. If it did, he would be crushed right now. He drove past it and parked into the common parking area, and as he got out of his car, the person who heads his old department pulled into the reserved parking space. Thomas decided to roll with the punches. He had a wonderful night with God and he refuse to allow the devil to put a damper on things. He locked his car and headed towards the door. He greeted the new department head and told him to have a wonderful day. He did not linger to chitchat, but continued walking at a swift pace. He had work to do, and he needed to get it done immediately. There were so many people depending on him, and he was depending on God for everything. The experience let him know that God is in charge and not him, no matter how hard he works. He realized quickly that without God, he is absolutely nothing, and can do absolutely nothing. He cannot even add one inch to his frame but he knows for a fact that God can. "It's nice to be reminded every now and then that you are nothing," he thought to himself and smiled.

Immediately after that thought, Thomas knew he had changed. Depending on God for everything is the way to go. "Okay, God. We are about to enter the building, so what will you have me to do next?" Thomas asked God. God told him to render unto Caesar that which is Caesar's and unto God that which is God's, so Thomas decided to do what God told him to do and to give his all while he is on Caesar's time.

He walked into his office and his secretary was grinning from ear to ear. She told him that she could not sleep so she prepared all of the folders and she is ready for his next instructions. She told him she is excited about this and feel that God will make this department very prosperous. She told him about what happened this morning, about the comments she heard when she went into the break room to get some coffee earlier. The other secretaries told her that they felt sorry for her, and she asked them why, and they said because she is the secretary of a temporary office. They feel that she will be out of a job before the month is over. She told Thomas that she wanted to give them a piece of her mind but then quickly realized she needed all of it. She felt sorry for them, and smiled at them instead. She decided not to say a word and left after she poured herself some coffee. She and Thomas decided God would lead them because they know without a doubt, that He is involved because of what He did yesterday.

"Are you ready to work and walk by faith today?" she asked and waited for an answer. "Mom, I was ready since yesterday, and I know that God is going to use us in a mighty way. Keep in mind that we are walking among the lost, so God expects us to be His witnesses. Are you ready?" he said showing most of his beautiful teeth through a beautiful smile. She said she was born ready. Their goal is to set up all of the accounts today.

When Thomas picked up the phone to talk to the first client, he heard hello. It was the contractor on the other end of the phone. He told Thomas that the home is ready and Mary can move in tonight. Thomas was happy. He told him that Mary will attend Bible study tonight, so she will probably start moving some of her things in tomorrow. The contractor told him that they will help Mary, and they will not charge her anything. They are so proud of what they did, and even threw in some extras. He wants Thomas to come sometime today to look at what they had done. Thomas told him he would after he thanked him and his crew for working so diligently. After he hung up, he called Mary.

Mary was so happy to hear from her brother-in-law. "You are the bearer of good news!" she screamed while jumping up and down. I have to go to Bible study tonight, but I will be ready tomorrow if it is okay with you," she said trying to whisper because the other ladies were looking at her and trying to listen to what she is saying. He told her that was what he told the contractor, and she laughed. After she hung up, she went to the back of the kitchen, got on her knees, and thanked God. She decided to sing Him a song, and it was so beautiful. No one could hear the song because nothing was coming out her mouth.

Today has been a very interesting day for her. She was used by God to help a family, and now God blessed her by moving up her move-in date up. What a mighty God. She will start packing her things up after Bible study tonight. She is so happy! "Thank you God!" she said aloud as she walked through the kitchen doors and entered the dining area. She cannot let anything come before Bible study unless God tell her to do something else was what she decided.

She knows that there is so much she needs to know. For instance, she needs to know who and who not to help. She knows that some who claim to be homeless are not homeless at all. They are the ones who do not want to work for a living. She knows if a man doesn't work then he shall not eat. Unfortunately, she sees too many of them, and the ones she knows are in better health than she is.

One of the first things she noticed was the same people was present in the dining area; no one left and on one entered. Then all of a sudden, people started coming in as if they heard her thoughts and decided to change things. "Okay God, are you doing this?" she asked God, and she heard a small still voice said yes, it is I. She told Him thanks and prepared her mind to work hard today for Him. She believes God is making sure she earns a nice salary in the form of tips, and she read that He is the One who gives His saints rest, so she will get her rest later.

After Sophie opened the door and entered her apartment, she noticed the blood on the floor. She knew it was her blood. She told herself, through tears, that she would never allow herself to be possessed by the devil again. She said, "I promise not to ever go to the club again." She remembered hearing voices in the club, but she did not know that they were demons talking to her. "I guess because I was drunk," she said. She decided that she needs an entirely new environment to change and heal. She now knows what she will use the rest of the money on. She will purchase a small house. A house that is located in a nice and quiet neighborhood.

She will not allow Eric to move in, and as a matter of fact, she will ask him to leave tonight. She decided that she will tell him why, and it would be the truth. She never had a problem with telling the truth, no matter how badly it cuts the other person. She realizes that he may not believe her because he is a lot like the unsaved Sophie, but it is okay. If someone had told her that she would have done this two days ago she would have denied it. She never believed in demons but she did believe in evil forces, which for the first time, she now know are demons. She realized that they were what she and the rest of the members of her group was worshipping. "How could I have worshipped something that wanted to take my life? That is dumb," she said aloud. She can never turn back. Besides, if she turns back now, the demons will return and bring others. They will again convince her to kill herself, and because there will be more, they will probably be successful, and she would die the next time. She cannot allow that to happen.

She pulled out the bucket from under the sink and filled it with warm water. She decided that she would use her sponge to wipe the blood up from off of the floor. She will tidy up the apartment after she returns from work tonight, but she cannot allow her blood to remain on the floor.

She decided that she would go to Bible study with Maggie tonight to thank God for healing her. That was a true miracle, and although she has already said thank you to Him, she wants God to know that she meant what she said by attending service tonight. She should have been dead, and she is fully aware of it. She saw mercy in action, and it makes her feel good that God thought enough about her to give her another chance, even after denying Him so many times. After she got up all of the blood, she put the sponge in the trashcan and walked towards the bathroom.

Stephen thought about his home life as a child. He never understood his parent's relationship. They would put on a show at church, and then after service was over, and after they were away from the members of the church, they would go their separate ways. He hated his dad for treating his mom that way, and he hated his mom for accepting that treatment. To him, both of them were fake, as fake could be, and even now, he does not have any respect for them. He is unable to understand why preachers stand in the pulpit and tell others to obey God, when they do not do it themselves.

He remembers his dad telling the family years ago that God told him to vacate, but his dad decided that he enjoyed his life so much, that he would disobey God and keep his marriage the way it was. He felt he was doing the right thing, and unfortunately, he could never see the truth, which he was not. Although he was a fake Christian, he loved going to church and studying God's word, but his mom was just the opposite. She loved being seen of men, and being glorified as the preacher's wife, but come to think of it, he was not that different. He also loved being seen, and wanted everyone to know that he was a preacher, especially those who did not know him. Sometimes, he wished that he would have kept his mouth shut because he was well known in their small town as being with many women, one at a time, but still many women while he was married to his mom.

Because of what he witnessed as a child, he does not like being around his family. He finds every opportunity to un-invite himself to their family gatherings. They were never able to figure out why, and he never told them for fear of saying something that he would regret. He was taught to respect his parents, although he did not agree with the way they were living. He decided that he would be a better man and do things that are pleasing to God, and God alone. He does not want to be like his dad, who scarred his siblings by introducing them to cheating. Of course, he did not tell them to cheat, he showed them how it was done, and made them believe it was okay since he was doing it. He did not want to sit on the front pew when he was young for fear of lightning striking his father, and accidentally striking him and the rest of the people near the pulpit.

He prayed and asked God to explain why he allowed it, and God told him to forgive him because he knew not what he does, and it was not until this morning that he understood. His dad really thought he was doing what was right by disobeying God. He knew he disobeyed God, but he felt he was justified at doing it because he believes that God does not condone divorce, although God clearly told him to vacate. He did what Adam did, in a way. Because of one mans sin, all suffered, and because of his dad's sin, all of them suffered. His mother will never recover from her many illnesses, and they believe she will die any day now. Two of his sisters were murdered last year, and his brother is dying of cancer in jail. Another sister appears to be doing okay for now, but he does not know for sure. He believes he is spared because God called him into the ministry. After thinking that thought, he had to repent. He was out in the world of sin. He was hanging in the clubs and doing everything that he thought he was big and bad enough to do, and then on Sunday mornings, he would walk up to God's pulpit. He is glad that he finally saw the light Sunday. If he had not repented, maybe there was a lightening bolt waiting for him the next time he step foot into God's pulpit.

He felt relieved for the first time in his life after he finally forgave his dad. It felt as if a huge burden was lifted off of his shoulders, and because of it, he would call his dad and apologize for not being there. He will also explain the reason to him, but first, he has to hurry and get dressed and head for work. He cannot afford to be late.

Sophie put on a pair of jeans and a white shirt. She wants to look nice because she does not want anyone to feel sorry for her, unless they are willing to put money in her pocket. As soon as that thought surface, she realized that God has work to do, as far as she is concerned. "Oh boy, how am I going to give up my boyfriends and girlfriends God? I need your help Father! I will have to make it on my own until I am married, and I don't know how to do this. I will have to do it because it is unacceptable Christian behavior, or at least that is what I have been told all of my life. Is it true? Okay God, You have to do it for me," she prayed. She put on comfortable shoes, put money in her pocket, locked the door behind her and walked over to Maggie's apartment. She knocked on the door.

"Are you ready to go?" she asked Maggie and she was told yes. They walked down the stairs and headed towards the deli, and as they walked down the street, they ran into one of Sophie's female partners. Immediately, she noticed jealously written all over her face when she looked at Maggie. She stared at Maggie and began to allow her eyes to move slowly from Maggie's head to toe, as if she was doing an inspection. The female lover told Sophie that she wanted to talk to her. She wanted to know who Maggie was, so Sophie introduced her to Maggie. "So, are you cheating on me?" she asked, and Sophie told her no, she and Maggie are very good friends, and that they grew up together. Maggie told Sophie that she must continue walking towards the deli and Sophie told her to go ahead, and she will be there shortly. Sophie asked her lover to walk with her towards the deli because she needed to talk to her. As they walked, Sophie explained to her about what happened that morning, and the lover did not believe her. She told her about God healing her, and she still did not believe her. Sophie decided to show her the scars, so she stopped walking and rolled both of her sleeves up to show her the bandages, and removed one of them to reveal the deep wounds. The female was shocked and could not believe she was still alive, but she still did not want to hear about God although the wound was extremely deep, and she knew that it was a miracle she was able to walk.

Her lover felt sorry for her. She now knows that at least some of the story Sophie told her was true. Sophie continued and told her again how God healed her. She told her about the demons telling her to stab herself, and if it were not for Maggie and the angel, she would have been dead. After she finished the story, she told her that she could no longer see her because she has to live a life that is pleasing to God, and being involved in a homosexual relationship, was not pleasing God. The lover looked disappointed so Sophie asked her if she would like to join her and Maggie for Bible study tonight, and the lover quickly declined and walked away as if she found the words that Sophie said repulsive. She felt Sophie would be back, but little did she know that God removed the sinful sexual desire from Sophie. He heard her prayer, and answered it immediately.

The girl walked away wondering how Sophie could do that to her. She truly believes that she has been good to Sophie, and without her, Sophie would not be wearing the outfit that she bought her. She took her to the finest restaurants. As Sophie talked to her, she remembered her mother whom she has not seen in over a year. The last time she saw her mother, she remembered telling her that she was gay, and her mother immediately took her to church and had the preacher and deacons pray over her. She remembered feeling better. The following week, she went to school feeling different, and then one of her friends convinced her to try the homosexual lifestyle just to see if she is truly straight. Her mistake was trying it again. She believed she was free, and she should have stayed free. She wants to break out of this lifestyle but does not know how. She wants to be normal again, but since everyone knows that she is gay, she does not know if anyone will be able to see her as a girl again. One day, she plans to go to church, but for now, she has to do whatever to stay afloat.

When Sophie walked into the deli, she noticed that it was busier than usual. She felt bad because they were short two people this morning because of her attempted suicide. She decided that she would work hard to make it up to them. She quickly put on her apron and walked behind the counter. She washed her hands and called for the next person in line. All of the rest of her co-workers were amazed that she was working so hard, especially since they assumed that she was on her deathbed earlier this morning. Because the place was so busy, they did not have time to ask her questions. But believe me, they will get around to it. There were plenty of rumors and none of them were true.

Eric worked so hard today. He had never worked that hard before, but he was glad because he learned so much. He noticed that his dad was a little tired, and he tried to convince him to give him the shop now, and retire. His dad told him that he does not know enough to take over yet, but ensured him that one day, the shop will be his. He told him that it would take at least a year just to learn the business side of things and years to become a good mechanic. That was not acceptable to Eric. He wants him to give it to him now, and for a second he had a thought about killing his dad to speed up the process. Now, that is low even for him. He decided not to bring up that subject again, at least not today. He hopes his dad would die soon. If his dad dies, he will have all of his belongings, including the house, which he knows belongs to his mom, but the business was left to his sons. Unfortunately, he wants the house too. Why should he have to wait until his mom dies to get the house? He does not want to live with her. He wants total rule and he knows without a doubt, his mom will not let him rule over her. She is just as manipulative and evil as he is. His mom loves that house. She loves the house more than she loves her children and husband. He decided that he better remain cool for now. He will have to wait until the right time to make his deadly move. He may have to kill his parents to get what he wants, but he hopes he can come up with another option. They are standing in the way of his dreams.

After this week, he will not have a place to stay and he is unsure if he wants to continue to stay with Sophie because she has been acting strange. He is not sure if it is safe to live with her anymore. She might go rabbit on him, and kill him and the rest of the tenants in her apartment complex.

He turned on the TV. The news was on, and he recognized the area. Someone was talking about the lady with a knife that has multiple stab wounds. They showed the apartment and he knows it was Sophie's place. Now he knows for a fact that he needs another place to stay. The witness said she said something about hearing voices telling her to do it. "Oh yes, I need to get my stuff out of there right now, and now is the perfect time to get the rest of my things out of that place," he said and got up from the couch. He told his dad about what he saw on the news, and told him that he will have to move in. He explained to his dad that he should move home because his place of work is next door and he can be available to learn at his convenience. He told him that it is perfect. "This plan just might work," he said to himself. If he is there all of the time, he can find out who his dad's contacts are. Where he keeps his money, and he can slowly establish himself in their house. He wants to know where everything is located in this house because soon, he plans to make it his.

Half-way though all of the folders of his clients, Thomas decided it was time to take a break. He is hungry and he needs to eat right away before all of his organs began feeding on each other. It is to the point now where he feels like he is getting a headache. As soon as he stood up to put his jacket on, his secretary walked into his office with food. "You are wonderful!" he said as he reached for the bag. She told him that she knew he was hungry, and said she was proud of him. She loves the fact that he cares so much about his clients and his staff. She will do almost anything for the person who she considers her son. He already gave her a raise, and a nice one at that. Because he is so busy, he asked her to interview and hires the rest of his staff. She knows just as much as he does, so he is fully comfortable with her abilities. He will see if he can encourage her to take one of the positions, but if she does not, he will raise her salary again. She is more than an assistant to him. She is his partner and mom. He asked her to not let him work past 5:00 p.m. He does not want her to work late either. She agreed and told him that she plans to go to Bible study tonight. After they finished eating, they continued with their duties.

Today was another profitable day and Mary's supervisor was happy. This was the first week since opening the restaurant twenty years ago, that it has been this busy. She kept it open because there were a few loyal customers, and she prayed that the business would become very profitable. She wants to leave it to her daughters after she dies. She did a little better than breaking even each month, but this week has proven to be extremely profitable. She does not know the reason, but she really appreciates it. She believes things are finally looking up. She will finally become rich one day if things continue.

Mary made almost $3000 in tips today, which is a true miracle from God. She is so glad that she does not have to record her tips. She does not want anyone to know how much money she made this week, at least none of her co-workers. Her supervisor pays minimum wages, unlike the other restaurants in the area. Most of them require their employees to record their tips and pay them a salary of about $2.50 an hour. If she were working elsewhere, she probably would not get a paycheck. She thanked God once again for making it possible for her to pay her bills and have money to buy things for the new house.

She wants to hurry to the school and pick up her children, then head on home to get ready for Bible study. She is looking forward to it. She owes God so much and she hopes she always remembers it. She never wants to go back to the old Mary. She knows that life will not be easy, but being on God's side is worth so much more than all of the things she went through and will go through in the future.

Right now, everything is wonderful, but it might not be that way tomorrow. Thomas already warned her that people would mistreat her because they do not like seeing God in her. People will not understand her, and because of it, she will not get the awards and other things she feels she deserves. She is beginning to see that happen now. The owner's daughters are upset because most of the people sat in her section and refused to sit in theirs. Some of the people will leave their section and move to her section when a space became available. Mary has always gotten more tips than they, but this is ridiculous, according to them. People are tipping well beyond the norm. They have seen people that left their table and tipped them a few dollars and gave Mary $50.00. For the first time today, they have begun to treat her badly by not speaking to her. Unfortunately, they are the daughters of the owner. At this very moment, one of the daughters is talking to her mother about letting Mary go.

The owner is torn between Mary and her daughters. Mary makes the best pastries and bread than anyone she knows. She does not believe she can ever replace her, but she wants to make her daughters feel that she is on their side. Most of the customers that eat at her place are loyal to Mary, and prefer her cooking and she knows it is the reason why she has customers, although there are new faces coming in each day.

The supervisor walked over to Mary and asked her to take all of her things with her tonight. She told her that the other ladies said she is not a team player, and because of it, she will have to let her go. She did not give Mary a chance to respond. Mary grabbed everything she owned and the owner went to her office to write Mary's last check. She said good-bye and walked out of the door. She knew that God would take care of her, so it was okay. She headed towards the elementary school to pick up her children. She had only thirty minutes left before clocking out, so she decided to window shop as she walks towards the school.

It also gave her time to talk to God. She does not know what she is going to do, although she knows that God will help her. "How will I find another job Father God? I still have to support my daughters. Thank you for allowing me to make so much money in tips this week. These past three days, I have made more than I have made in years in tips alone. I thank you Lord. God thank you for good health, for giving me the ability to walk, talk, hear, sing, and for everything. I know I wake up every morning believing I am suppose to be able to do those things, but I realize that it is because of your daily grace and mercy that allows me to do it. You don't even have to wake me up each morning, but You do, and I say thank you. I need you Lord. I really need you Lord. Please have mercy on me. In Jesus' name I pray, amen," she said to God.

Walking towards the school, she noticed a cute house. As she got closer to the house, she noticed that it has the same address as the house Thomas gave her. "Wow, that is the house!" she said and started jumping up and down as if she is a little girl seeing her Christmas presents for the first time. "God, you are good! Thank you!" she said aloud. The house is a block away from the school. The house is perfect, what a blessing! What a blessing!

When she crossed the street, she looked both ways and a restaurant caught her eye. It was a fancy restaurant, and she noticed they had a help wanted sign attached to a stand next to the sidewalk. She decided to walk there first because there is twenty minutes left before she has to pick up the children from the After School program. She walked in and noticed the restaurant was crowded. The décor was lovely and from the looks of things, it is a very exclusive restaurant. She asked for an application and noticed one of the cooks staring at her. He came over and gave her a hug and asked her how she was doing. She told him that she was doing well, but was let go and he said well, he needs her help. He knows she is a good cook and she is well known in the neighborhood for her baked goods. He told the receptionist to take the application back because she is hired as of that very moment.

At that moment, she realized that he is more than just a cook. She followed him to the kitchen, and as she walked through the doors, she noticed that it was very impressive and clean. He told her that he wants her to be in charge of lunch. He reminded her of the exceptional jobs she did for all of the weddings he attended. The service was exceptional and so was the food. She smiled and thanked him. She confessed that she prays before she prepares everything. He told her to continue to do that because it works, and admitted that he does the same thing. She told him that she does not feel comfortable, and he told her that she would get the training she needs. She will attend school, and on the days that she is not attending class, she will receive on-the-job training from him and the co-owner, which is his dad. As he continued to talk, she began to piece together that he is the owner and his dad taught him everything he knows. Her work schedule is Monday thru Friday, from 7:00am until 3:30 pm. He told her that the staff would help out with dropping off and picking up her children from school. He gave her five chef gears and told her he will see her and her children first thing tomorrow morning. She told him that tomorrow is not good because she will be moving into her new place, and he was pleased because it is so close to her new place of employment.

He told her that it is amazing how God worked things out. He confessed to her that he has been praying for months for a person who is capable of doing what he wants her to do. She will report to work first thing Friday morning. He asked if she needs help and she told him no, but thanks anyway. She hugged him and walked out of the door to pick up her children. She believes he knows her from the restaurant but she does not remember him.

She was still happy when she arrived at the school. The children were happy to see her, and she was happy to see them. She wanted to get home so she can get the utilities transferred over into her name. Thomas told her to take her time. She knows he will honor his promises. He is a good man and the best brother-in-law that any person could ask for. As she and the children walked towards the house, and she explained to them that they will be walking from school and to that house tomorrow afternoon. They started jumping up and down for joy.

They finally arrived at their apartment, and she told the children to wash up while she heats up their dinner. She told them that they are going to church tonight and she wanted to be ready when their uncle comes to pick them up. The children did as they were told. After she put their food on the table, she started packing their clothes in suitcases. For the first time, she is grateful that she does not have much. Her apartment is practically empty because she could not afford to buy anything until now. After she buys groceries, usually there was no money left for anything else. When there was money left, Eric would steal it. Most of the furniture in the apartment was there when she moved in. She has enough money now to buy furniture, so it's okay. The only thing she plans to take is her kitchen things, clothes and linens. It will only take a couple of hours to pack everything up, so since she does not have to go to work tomorrow, she will do it tonight after church.

She acknowledges the fact that God is good to her. One door closed, and another door opened immediately. He closed that door, and opened another one. She will not blame the mother and her daughters. If that had not happened, she would not have gotten another job. A much better job that is close to her daughter's school, her church, and her work. She loves her new life. She does not know what God has in store for her, but she trust that it will be a wonderful journey. She will go to chef school, she is elevated to a higher position, which is kind of scary to her, and she will live in a beautiful home which is down the street from her new work place and children's school. One of the best benefits of moving is the home is paid for. She does not want the momentum to slow down, so she knows she must give her all to God. He has made it easy for her to study and work for Him, and she is going to do it. She remembers when she wanted to go to church so bad, and Eric convinced her not to and the more he talked the more the desire increased but fear crippled her. Now, she is not going to let anything get in the way of her praising the Lord.

Eric feels that his day was productive. He learned more today than yesterday. It is time for him to head on over to Sophie's place. He did not check up on her because he was in bad shape last night and hopefully she is still not hearing voices. One of his friends told him that Sophie is no longer in the hospital, so she must be okay. He hopes she is okay mentally and physically; besides, he was in worst shape than she was. At least she did not have a hole in her side. He wants to find out where she is keeping her money before this week is over. He is pretty sure she will not allow him to live in her new place, if she decides to get one.

He told his dad he would see him tomorrow morning. As he walked down the street, he dreamed of living in his parent's home alone. He wants them out of it. He knows they would prefer that he was like Thomas, but he is not. He is Eric, and to him, the most gorgeous man alive. He has the ability to attract the rich and poor alike. The problem is he can't seem to hold onto them. The longest relationship he has ever had was with Mary. He had to make her feel that he knew what was best for her. After she had the first child, he knew he had her. She provided him with shelter and food whenever he needed it. In a way, he is glad it ended but he does not know why.

Now, he can concentrate on bigger and better things, such as getting his hands on his parent's property. He wants them to die soon, and he would hate to help out by causing them to have an unexpected accident. But, he just might if they take too long to drop dead. He just has to come up with a good plan, and plan that will not cause others to think of him when they are looking for their killers or the reason for their unfortunate and untimely death. He does not want to hire anyone to kill them because they just might tell someone and he may end up as someone's girlfriend in prison.

When he arrived at the apartment building, some of the tenants were standing outside talking about the events that occurred earlier that morning. He heard someone mentioned Sophie's name, so he started walking over to the group and asked them what happened. They told him all they knew and added other details as needed to make the story make more sense to them. Eric did not believe them because although they were telling the truth without realizing it, the story sounds too farfetched to him. He felt he knows her, and he knows she has it together and would not freak out because she was hearing voices. He hears voices all of the time.

Although, she did act a little strange at the club that night, he believes it was because she was drunk. He walked up to the apartment, and could not enter because she was not home, and he does not have the keys. He felt a little hungry, so he decided to walk across the street to eat, drink, and wait for her to come home so he could get his things and try to find her money.

Sophie worked really hard at trying not to notice the stares from her co-workers today. She tried to answer all of their questions the best way she could, but no matter what she said, some of them would never understand. She asked Maggie to help her explain. Maggie advised her not to tell them everything, and reminded her that there are some things that you should keep to yourself. Sophie thought she could prevent them from doing what she did, but the more she talked, the more some of them thought she was crazy. She finally gave up and told them that she was crazy, and they believed that part of her story. She decided not to tell them about the voices. Maggie told her to stop talking, so she finally took her advice. After Sophie stopped talking, Maggie said to the group, "Have you ever been in love with someone, and he did you wrong?" All of the women either said yes or nod their head to say yes. "How many of you ever tried to kill yourself?" asked Maggie looking at each of them? Most of them confessed that during that period of their lives, they were stupid. She asked the rest of them if they ever thought about suicide, and they said yes. "Well, Sophie decided to do it, so why so many questions?" she asked. All of them hugged Sophie and told her that they now understand, but some of them still think she is crazy. Maggie was never stupid enough to kill herself over a man, but the story worked. She had to admit that she was close to it, but if it were not for Grandma, maybe she would have reached that level of stupidity.

Sophie thanked Maggie for digging her out of the hole that she buried herself in. She did not know how to appear not crazy, so she kept talking and the more she talks, the worse it got. For the second time in her life, she was grateful that Maggie is a friend. The hard part for her is to unlearn all those things, which she once believed was true. Maggie explained to her that once a person decides to become a Christian, they have to grow to maturity. "It takes time," she said looking serious. "That explain why so many Christians behave the way they do, why they can be so cruel and unloving," Maggie said. "Oh, okay," said Sophie. Sophie decided not to let anyone interfere with her going to church tonight. She really needs to understand what is going on and what she could expect. She has so many questions about God, and she wants to know everything.

The bus was crowded but they managed to find a seat near the back, and they continued to talk about God overlooking the stares from the other passengers. Sophie asked so many questions and unfortunately, Maggie was not able to answer most of them. She told Sophie that she must develop a relationship with God, and He will answer all of her questions about the whys and everything else, and she will be able to ask the pastor. If she wants a cure, Jesus is the only doctor that can cure all ills. No matter what those ills are. When the doctor or man say no, Jesus can say yes, and when He cures, it is permanent. If you need to stop doing something that you cannot seem to stop doing, Jesus is the answer to that problem too.

She told Sophie that she has a long way to go, but seeing demons caused her to run to God again. At one time, she did not want to be labeled a Christian. Sophie agreed, but she does not know if she is strong enough to stop doing everything that others consider bad. She decided to take things slowly. Her thoughts are drifting back to the club, and she thought for a second that maybe she would not see demons there. Maggie looked at her and asked her what she was thinking. She said, "Nothing," Maggie knew she lied.

When they got off of the bus. Sophie asked, "What if I go to the club every now and then, do you think the demons will come back? I will not be sinning if I go, I will just go there to have a drink or two. I will not get drunk," she said. Maggie could not believe her ears. "I don't know, but I will not go with you," she said. "Do you actually believe God is partying with you in the club? I don't know if demons will get into you, but if they do, you will be worst than before? The answer is yes. Do you want to take that chance?" she asked looking directly at her. "I was just asking; calm down," she said, "calm down." Maggie felt the confused spiritual conflict going on within Sophie, and decided that she needed direct intervention from God in order to last. She needs strengthening right away, if not, she will be out there again. She told her that she would pick her up tonight so she can ask questions. "Sounds good to me," Sophie said knowing that she needs help. She has to be released from bondage, and she needs to know how she can do it. She has every intention of going tonight. She wants to talk to someone that can answer her questions right now. "God don't expect me to give up everything immediately, does He?" she said being serious. "I now believe in Jesus, that is a start, right God?" she asked realizing that she is now save. She is glad that she does not have to worry about going to hell. She didn't expect an answer. She remembers the voices of the demons, and she never wants to hear from them again. She hopes to one day hear the voice of God.

They ran up to their apartments to get ready for Bible study. Both of them are looking forward to it. Sophie is still grateful that God healed her this morning, and added time to her life. She wants to know more about this Jesus she now believes in, but she also wants to retain some of the things she enjoy, such as going to the club. She knows that the confusion is not of God. She knows that if it were not for Jesus, she would be dead and in hell now. She knows for a fact that she loves Jesus, and wants to work hard for Him one day. "Wow, am I now a Jesus freak?" she asked herself.

Cory believes this is the worst day of his life. Usually, he is on the top of the world, but today, he feels that he has bottomed out. He does not know what to do or think. He needs to think, but it is difficult. He is constantly thinking about both dreams, and he must admit, they scare him to the point of being immobilized. So far today, he has not eaten anything, and he does not feel hungry. He is stressed to the point of getting a severe headache. Every time he moves, it hurts. He needs relief now, so he can come up with a solution to his problem. He needs to talk to someone, but his head hurts so badly, that he cannot even do that. He knows what to do, he will lie down for a couple of hours, and then he will get up and think.

As soon as he lay down, he began to hear voices. The voices were loud and clear, and because they were so loud, they were disturbing him. He did not know where they were coming from because he is not able to see them. He wonders if people are outside making noise, or if someone decided to throw a party, but it still does not explain why it seems that all of the voices are coming from within his bedroom. Now, he is beginning to see a dark object in the form of a person coming towards him. It looks like a tall skinny man wearing dark clothing with something in his hand. As the man got closer, he could hear something that sounds like chains rattling, and then all of a sudden, he saw his helpers and they all grabbed him. All he could do is scream.

Thomas had a wonderful and prosperous day today, and he is still thanking God for it. He completed all of the tasks and all of the clients' information is entered into the computer. All of his clients are now making money on their money, and of course, they are not complaining. It is a miracle that everything is completed, and he knows God did it. He and his secretary performed all of the tasks, but it was the Holy Spirit who actually did all of the work through them. They hired their remaining staff, and

The Fullness Thereof

they will start Monday. God is so good, and they do not ever want to forget it. Thomas is tired, but he feels good that everything is complete and perfect. He is looking forward to Bible study tonight and he and his secretary decided it was time to go. He has to pick up Mary and the children on his way to church this evening. He loves God, and every time the church doors open, he wants to walk through them to hear a word from the Lord. A word that always speaks to his situation and gives him comfort, no matter what is going on around him. There is so much he does not know, and because of it, he wants to learn everything although he knows that it will not take Jesus long to come back for his bride. He desires a closer walk with Him, and he will do anything to get it. He shutdown his computer, turned off the lights, and locked the door behind him.

When he arrived at Mary's apartment, she and the children were ready to go. As they drove towards the church, Mary told him about her day. He was happy to hear it. "When God moves, He really moves in a big way, doesn't He?" he said remembering some of the miracles that he witnessed. "Yes, He really does!" she said and they started laughing. The drive to the church was only 10 minutes, and as they pulled into the parking lot, there were about twenty cars. He told her that they were just in time for devotion. She was familiar with devotion. She enjoys praying, reading scripture, and singing. She remembers being told about the purpose years ago, which is to prepare the people to receive the word of God. The children were also excited and were rejoicing when they recognized some of their classmates.

They walked into the church and soon realized the cars must have been packed with passengers because there were so many people inside the church. Thomas told her that he forgot about the bus. They sat down on one side of the church, and the children sat down on the other side. As soon as they sat down, devotion started.

On the other side of town, Sophie and Maggie walked through the church doors. As soon as they sat down, the deacon told them to separate to their individual classes. They did not have to move because the adults sat in the sanctuary. The teacher told them to turn to Romans 1 and everyone stood up and read the verses.

When they sat down after reading the verses, both of them were astonished that the reason why people become homosexuals was in the Bible. Like so many others, they believed that people were born that way at least that is what scientists are saying. They soon realized that they were lied to. It is amazing how the media can cause so many people believe a lie. People turned their backs on God because they want to do things their way and not God's way. "Who would have known this?" both thought and looked at each other. Sophie is forced to see things about her lifestyle that she heard about, but did not believe. He mom told her this same fact, and she did not believe her. She thought her mom was just saying that to get her to stop, but now since she read it in the Bible; she knows that her mom told her the truth. They both agreed that this lesson is going to be very interesting, and they can't wait to learn more.

Eric wondered why Sophie did not return to the apartment yet. He has been waiting at the restaurant for hours, and still no Sophie. He may have to go home tonight. He walked across the street, and was told that Sophie was there earlier, and she and Maggie left not long after they arrived. The older lady told him that they were talking about going to church. Eric could not believe his ears. "Oh no, not another one of them?" he said shaking his head in disbelief. "I can't believe someone would talk her into going to church," he told the lady frowning as if a sour ball was in his mouth. She looked at him and said, "Son, I don't know you, but let me tell you this. Without the Lord, you will not make it in. You need the Lord to get into Heaven. Heaven and hell are real, and if you don't believe it, soon you will find out that it is true. If I was you, I will go to church right now. I am going, do you want to go with me?" she asked him. He declined and quickly walked away from her after calling her a Jesus freak. She yelled back, "And proud of it!"

He could not believe it. "Why so many people are jumping on this Jesus band wagon. Don't they know that He was only a man?" he said aloud while walking fast. A teenager heard him and yelled, "Mister, Jesus is real. He is my Lord and Savior. He saved my soul and turned around and healed my mom from cancer!" Eric tried to stop up his ears and hurried to the bus stop so he could sit down on the bench. As soon as he sat down, a child sat down beside him. She said, "Sir, I love Jesus. I saw Him you know. Jesus is so beautiful. Did you see Jesus, Mister?" Eric looked at her with disbelief showing all over his face. She looked at him as if she could see right through him and said, "Sir, Jesus told me to tell you that you will die before tomorrow morning." He could not believe his ears and asked the little girl if she was a witch. She said, "No, I am a child of God. I was told to give you a message. The death angel is sitting on the other side of you. Good bye mister." She got up and walked away. Eric sat there and watched her walk away. "What a scary little girl," he said. Eric started cursing and blaspheming God and as soon as he got the seventh word out of his mouth, Eric saw the truck rolled up on the curve and coming fast towards him. The truck came out of nowhere. It hit him head on.

Everyone on the street saw Eric flying backwards as if a strong force was sending him to hell. No one has seen anything like this! It could not have been wind because no wind was blowing, but they knew something was causing him to fly backwards. As they continued to look, they noticed that the ground opened up, and then all of a sudden he disappeared. The ground closed and the pavement looks as if nothing happened. If someone had told them what happened tonight, no one would have believed it. They are only able to believe it because they saw it with their own eyes. The ones who knew him said they would not miss him. To them, he and his family was bad as bad could get.

They remember when Eric was young, how he would kill their pets. He would leave the dead pet and a note on their porch or in front of their apartment. His parents never did anything about his bad behavior, but instead, they encouraged it by not doing anything about it. Because they worship the devil, they will get what they deserve. They saw Eric reaped what he sowed tonight. Everyone gets what he or she put out. If you put out love, you will receive love. Eric put out hate and he was justly rewarded.

Mary is having so much fun! She is learning so much and she is feeling the Spirit of God all over her. She loves this feeling. This church feels like home to her. It is amazing how she feels that she belongs here. Although this is the first time she has ever been in this church, she feels like she has been going here for years. She loves Bible study because she is able to ask questions, and the teacher told them that no question is dumb. He also told them that in order to divide the word of God; you must fully understand the scripture, so he wants everyone to understand what the word is saying. After Bible Study was over, everyone came back into the sanctuary and recapped what each class learned. Then everyone joined hands and prayed. She hated to leave, and as everyone hugged everyone else, she discovered that everyone enjoyed themselves.

On the way to Mary's apartment, Thomas, Mary, and the children discussed what they learned tonight, and the excitement in all of their voices was great. Mary promised the children that they would try to attend all church services. She wants them to grow strong because she knows scripture is the ultimate weapon needed in spiritual warfare. The closer she and they are to God, the better. She wants to be so close that whenever she moves, she wants to feel the presence of the Holy Spirit. His presence is very addictive, and she wants to feel it all of the time. She heard that there is no power like Holy Ghost power, and she knows for herself that it is true. There is no greater power than that of God. Absolutely no greater power than God!

They are now in front of the apartment, and all of them are still having fun. Mary thanked him again for picking them up. She also thanked him again for the house, car, and money. She and the children will meet him at the church on Sunday.

She talked to Thomas' fiancé at church. She hopes that Thomas saw what she saw in her. She was there to check out the budding relationship between her and Thomas. She knows she talked to Thomas' parents, so she calmed her fears tonight by telling her that she is Thomas' sister and not his guardian. She told her that she believes in staying out of grown folks business, and if she or Thomas invites them into their business, she will bring out the Bible to answer their questions. She did not stay long. As a matter of fact, she left before the lessons began. It was obvious that she came to Bible study for the wrong reasons.

Everyone started laughing and they hugged each other. The children reminded them that it was very late, so she hugged Thomas and told him to watch and seek guidance with regards to his fiancé. "That I'll do," he said and he must admit, he noticed something that he did not like about his beautiful fiancé. All of the children hugged their uncle and ran up the stairs to their apartment. Thomas told her that the moving truck would be there very early in the morning before he pulled off.

Thomas was so glad that Mary and his fiancé talked. His fiancé is a minister and although she has sisters, her and her sisters are not close, but he does not know the reason why. She told him that it is because she is working for the gods and they are not. He remembers asking her if she meant God, and she said yes. She and Thomas attend different churches, and he knows that she attended Bible study at his church so she could talk to Mary. He never attended her church, and she does not want him there until they are married, but she will not tell him why. The reason why she attended Bible study tonight was to find out what was going on with Mary and Thomas. Thomas' mom asked her to find out all there is to know about what Mary is up to.

She told him her sisters are unable to understand why she hangs out at church more than they do. They attend every fourth Sunday and don't believe attending church so often is necessary. It's really amazing that so many families are so messed up. "Satan is on his post in deceiving the entire world," he said to himself. "We Christians need to get on our post too," he said aloud as he pulled into his parking space. He

The Fullness Thereof

wants to meet and talk to her sisters, but every time he brings it up, she comes up with excuses. After he is married, he and his fiancé will move into a very nice home. His fiancé already found the house, and now it is being painted inside and out. The builder said it would be ready in another month. It will be ready just in time. After it is completed, he will pay cash for it. This last test and seeing what Mary went though taught him a valuable lesson. That lesson is to try to stay out of debt. There is no guarantee that he will have a job tomorrow. He plans to take a shower and go to bed.

As Sophie listened to the teacher ask the children questions, she thought about homosexuality. She never considered herself as being a homosexual although she is involved with men and women. She knew she was not born that way but she was curious. She did it because others were doing it and she felt it was okay. She did not know it was in the Bible. She knew God destroyed two cities because of it, but that was just two cities. Everyone is doing it, and besides, society does not see a problem with it. Now she feels awful. She is grateful because she knows the truth and God removed that sinful desire. She is glad that it is not too late for her. She now has everlasting life, and no one can do anything about it.

Now the preacher is talking to them. He told them that once they turn back to God, He would forgive and clean them up again. "God is waiting for you to tell Him all about what you are doing. He already knows, but He is just waiting for you to confess your sins to Him. He is waiting for you to ask for forgiveness, and He is just waiting to forgive you. He will make you clean again. He will help you if you are having problems overcoming your sin. All you got to do is ask and believe. Now, this is important. Once you pray, you must believe that God has already taken care of it. You have to act on it, for instance, you have to make an effort to change, and God will take over. If you don't make an effort, then you will not change. You take one step, and God will take many steps," the preacher said. He asked if anyone needed prayer, and before he finished saying the word prayer, Sophie was on her feet.

He asked her to move forward, and she went to him and whispered that she needs help with everything. He asked for all of the ministers and deacons to surround her. They prayed for her and she collapsed to the floor. When she was finally able to get up, the men helped her to her feet. She felt different, and started jumping up and down praising God. She realized that the preacher was right, she felt like a new creature in Christ. She said "Thank you Jesus! Thank you Jesus! Thank you Jesus!" Everyone was shouting and praising God for the next twenty minutes. Everyone held hands and prayed. They walked out of the church smiling and greeting each other. Sophie promised God again that she would serve Him only. For the first time in her life, she knows that there is only one God. "There is no God that can make you feel like this! I love God, Margie. I really love God!" she shouted and it was obvious that she is filled with joy. "I can't turn back. I just gave my life to Christ, and I am not going to turn back. I came in with different thoughts and I am leaving as a new creature," she said through tears of joy. Maggie's teary face was beaming with joy. "I know girl," she said, "I know." Although it was getting late, they decided to walk home. For the first time in their life, they noticed how beautiful the sky, the trees, the flowers, and everything else God made is. Today was a new beginning. They took their time, and when they opened the doors to their apartments, it was 11:58 p.m.

At exactly midnight, the creatures took Cory to a place that he did not recognize. It was dark and stinks. It was a place that was not fit for any humans to be, but he does not know where he is. He asked, and no one said a word. He was given an object, and because it was dark, he could not see what it is. Then all of a sudden, things became a little clearer. There was fire and rocks everywhere. The object that he was given was a pitchfork, and for some reason, Cory believed that he was in a dream. He decided to work because he felt it would be over soon, and it was not as if he had a choice. His captives were much bigger and meaner that he could ever dream of being. He noticed that there were so many others there.

The place reminded him of a huge, hot cesspool. It is awful, and as soon as he was about to relax deeper in his comfort zone, someone that he recognized came up to him and said, "What's up man, welcome to hell!"

Chapter Five

Thursday

Mary got up early to finish packing. She decided to let the children eat at school. She does not know what to do with the food in the refrigerator. She forgot about a stove and refrigerator. She will have to buy one of each today. She packed up all of the can goods and put them in boxes. She has only 30 minutes left before the trucks are due to arrive. She decided to take a very quick shower and get the children up so they can get ready for school. She decided to put them in a cab rather than ask her sister to pick them up. She is still having problems with her sister's decision to allow a complete stranger to move in with her and her children. She will just have to continue to pray for her. The shower took less than five minutes. She quickly got dressed and got the children up. She told them to hurry because the movers will be here shortly. The children done as they were told, and as soon as they were dressed and ready for school, the movers arrived.

The children were very excited. The children noticed that one of the movers is Uncle Thomas. They ran downstairs to meet and hug him. He hugged and kissed them on the cheeks. "It feels good being loved!" Thomas said to the crew smiling from ear to ear. This week was the first time that he has ever spent this much time with them. He plans to be the best uncle ever. He can say he truly loves them. They are his blood and he will take care of them. "Are you ready for school?" he asked. They told him yes and their mom was going to call a taxi to take them to school. He told them to run upstairs and tell her not to do it. They were going to ride in the truck with him. The school is down the street from their new home. They told him that they saw it yesterday. He smiled at them and they ran upstairs to tell their mother. She dialed the cab company again, and cancelled the request.

It took less than thirty minutes to load all of the things in the truck. During the final check, Thomas noticed that food was left in the refrigerator and freezer. Mary explained that she does not have a refrigerator or freezer, and Thomas told her that she does. He put in all new appliances in a few days ago. "You don't even have to go to the Laundromat again because you have a washer and dryer too," he said showing most of his beautiful teeth his smile. She hugged him and said thank you as tears came rolling down from her eyes. "Oh, by the way, one of the movers wants a date," he said. "But since I am your big brother, I told him he has to wait until your divorce is final, which is probably next week. He is a good man. He goes to church more than I do, besides, he knows that if he hurts you, I will kill him," he told her smiling.

Standing with her hands on her hips, she informed him that she was older than he is and she does not know the man, besides, she was not interested. She does not want any more headaches and heartaches. He understood and grabbed her hands. He walked her over to the window and pointed to the very handsome and well-mannered gentleman who is dressed nicely. "No way! You know that man is not interested in me," she said looking at him as if he was crazy. He assured her that he is. "He is a good man, so all I ask is that you pray about it" he said giving her that serious big brother look. She said she would, but deep down, she does not want to have anything to do with him. She is simply not interested in anyone except Jesus right now. She knows that He is better than any man she knows, and He alone is fully capable of taking care of her and her family.

Sophie got up early and realized that she wanted to read her Bible, but the problem is that she does not own one. She decided to purchase one this morning. Since last night, she developed an overwhelming thirst for the Word of God. She wants to know everything about God. She can still feel Him! She will also purchase a small house with the rest of the money today. She saw one near the church last night. It was small and it looks like it was vacant for a while now. She asked one of the church members about it last night and he said the house belonged to his cousin. He told her how much he wants for it, and she has enough to purchase it, but she will not have any money left. She will definitely have to continue to work. It will be a new beginning for her. She will ask Maggie if she wants to move in with her. She was glad that she purchased the furniture days ago. She decided to call him right now.

She dialed the number and a young lady answered the phone. She told the lady that she was interested in purchasing the house after apologizing for waking her up. The lady said it was okay, and she will put her dad on the phone. She asked her to hold on. He greeted her and told her that he expected her call. He said he had a dream that someone was going to call to buy the property. She was shocked. He told her that she could move in tomorrow. He told her that he is also a lawyer and will draw up the paperwork as soon as he gets off of the phone. He told her that he made all of the repairs and the house is in excellent condition. He said he would put new appliances in today. She asked him where he stayed and he told her. He told her that he is on his way to work and he will drop by her apartment right now to pick up the money. He said he would give the deed to the house as well as the keys. She agreed because it felt okay. She thanked him and hurried off to the shower. She is looking forward to moving.

Maggie dried off and got dressed. She made some tea before she got in the shower, so she knows that it is at the right temperature right now. She will sit in her chair, sip her tea, and read the Bible. She loves this quiet time with God. Earlier this morning, her grandmother called and told her that she is giving away her great grandma's house. She loves that house, so she does not understand why she is giving it away. "Do you want it child?" her Grandma asked, and Maggie told her grandma yes, she loves that house. Her Grandma heard the excitement in her granddaughter's voice, and she is glad that she made her happy. She started jumping up and down, but then she thought about Sophie. She is concerned about leaving Sophie in the apartment building alone. She expressed her concerns to her grandma. Her grandmother said, "Work out you own soul salvation with fear and trembling. You can only pray for her baby. From the sound of things, she is on her way to becoming a true Christian, and so are you. Sometimes, God will separate you from others so He can work on you individually. Your strength comes from God, and only He is the one that can work on Sophie. Remember that, okay?" "Okay grandma, I will move in this weekend," she said feeling so much better. Grandma explained to her that all of her children and grandchildren own their own homes. She had to promise to not sell the house. All houses must be passed down through the generations. It is one of the great inheritance one can have besides learning about the ways of God and how to please Him. She agreed. She is very thankful that she has a grandmother full of godly wisdom. She thanks God for her grandmother and was told that she is just like her from all of her aunts and uncles. "What a compliment," she said. "I love you Grandma," she said before they hung up.

Cory thought he dozed off, but when he opened his eyes, he was still in this hot dark place. He now knows that he is not dreaming. This was not a nightmare. Now, he started having regrets. For the first time, he realized that what he thought was fiction is now fact, and because of ignorance, he is living in a place where he does not want to be. He remembers Joseph's sermon that he preached a couple weeks ago entitled, "Going Home to the Other Side." Where he is located is not the other side, but it is the side where people like him ends up, according to most of the people that he talked to. He remembers hearing the old mothers telling him that if he does not change his ways, he was going to hell, and he would curse them out. He looked around and he does not see any of them, but he does see some of the ones who others considered mean and traditional. The ones who would look around to see what others were wearing, rather than being glad that the person who looked like a prostitute was attending church to hear a word from God. There were so many there with him, but he was still lonely and miserable.

Joseph's sermon described a place where he wished he were at right now. It is a place where the streets are paved in gold, and he could walk down those streets arm-in-arm with Jesus Christ. A place where there is no crime, and no one is talking bad about their brothers and sisters, but are saying words that are full of love. A place where there is no sun because Jesus Christ's is there to provide all the lighting that is needed. A place where there will be worship all day and all night, rather than torment. He wished that he had believed because he is now in a place of torment.

As he looked around, he sees some of his family and church members. They were the ones that he tried his best to be like. "Wow, that is the person who I danced with at the club," Cory said, and as he looked around, he saw most of the people that he partied with and who believed in the same things that he believed in. He also sees the ones who encouraged him to get all he can while he can, and to take no prisoners. They are the ones who told him to steal from others and keep for himself, and he did exactly what they said, but look at him now. He does not have his worldly possessions with him now. As he reflects on the "Other Home," he can imagine the luxury that they must be living in. They were the ones who were not overly concerned about worldly possessions because they said they were building treasure in their "real home." If only he believed in Jesus Christ, then he would have been in a place where he can be happy all of the time. He wants to live forever in a place where there is peace and joy, and as he continues to think, he believes he hears laughter.

He thought he saw something, so he asked one of his tormenters could he walk to the end of the rock to take a look, and after a long pause and feeling the sting of an object that looked like a pitchfork, he told him to take a short look and come back quickly or else. He walked over to something that looked like a gulf that separated the two places, and he can see one of his Christian cousins in Abraham's bosom. He knows it is Abraham, but he does not know why he knows. He was being taken care of. He picked on this person since they were children, and did not go around him when he was dying. Cory began to cry. His time was up, and his tormenter was now by his side making his life miserable by doing things to him that no one could imagine. He felt he had a wonderful life while he was living, but he now knows that the Bible is true, the wages of sin is death, and the gift of life can only be gained through Jesus Christ. He wished that he believed, but now it is too late. He will now live forever in hell because none of his sins was forgiven.

Eric's dad started worrying about him. He called Sophie and was told that she did not see Eric. She asked him where he stayed because she needs to drop his clothes off because she is moving tomorrow. His dad gave her his business address. She told him she would ask some of the people in the neighborhood if they saw Eric. He told her that it was not necessary because he has contacts in that neighborhood. She told him that she would ask anyway. After hanging up the phone, Eric's dad called the owner of the diner located across the street. She told him that she saw what happened to Eric last night, but she knows he will not believe her. He told her to try him, and she told him exactly what she saw. He did not believe her and told her that she watch too much television. He called other numbers and some of them do not know anything and others told him the exact same thing as the lady who owns the diner across the street from Sophie's apartment told him. He does not know what to think. If Eric is gone, he does not have any sons. He will not have anyone to leave the business to, and he does not have anyone to take care of him in his old age. He has to tell the wife.

The movers moved everything in Mary's home. She feels so good and started to cry. The one who wants a date walked over to her and allowed her to put her head on his shoulders. She cried for over thirty minutes and he waited patiently for her to finish. She did not realize that it was he until she finished. She felt sorry for him because his nicely starched shirt is now wet with her tears. She apologized and he assured her that it was okay.

He told her that he was blessed and he knows exactly what she is going through. He asked her to sit, and he told her about his life. After he finished, she knew he could relate to her. She also realized that she was better off than most people. At least she was wanted, but Jose was not wanted as a child. He told her that she belongs to him and God told him so.

Within minutes, she heard a still small voice telling her that what he was saying was true. She told him that it is amazing how God works. She was not looking for a man but when she was looking for one, she found the worst creature that ever lived. Now, she does not want one and God sent her a wonderful and godly man. She started laughing and he joined in. He agreed with her. He told her that he must go to work now. He is a professor. He teaches biblical studies at night and networking classes during the day. He told her that he would see her again once her divorce is final. She told him okay. When he walked out of the door and got in his car, she got a feeling that God has a plan for them. She does not know what it is, but she got a feeling that it is important. She asked God to reveal it to her. She was told that he is also a preacher.

The nice man dropped by Sophie's house and gave her the deed and asked her to sign the paperwork giving her ownership of the property. His brother was acting as the closing attorney and she went across the hall to ask Maggie to be the witness. The closing lasted for less than forty-five minutes. Maggie was happy for Sophie. After everyone left, Maggie said she has to hurry and put on her shoes so they can walk to work. Sophie told her to hurry because she has a deal for her.

It did not take long for Mary to organize her new home. To her, it is the prettiest home she ever saw. She walked to the store about an hour ago and bought groceries. Now, the freezer and refrigerator are full. She brought curtains and hung them up. Thomas gave her enough money to buy furniture, and told her to put the money she has in a savings account. She noticed that one of the furniture stores is going out of business. She went in and brought fine furniture for every room in the house and still had money left. She thanked God after the cashier gave her the change. They told her the furniture would be delivered in about two days. She and the children will have to sleep on the floor until the furniture arrives, but that is okay with her. She is grateful that she has a roof over her head. Without God using Thomas, she would not know how she would be able to pay the rent after losing her job. She is literally starting over and this is the first time she has time to really think about it. She will start another career next week. She still has money in her pocket. Her divorce will be final soon. She will start dating again next week. She has a new house that is paid for. She does not have any bills. She has a car that is paid for. The school is right down the street, and

The Fullness Thereof

even if she is not home, the kids can walk home and do their homework. God is definitely in the blessing business.

She will have to start training her daughters. They will get their first cooking lesson today. She will wait until they get home and they will prepare dinner together. The garage has a keyless lock so she will give them the combination so they can let themselves in. She will also give them the key to the house. Her neighbors have already come over and welcomed her to the neighborhood.

The older couple told her that they would keep an eye on her kids. Their grandchildren are over on the weekends. They seem to be nice people. She still wants the children to be independent. They need to learn to do things for themselves, but it is nice to know that others will be watching over them. She will add her neighbors to her prayer list. Some of them invited her to their church, and she discovered the older couple attends the church that she is now going to. The older lady is a retired schoolteacher, and the more she talked to her, the more she loved her. She got down on her knees and talked to God. She told Him that she is so grateful. She prayed for all of her neighbors, her family, friends, and enemies, and even prayed for Eric.

Sophie and Maggie talked all of the way to work this morning. Maggie told her that she is proud of her but she had to decline her offer about moving into her house. She told her about the conversation she and Grandma had that morning. She told her that she has to buy furniture because the house was empty, but she wants to do it on her own. Sophie told her that she found the money in the apartment and spent all of it on furniture, clothes, and the house. She told her that she wished she had some left over to give to her. She told her that she was grateful that she saved her. Maggie corrected and told her that it was Jesus who saved her. She told her to never give man God's glory. It is God who does the saving and not man. She told her that she is glad that she is now a Christian.

"Now, you know what you must do? All of us are ministers and witnesses of God. You have to tell others about Jesus, but if they are not interested, then just shut up," Maggie said. Sophie said she understood. She told her how it feels to be a changed person. She told her that she cannot go back to that old life, and how strange it is not to have any of those desires anymore. She told her that it was touch and go yesterday because she wanted so badly to go to the club. Maggie said, "Yeah, I know." "I am glad I went to Bible study last night," she said. "I am glad to. You know, I was going to discontinue our friendship. The Bible says what fellowship does light have with darkness, so I am trying to get closer to God. I have to hang with those who are traveling in the same direction as I am now traveling in. I am glad we are traveling in the same direction," Maggie said, and if you need to ask, we are traveling in the direction that leads to Heaven. "Me too," Sophie said. "I want to know all there is about God," Sophie said. "Me too," said Maggie. "Well, we are here now," said Sophie. "Oh, by the way, I am thinking about going to college," Maggie said. "Good idea, I just might go too," said Sophie.

Thomas felt good about helping Mary move in. He was glad that everything was done yesterday; it made taking off this morning easier. His office was so peaceful. He gave his secretary the rest of the weekend off. He told her that she would be training the new recruits Monday, so she needs to get some rest. She thanked him as she walked out of the door. He purchased some paint. He wanted to paint the office. She put a nail in the exact location on the walls where she wanted him to hang the pictures. He put on his coveralls and covered the floor and furniture with plastic. He turned on Gospel music and went to work. He plans to continue until his and his secretary's office are painted. The new recruits will occupy cubicles outside of his secretary's office.

The other managers told him that he should leave work like that to the hired help. Because Thomas does not own this business, he considers himself to be one of the hired help. He smiled at them and told them to have a wonderful day. They shook their head with disbelief. They talked among themselves thinking that Thomas needs to work on getting clients rather than do manual labor. They started bets with one group giving him a week to fail, and the other group giving him a month. Little did they know that Thomas has already out performed them. His clients recruited other clients, which made his division the largest money making division in the entire company.

Thomas had a vision last night. He saw himself owning his own company. He will look for the building in his vision tomorrow morning. As soon as he gets off work, he will look though the real estate book in search of the building. He no longer has fears about being a business owner. He saw God in action, and is a witness of what God can do. A couple of days ago, he did not have any clients. Yesterday, God gave him many clients.

Time went by quickly and both rooms were finished before 5:00 pm. Thomas kept on the coveralls and got his things to leave. He will hang the pictures and move the furniture tomorrow morning. He will not work this weekend. He does not plan to work any weekends anymore. He will be married soon, and he refuses to be one of those workaholics that women so often complain about. He wants to enjoy his wife. He will call and make arrangements at her favorite restaurant tonight and tell her the good news. She had been telling him since she met him, that he needs to open his own business. Obviously, God agrees with her. He is only stepping out because God is telling him to. He will call her as soon as he gets in the car.

As soon as Thomas got in the car, his phone ranged. It was his dad. He told him what he was told about Eric. "What, are you sure?" said Thomas concerned about the wellbeing of his brother. "Will God do that?" his dad asked and for the first time, Thomas believed that there is a chance that his dad might believe in God. Thomas could not answer him. Thomas told him that he would ask around. Thomas drove to the neighborhood where Eric had disappeared and talked to an older lady. She told him the entire story. She also told him what she told Eric prior to the incident. The lady is one of the ladies that attend Thomas' church, and she is known for telling the truth. She told her that a neighbor's daughter also talked to him just before it happened, and she walked Thomas over to where the little girl stays. The little girl told him everything, including what she had told Eric. Thomas was sorrowful because he knows that Eric was not saved. The little girl saw his expression and said, "It's not your fault Mister. All of us have a choice as to what path we want to follow. Everyone in your family except you chose to follow the devil. You are the youngest, and you chose to follow Christ. You prayed for him but the choice was still up to him to make. You did what you could do, so don't cry," she said as she continued to look at him as if she could see his very soul. He looked at the little girl and marveled because of the wisdom that she possessed. He hugged and thanked her. He and the older lady walked out of the apartment.

The older lady told Thomas that the little girl has always been like that. She has terminal cancer and her parents were told that she has less than a year left. The doctors told her parents were told that ten years ago. Thomas thanked the lady and decided to take her and the little girl's advice, which is to move forward in the Lord. He can't do anything for or about Eric. Eric made the wrong choice. He hopes his mom and dad will change after discovering the truth. He will still remain hopeful.

When he got back in the car, he called his dad and told him that he was told the truth. He told him that God is real, and if he and his mom do not believe in Jesus they will also die and go to hell. His dad told him that he will see him in hell and hung up the phone. Eric called his girlfriend and invited her to dinner. She told him to pick her up and that she is hungry. He called the restaurant and made reservations. He will change when he gets over to her house. Today has been an unusual day, and he hopes it gets better.

Thomas called Mary and told her about Eric. She sat down. She decided not to tell the children. She does not know what to think. She knows that she should not be happy. She wished that he accepted Christ before he died. Thomas told her what the little girl and older woman told him. He told Mary to follow their advice, and she agreed to do it. She will still go back to her maiden name. Without a body, no one will believe that her husband is dead. They did not have any insurance to bury him anyway. She decided to continue showing the children how to cook dinner. No need to moan, what's done is done and there is nothing she can do about it. She hopes his family will see the light and change.

After the children ate, and went to bed, Mary decided to stay up a little while longer. She wanted to reflect on all of the recent events again. She is overwhelmed because things happened so fast. She is looking forward to going to work tomorrow, although she usually doesn't like changes. It is something different and she asked the Holy Spirit to help her. She got her Bible, sat down, and started reading. She will continue to do this just prior to going to bed each night. The house is so peaceful, and it is nice not hearing the neighbors while she read.

Sophie told Maggie to go ahead. She needed to stop by the bookstore to get a Bible. Maggie hugged her and got in the taxi. She ran down the street to the bookstore for fear of them closing before she got there. She arrived almost out of breath. The sign says the bookstore closes at 11:00 pm, so she did not have to run. There were so many Bibles to choose from. She did not know which version to get so she got the King James Version because that is the one they read in Church. One of the attendants suggests that she get another version also, so she did. She asked the attendant if she would call her a cab, and she did.

When Sophie got home, she ran up the stairs and started packing. She does not have much because she rented a furnished apartment. Besides her clothes, she has a few dishes. All of the things, except her clothes could fit in one big box. The phone ranged and when she picked it up, she recognized the voice of one of her male boyfriends. He asked if he could come over and she told him no. She told him that she tried to kill herself the other day and he did not believe her. She started talking about Jesus and five minutes into the conversation, he told her that he has to go. He told her that he decided that he has to end their relationship because he thinks he wants to reconcile with his wife. She told him that it was a very good idea. She decided to call the others, and one by one, she talked to them about Jesus. It was amazing how every one of them broke it off with her. After she hung up, she started laughing. "Boy, God will either draw you or repel you, if you are not right," she said and continued laughing and praising God. "Thank you God!" she shouted and could not believe how easy it was to get rid of them.

She decided to take a shower, get comfortable to read her Bible in her bed. She wants God's words to be the last thing she remembers before falling to sleep tonight. She is so grateful that He saved her. She is so grateful that God redeemed her back to Himself. She is so grateful for another opportunity to get it right. She heard what happened to Eric, and she is so glad that she accepted Christ. She was in worst shape than Eric, so she has so much to be thankful for. She heard God's voice and answered His call. If Eric heard God's voice, he would not have answered His call, which is why he is where he is now. According to one of the eyewitnesses, he cursed God just before the ground opening up.

Leonora Austin

Chapter Six

Friday

Pastor Watkins called Joseph and Stephen and asked them to go over to Cory's house to check on him. He told them that Cory is in trouble, and he may not be among the living anymore. He tried calling but no one answered, so both of them agreed and headed towards Cory's house.

When they got there, they noticed that the door was not locked. As they walked through the door, they noticed that everything was not in its proper place, which is unusual because Cory is a neat freak. He is not the type of person to have an untidy house. Stephen called his cousin's name, and no one answered. Joseph walked into the bedroom and called for Stephen to come in also. Stephen walked in, and both of them knew immediately that Cory was dead. The expression on his face let them know that something awful had happened. They have never seen such a frightening expression before.

Both of them began to weep because they knew that Cory was a false prophet. Joseph said to Stephen, "Man, we tried but he would not listen. God does not force us to believe in Jesus, and he allows us to make up our own minds regarding which path we want to take, and Cory decided to take another path." "You are right, and I know it, but I wished that he had more time to get it right," Stephen said through sobs. "You and I both know that we do not know the date or time when Jesus will return, so we must always be ready. God gives us sufficient time to make up our minds, but some chose a path that leads to destruction, and some do not, but when you say you are a preacher, and are leading God's sheep in the wrong direction, then the punishment for that person is severe, and you know it," said Joseph. "I know and I tried to warn him, but he would not listen," said Stephen wiping the tears from his eyes. Joseph dialed the number for the coroner to come and get the body, and then he called Cory's parents. They decided not to pray because it would not do any good since he was already dead. They called Pastor Watkins and told him what they saw and done.

Mary and the children slept on the floor last night, and she woke up a little stiff. She thanks the Lord for allowing her to sleep under the roof that He gave her. She loves and thanks God often for his many blessings. She decided to walk into the living room with her Bible and sat on the couch. When the furniture arrives, she plans to put the couch in the back room, which she plans to turn into a sunroom. She loves her beautiful house. It is so wonderful living in something that is paid for. She does not have to worry about debt. Her only concern is being able to pay the yearly taxes, but she knows that God will take care of it because He gave her this house. After she reads some verses, and after she fully understands what she is reading, she will wake the children up.

She started reading Proverbs 31. When she got to verse 10, she remembers hearing something about the virtuous woman. She wants to become one, so she continued reading. As she was reading, she started cross-referencing scripture with other scripture to get the full meaning. She realized that she is worth more than rubies because this woman possesses godly wisdom. She is filled with and is led by the Holy Spirit. She found out that to get spiritual wisdom, you must first get Jesus in you. He is the way, the truth, and the life. After you believe on Jesus, you must ask for the Holy Spirit is what she often heard. She prays that the closer she gets to God, the more others will see godly light in her. That light they see can only come from God. What makes this woman stand out is that she is filled with the Holy Spirit. She believes the problem is that most of us don't want to be filled. We want some of Him and want to be able to call upon the Lord when we need Him, and when we think we don't need Him, we want to put God back in our box. This woman possesses so much talent, so she assumes that Solomon is talking about more than one woman. She is the type of woman that others will seek out because of her wisdom, her kindness, and the love she has for everyone. She is Christ-like and loving. She can cook and make a living. She is absolutely wonderful. She got down on her knees and prayed for God to make her virtuous.

She woke the children up and they quickly got on their feet and ran off to the bathroom. They were excited and told their mom it was nice to be able to sleep without hearing so much noise. It did not bother them that they slept on the floor. They were excited about walking down the street to their school. They were glad that for the first time in their life, they have a yard to play in, which is a yard just like their cousins' yard. They feel like they are older because they are now going to be able to let themselves in their home. They were able to practice yesterday and both of them remember the combination number. They must remember not to give the combination number to anyone else, nor will they enter it if someone is standing with them. Their mom told them that they are to be responsible, and they do not want to disappoint her. As they got dressed for school, they heard their mother humming a familiar tune they heard in church. She usually hums when she cooks, and they notice she does it more since their dad left. They don't miss him because he never talked to them. They also did not like the way he treated their mother, and how he stole money from her. They saw him do it most of the time. They are glad he is gone because the house has now become a home.

Mary told them to come to the table to eat breakfast. She told them to join hands and she prayed over the food. This is the first time Mary ate breakfast with her children in months, or perhaps over a year. Usually, she gets dressed while they ate. She is determined to make things better for her children, and because God is now in her life, she knows it will be better. She wished things were like this from the beginning, but she wonders if she would have appreciated it as much as she does now.

As she thought about human nature, she believes that it is unfortunate that we don't give God the praise until after he has brought us out of a terrible storm. As soon as things become good again, we often forget about God until another storm starts brewing. She has to always remember to praise God during the good times and bad times. She is determined to keep God first in everything, and to include Him in all of her many decisions. For the first time in her life, she realizes that God knows her past, present and her future. He knows exactly what she will do an hour from now, so she should ask Him for advice. That would be the smart thing to do.

As they ate their breakfast, Mary saw the smiles on her children faces. She has never seen them this happy before. She thanks God for it. She promised to continue to pray for them. She wants them to grow up to be godly adults in this very sinful world.

After the children ate their breakfast, each of them washed their dishes and put them in their proper place. It's time to walk to school. As they walked, Mary reflected on the recent events again. She could not believe how quickly things happened. How her life has changed in less then a week. She has to be a witness. A witness to the fact that if you allow God to change your life, He is capable of making your life completely over in a matter of moments, only if He chooses to do so. If she had planned this, it would have taken years. "What a God we serve," she said. The children heard her and said, "Amen." They all started laughing. They hugged her and ran into the school.

Mary headed to work. She reminded God of His promise to never leave nor forsake her. She is looking forward to this and is a little nervous. She knows God has everything under control, and she will fully trust Him.

Thomas woke up, and did not remember the alarm clock going off. He has only fifteen minutes to get dressed and out the door for work. He wants to finish hanging the pictures on the wall, and move the furniture to where they are supposed to be. He is so happy that God blessed him to be a blessing to Mary and others, and how he blessed him to become a business owner. His boss called him late last night and told him he wanted him present at the meeting this afternoon. He was glad that he sat everything out last night. He rushed to the shower.

Sophie got out of her bed and dropped to her knees. She thanked God for another day and asked him to help everyone today. She stood up and decided that she wants bacon and eggs for breakfast. She usually does not eat breakfast. "Boy, have I changed?" she said. She decided to hurry up and get showered and dressed so she could go across the street to the diner to eat breakfast. She decided to call Maggie to see if she wants to go.

As Maggie was finishing up, the phone rang. "Good morning," she said. "Good morning to you. I am calling to see if you want to go across the street for breakfast? I woke up hungry with the thought of bacon and eggs on my brains," said Sophie laughing. "Wow, you eating breakfast?" asked Maggie sounding surprised. "I know, I can't believe it either," she said. "I ate breakfast earlier this morning," said Maggie. "Maybe tomorrow, I will go with you," said Sophie. "Okay, got to go. I will see you at work," she said. Maggie continued tidying up her apartment. She wanted to come home to a clean apartment.

As Maggie walked to work, she suddenly got an overwhelming desire to pray. She decided to pray, although she does not know whom she is praying for. She was glad the sidewalk was not very crowded because she knows they would probably think she is crazy. In a way, they would be right because she is crazy about God. She does not know what the future holds. She is looking forward to the day when Jesus returns. When that day comes, she does not have to walk to the deli. She does not have to experience any pain and suffering. She hopes that more people wake up and turn to Jesus before it is too late. To bad Eric did not convert to Christianity.

Thomas arrived at the office with one minute to spare. The meeting is a couple of hours from now, so he will hang the pictures and move the furniture back in its proper place. He was not told what to bring to the meeting, so he decided to take along a report of the amount of clients he has along with overall account information. It will take less than thirty minutes to hang the pictures and move the furniture. He prayed to God when he got up this morning, and on his way to work, so he will allow God to control his actions in the meeting. He is confident that everything will be okay. He was glad that he arrived on time today because for some unknown reason, all of the managers were present. They don't usually arrive until later in the day. "Something is going on," he said to himself. One of the managers came into his office and told him that rumor has it that another department will be eliminated. If the rule still holds, Thomas department will be the department that will be eliminated. That unwritten rule states, "the first hired, the first fired." He will put his hands in God's hands. Thomas did not have a response for his co-worker. He told him he will wait for the meeting, and continued doing what he was doing. After he moved the last piece of furniture in its proper place, another manager came into his office and told him the meeting will start in five minutes. Thomas was glad that he already pulled the information. He put on his jacket and walked with the other managers to the conference room.

Maggie finally arrived. Her walk today appeared to be longer. She guessed it was because Sophie did not walk with her. For some strange reason, she did not feel alone. As she walked through the door, she looked back and saw Sophie getting out of the taxi. She waited for her and Sophie told her the breakfast was very good. She decided not to buy groceries until she moves into her new house. Maggie agrees with her. As they walked into the deli, everyone appeared to be working hard at putting everything in its proper place. The supervisor asked them to prepare salads although they arrived ten minutes early. Their regular shipments of salads did not arrive, and will not arrive today, so they have to prepare them from scratch.

Thomas walked into the conference room and decided to sit in one of the chairs against the back wall. Most of the chairs at the conference table were taken and because other managers were walking in after him, he decided to sit elsewhere. His ex-assistant occupied his usual chair. Before the other managers took their seat, the director called the meeting to order. He said he wanted to get this over with. He told them he was going to eliminate two departments. He said some of the departments were not making enough money to justify their existence. He wanted each manager to tell him how their department is performing starting with the newest department, which is headed by Thomas. Thomas stood up and walked to the front. He stated that his department is less than a week old. He told them the amount of clients he has so far, which far exceeds the other departments. In less than a week, the money amount his department is responsible for is a couple of billion dollars, which also far exceed the other departments. He gave the director a copy of the report and asked if he had any questions. The director knew the newly formed department was making lots of money but he did not have a clue as to how much. He was so impressed by the numbers that he told Thomas his department is safe. He asked him how he did it, and Thomas told him that it was God. Thomas was told to take a seat, and the director thanked him again. As he walked to his seat, he saw the expression on some of the manager faces. They were shocked. Most of them expected him to fail and even went as far as to place bets against him. They knew he does not have a full staff yet, so they were confused.

Some of them admired Thomas because he will roll up his sleeves and work along side his staff. The rest of the managers will not do that. They give orders and expect their employees to perform duties that they are not skilled at, without their assistance. If their employees do not work as hard as they think they should, they would often fire them without first giving them proper training. Thomas is different. He believes in working and making sure his employees are fully trained for their job and for the job they desire. He believes in giving everyone a chance and always encourages his employees to voice their concerns and give suggestions for improvements. Some of the employees from his last department want to come to his newly formed department now. Earlier this week, those same employees said they did not want to go the newly formed department, and that they wanted to support his then assistant. He told them the truth, which is it is too late. He already hired a staff.

After the meeting was over, the director decided to eliminate three departments instead of two. One of the departments is a cash cow, and he blames them for causing the corporation to not be as profitable as their competitors. The ex-associate managed to keep his department because it is in very good shape before he became manager. He received a strong warning, which was to become more profitable than his predecessor.

The Fullness Thereof

He gave him less than six months to double his clientele, and he knows that it cannot be done without divine inspiration. Thomas felt sorry for him because he knows that this guy is all talk. He already told Thomas that he does not want any assistance from him, and Thomas told him he would honor his wish. He wants the best for him, but he also knows that it is better to deal honestly than dishonestly.

Thomas thanked God once again as he walked to his office. He told his secretary the good news. She gave him the thumbs up and smiled at him. She put her hand over the phone and said she already prayed. He smiled at her and walked in his office.

Mary been on the job for more than six hours and she has learned so much. There is so much that she needs to learn, and for the first time since she has been working in the restaurant, she realizes that she does not know as much as she thought she knew. As a matter of fact, she feels she does not know anything. This restaurant is very technical. The staff is professionals and knows more than she knows, as far as technique is concerned. The owner told her she knows more than what she thinks she knows. The staff is professionals but they do not know as much as she does. They depend on their techniques and she knows the business, but does not know she knows. She will start attending the same school that the staff was trained at next week. She will go to school the first half of the day, and will work at the restaurant the second half. He told her that he plans to open another restaurant, and he wants her to be co-owner.

As they continued to talk, Mary was informed that they are relatives. They have the same biological dad. He knew about Mary but she did not know about him. He asked her to ask her mother. She called her mother, and her mother told her the truth, which was Roy was telling her the truth. Her mom did not know she was working at Roy's restaurant, but she heard that he has one, but she did not know that it was in Atlanta. When Roy was a baby, he and Mary would take naps together. As they continued to talk, she remembered some of the incidents he talked to her about. Roy told her he does not have many people that he trusts.

This was the perfect opportunity to talk about God, so Mary decided to find out if Roy was a Christian. His actions are Christian-like but she wants to hear that he believes and serves Christ. She was very please to find out that he is, and that he loves Jesus more than anything in this world. He refuses to open on Sundays because he wants all of his employees to go to church, if they so desire. He told her that he goes to church, and as they talked, she found out that he attends the same church that she is now going to. He reminded her that he allowed her to bring the children in the restaurant and provided transportation because she is related to him. She admitted to him that she thought it was strange that he did that, so now she knows why. Roy also has children and he wants his children and her children to grow up together.

To her, this is good news, but it is too much to process right now. Things are happening so fast, and she knows that it is God opening up the window and pouring out a blessing that there is no room to receive it. It is so overwhelming. She is filled with joy, and started hugging him and praising God. She is so happy that she has a brother. She promised to look after him, and to do her best to ensure the business is successful. But most importantly, she promised to keep him and their family in her prayers. His wife died a year ago, so he is also a single parent. She is looking forward to getting to know him and her niece and nephews.

She asked him about their dad, and he told her everything, including the fact that he is one of the chefs in their restaurant. She was surprise to find out that he is alive. She found out that her dad would often visit the school to watch her performances in plays, and how he would walk over to the school and look at her while she played on the playground. He can name every play she was in. She told him thank you, and asked if he can introduce her to their dad. He said, "It's my pleasure, Sis."

When Mary walked through the double doors, she saw the older man with a smile like her youngest child on his face. She walked towards him, and he stretched his arms wide and said, "Come here baby girl." She walked into her dad's arms, and thanked God for his precious gifts. She could care less about the past. She looks forward to the future. She was glad to find out that he is also a Christian.

Maggie and Sophie worked hard all day, and were glad to finally get a break. The afternoon crew was leaving and the evening crew was now coming into the deli. She was appreciative for the breather. Because it was so busy, none of them had lunch. Maggie decided to make her and her fellow employees sandwiches. All of them were hungry. They decided to eat a few bites of their sandwich, one at a time. One would go to the back while the others would wait on customers. They could not believe that it was so busy. The good thing was that time was flying. In a few hours, Maggie and Sophie will be walking out of the doors and heading towards their apartments. But for now, they have customers to wait on.

Thomas was so happy that he would have the opportunity to go to work tomorrow. The overall atmosphere of the business changed. Most of the employees thought the newly formed department were going to be abolished. As a matter of fact, most of them whispered to their managers that because they believed it was not prosperous yet, it should be cut. They were surprise to find out that it is the most prosperous department in the corporation. "But how?" all of them wonder.

All of them are looking at Thomas a little differently now. They felt because he is honest, he was not going to be successful. They believed that those who were members of the "good ole boy network" were the only ones who would be successful. They found out today that their beliefs were false. Some of them are now without jobs. The director decided not to find other positions for the employees that were laid off. He wants the departments to do more with less. He wants them to make more money for the corporation with less staff members.

Thomas is looking forward to the day when God tells him it is time to start his own business. He will wait until God says to leave this place. He knows that God will move him when He is ready. He feels that he is still at this corporation because God is using him to show His power. Some are already noticing it, and hopefully, because of it, they will change their ways. He prays that they do before it is everlasting too late. He is so glad that making money did not come before the things of God. He has seen so many that grew up in the church, and is now turning their backs on God. To him, they are spoiled. He had to sneak and hide, to read God's word, and they went to church with their parents. Because of all the promises contained in the Bible, he often wonders why they behave the way they do. "Why do we take you for granted, Holy Spirit?" he asked God, and waited for Him to answer.

It amazes him how so many spend so much time trying to acquire wealth, but they do not include God in obtaining wealth. So many get worldly wealth, and forget about others who need help. He vowed to share his wealth with those whom God tells him to share it with. He knows there are those who do not want to work, but are able to work. He believes in giving people opportunities to work and earn money to provide for their families, but he does not believe in constantly feeding people who refuse to do anything about their circumstances. He decided to call his fiancé to tell her he loves her.

When he hung up the phone, he looked up and a figure was standing in the doorway. The figure startled him because he did not expect it. As he stared to examine the figure, he finally recognized who he is. It was his ex-assistant. Before he could open his mouth to greet him, the ex-assistant said, "So, how do you do it? How do you avoid getting the axe? Tell me your secret." "I don't have any secrets, and you know that. If there is a secret, then I must tell you that it is God. I don't consider Him a secret, because He is not a secret at all," Thomas said. Thomas thought this was a perfect opportunity to talk to him about Jesus, but the ex-assistant did not want to hear it. "Man, I heard about Jesus all of my life. I grew up in church, and I believe if I want something, then I should do the same things as our forefathers did, which was to take it. You never get anywhere in this world by being honest, you know that. That is why I am over your old department. Now, I need you to help me to keep my job. You already know my credentials, and you know that I can talk my way into getting what I want," he said. He went on to explain that he believes they are out to get him, but he plans to get them first.

Thomas decided not to talk to this fool right now, and he waited until he fully stated his case, but he knows that he is not able to help him. He offered a few days ago and he refused. Besides, he will be busy himself trying to make his department more profitable. He already knows he cannot trust this person. He was glad that things turned out the way they did as far as his true colors being revealed. He hopes that he changes because he needs this job, and has a family to feed. After he finished, Thomas said, "I wish I could help you, but I can't. You and I were in the same meeting, from what we heard, you and I will be busy making sure our employees will still have a job next year." "Yes, I know, but you have outside connections, don't you?" he said. "You and I have the same investor connections man," Thomas said. "Yeah, you are right. I didn't think about that," he said.

"Nice talking to you. I got to go and get another job Thomas. I am sure one of those investors will give me a job, but before I go, I plan to do something to the corporation. They will always remember me," he said.

When he walked out of Thomas secretary's door, he yelled to his assistant to bring him all of the accounts. She grabbed them out of the filing cabinet and gave them to him. He stuffed them into a large metal trashcan and placed the trashcan in the middle of the floor. He pulled out his cigarette lighter and set the files on fire. He went into his office and grabbed his belonging. As the director and the other managers ran towards him, he ran out of the office yelling profanities at them. Thomas believes the directors and managers will remember the assistant that they grew to love and trust. After someone extinguished the flames, everyone stood around the trashcan shaking their head. The other managers wished they had asked for the files after the meeting was over, but they did not expect this because they allowed this fool to keep his job.

No one had a clue that this would happen. His department was going to be divided between several departments within three months, so they needed those files. They hope that the information was computerized, and as soon as they made that request known, the secretary that was just laid off, logged onto her computer and deleted all of the files. She told them that none of the data was saved. Thomas has a copy of all of the files, but he remained silent. The other departments were told to recreate the files by any means necessary, and if they fail, they are putting their jobs at risk.

Thomas saw the expression on the faces of the crooked managers. They got to where they are by snitching on other managers. They did not get laid off because they lied on or told on the ones that were laid off. Everything is a mess now. These people need Jesus, but they do not know they need Him. He decided to leave for the day. He locked the office and walked out of the door in the midst of chaos.

Mary was so happy to talk to her birth dad. He told her everything and when she looked at her watch, she realized that it is now nighttime. "Oh no, it's late. I have to talk to you tomorrow. I am glad I told the children to walk home and let themselves in. I will see you all tomorrow, okay?" she said. She hugged them again, and ran out of the restaurant. Roy ran out of the door and yelled that he will give her the information regarding class tomorrow. He will see her tomorrow. She yelled, "Okay, I love you." He felt so good. He finally has a sister. He was grateful that his dad raised him. After hearing her story, he decided he would never complain about his childhood again. He was blessed, and now he really knows it.

When she finally arrived at her house, she saw the children studying through the window. She was so glad that she taught them to let themselves into the house. They know where she works, but she does not know if all of the staff knows her name. She walked in and the children were glad to see her. The furniture will arrive tomorrow, and she is so glad. She will sleep on the floor tonight, but it is still okay. She is grateful for the roof that God provided, to cover them. She knows that she is blessed. The children told her that they made sandwiches and ate them. They told her that they are not hungry. They finished their homework and want to watch television. She decided to watch television with them. She will tell them about their grandfather and uncle tomorrow. She will use the pillows to get comfortable. She got a few of her thickest blankets, and she and the children lie on top of them, and put the pillows against the walls for support. They plan to stay up all night.

Maggie is so tired. She could barely keep her eyes open so she decided to go to bed. As soon as she got into bed, the phone ranged. She picked it up and Sophie was on the other end of the phone. She told her that she was tired and was going to bed. She did not want to go to the movies because she knows she would fall asleep. Sophie told her that she did not want to go along, so they made plans to go tomorrow afternoon. Sophie confessed that she is tired as well. She decided that she would go to sleep early as well. She will be moving tomorrow. "Oh, I forgot, we can't go to the movies tomorrow, both of us are moving," she said. "Yes, I know. I am so glad that I don't have much to take, so my move will not be long," said Maggie. "I don't have many items here, but my furniture will be delivered tomorrow morning. I got furniture coming from four different furniture stores. I hope they do not arrive at the same time. I want to put each piece of furniture in place as soon as they bring it in. I bought some beautiful things, so you have to come and see the house after things are put in place," Sophie said. "And you must do the same. My grandmother's house, or should I say, my house is beautiful. It has the columns, the big porch, the big kitchen, the iron bathtub with foots and so much more. I plan to decorate it slowly. I don't plan to go into debt trying to furnish the entire place at once. Girl, you are blessed that you found that money," Maggie said. "You know, I was thinking about that. I hope the person who hid it is dead. I hope that they don't hunt me down to get that money back," she said. "Just pray," Maggie said.

"Too bad I did not know God prior to spending the money. I should have paid tithes," she said. "If you had known and not do it, then you would have been responsible," she said. "Girl, before I go to sleep I want to say thank you for being a wonderful friend. I want to thank God for you, and I love you. I consider you my sister, as well as my best friend. I pray to God that you and I remain close, especially since we are members of God's family now, and I think that is so wonderful and exciting," Sophie said with tears steaming down her face. "I am glad too. We must always remember to put God first and to talk to others about Jesus. I hope that everyone becomes saved, although I know that everyone will not believe. Good night girl, I love you," said Maggie. "Good night, I love you too," said Sophie.

Thomas always enjoys spending time with his fiancé regardless of the things that he heard about her, which he is still trying to determine if they are true, so he took her out to dinner, just to talk. He found out new things about her, such as, she does not like the fact that he is so free with his money. She wants him to hold onto most of it. She believes that everyone should work hard for it because that is what she did. Thomas tried explaining to her that when God blesses him, he is required to be a blessing to others. He admitted that he never did for anyone as much as he did for Mary. He reassured his fiancé that Mary is only a sister. She has a lot of growing up to do to be a good minister. He was hurt that his fiancé thought something other than the obvious. He truly loves her.

After he dropped her off, he had to really search for answers. He prayed and asked God if she is the one He wants him to be with. He does not want to be with someone who is going to have a problem with him using what God gives him to bless those who God tells him to bless. His fiancé made it obvious that he will not be able to do that once she marries him. She appears to be a godly woman but she is not as spiritually mature as he is. She also told him that once he marries her, he would not spend time with his secretary. She knows that he considers her to be his mother, and besides, the woman is over sixty years old. His fiancé said she did not care. She wants him to spend time at home, and if he were spending it with someone other than his mother and father, or her, then she will have a problem. She does not want him spending time with Mary and her family either. He kept reminding her that she and the children are also his family. She told him that she does not care. He decided to pray and ask God for an answer immediately because he is scheduled to marry this woman soon.

After talking to her for hours, she told him that the rules that she will impose on him are also for her too. She told him that she grew up in a family where her mom was the boss. Her father could not take it any longer and left her mom when she was 18 years old. She decided to stay with her mom, and took her side. She refuses to talk to her dad, although he makes every effort to include her in his life. She tells him often that she is not interested. Thomas did not know this. All of this is new to him. He told her that she is wrong and explained why. He asked her if she is interested in counseling sessions with his pastor, and she told him no. She feels that she does not have any problems, and if there are problems then he is the cause of all of them. He decided to remain quiet and rely on God to tell him the truth.

This is the woman that he wanted to spend the rest of his life with. The problem is that he does not know this woman. He is so glad that all of this is being revealed to him before he walks down the aisle. She is not as godly as he first believed. He believes it was the devil that called her to be his minister, just like Mary implied. The Bible was right when it says what is in you will come out. Her true self is coming out right now. He could not wait to drop her off. His brain is now going into overload. He decided to end the date by telling her he is getting tired and needs to retire early.

He paid the tab and they walked to the car. He opened the door and helped her into the car, went over to the driver's side, got in and drove off. She continued to lay down the ground rules, which will begin after they are officially married. She told him that because he is so busy she would make all of the decisions because she is smarter. She told him that she would also pick out the house and the furniture because he does not have good taste because she believes his apartment is ugly. She told him she told the contractor that she no longer wants the house because it is not what she really wanted in the first place. She said she wanted and deserve better than what she was getting. She also told him that she will also pick out his clothes and will tell him who and who not to socialize with. He thought she was joking, but as she continued to talk he realized that she meant every word she is saying. He did not say one word until he walked her to her door. He hugged her and said goodnight. His head was reeling as he walked back to the car.

He does not believe he could tolerate the person who he believed was the love of his life. They are total opposites, so he asked God again if she is the one. He heard what Mary had told him earlier, but he did not want to believe it. He now believes it, but he will pray when he gets home, and decided that he will continue to ask God to answer him. He does not care if he has to do it all night. He has to know! Surely, she can't be the one for him if her beliefs are as they are now. She fooled him!

Chapter Seven

Saturday

Sophie packed up her belongings and called a taxi. She feels so refreshed and knows she has a long day ahead of her. She is so glad that she went to bed early. She is so glad that she is moving into a new house. A house that is paid for, and in a few hours, it will be fully furnished. The money did not make her rich, but it was able to pay for a house and furniture. While she emptied the refrigerator, she heard the taxi driver blow his horn outside. She looked down and saw Maggie getting into the taxi. She believes that Maggie is blessed. Her grandmother left her a beautiful house that is much bigger than hers. The house is in excellent condition because her family keeps it up. The house has to stay in their family, and she believes it is a good idea. If Maggie gets married, her husband will have to sign something stating that he will not have any claims against the property.

Maggie woke up very happy. She called the taxi before taking her shower. She knocked on the door of the building superintendent and gave him the keys to the apartment. She carried all of her items downstairs and waited for the taxi. She was not afraid, although it was still dark outside. She is so grateful to be enroute to her lovely home. She thanks God for His wonderful blessing, and is looking forward to her new life. She may not have nice new expensive furniture like Sophie yet, but she will eventually furnish it. She is grateful. To her, this is a brand new start. She will start school soon. She is looking forward to the future, which is a future where God is more important than everything else.

At last, she has arrived. She is surprise because her family is already there. They ran down from off the porch and hugged her. There were aunts, uncles, her grandparents, and her cousins. It looks like a family reunion. What was amazing that they came bearing gifts! There were so many gift certificates, money, things, and furniture. They even cooked breakfast. She walked in and found the house furnished with beautiful furniture. She thanked God. She is so happy. They plan to enjoy each other's company all day and night in celebration of her and their family getting closer to God.

Sophie started getting worried that the taxi company forgot about her. As she dialed the number again, she heard the horn. She looked out of the window and saw the taxi. She yelled that she is coming down. She ran downstairs and told him that she needed help with some of her belongings. He told her that he would have to charge her extra because he does the driving and is not responsible for anything else. She told him that she does not have any extra money. He told her that he knows she just got paid. He was right, she did but she planned to use the money for other things, such as, to pay her utilities. She decided to pay him. It took over thirty minutes to load the items in the car, and to turn in her keys.

She finally arrived at the house. It is not what she really wanted but the price was good. It looked better before, but now she is a little disappointed because it does not match the furniture. She decided that her thoughts were wrong and immediately repented. She thanked God for his many blessings. She opened the doors and found the house to be very pretty. The inside looked much better than the outside. She thought about something she remembered in Bible study, how God transforms His children from the inside out. God is more concerned about what is in the heart than what she looks like on the outside. The inside will definitely match the furniture. She paid the taxi cab driver and thanked him. She decided to put all of the things away before the furniture arrives. As soon as she was halfway finished, one of the furniture trucks arrived. She knows that today will be a long day, but she is not going to complain.

Thomas woke up still praying to God to give him an answer. He does not want to marry the wrong girl. The phone constantly ranged all morning and when he looked at the caller ID, he knows that it was his fiancé. He did not want to talk to her, but to stop her from calling; he decided to talk to her the next time she calls. He did not have to wait long because she called again. She has been calling every five minutes. He picked up the phone and immediately she wanted to know why he did not pick up the first time she called.

He asked her what changed her because he felt he really needed to know. He really did not understand the sudden change, and she told him that she was always like that. She said she was tired of pretending to be this other person. She said she wanted to step out on faith to show him that she is an asset to him. Her beauty and brains will make him go further than he can ever dream of. She also offered to be a partner in his new business. He reminded her that he does not have his own business yet. She said she knows and that she will help him open the business because she has plans. She told him he should step out and do it, rather than waiting on God to give him the go-ahead. He told her that he disagrees, and she was not interested in finding out why. She told him that she knows she is right. He did not want to argue with her, and he did not want to talk to her. He still needs to find out if she is the one that God wants in his life. He hopes that God says no, although he really loves this woman. If she is the one, he may have to postpone the wedding until she agrees to counseling. She needs it, and if he continues to listen to her, he will need it also. He decided to listen, and not say much. After hours of listening to her ideas, she asked if he wanted to go to do something today, and he said no. He told her that he was very tired and he plans to go back to bed.

He did not lie. He is very tired. He stayed up talking to God. God was so quiet, and he still did not get his answer. He decided that he would continue to wait on God. He will stay in and will not call anyone today. He just wants to talk to God. He asked his fiancé not to call back. He explained to her that he needs to talk to God about their future. She lied and said she understood. She hung up the phone without first saying goodbye. He went back into his bedroom and got into his bed. He wanted an answer from God, and decided to wait for it, no matter how long it took.

Mary woke up with the television still on. She went into the bathroom and said her prayers in the shower. She got dressed and woke the children up. The trucks should arrive soon so she decided to prepare a quick breakfast, and as soon as she finished cooking, the doorbell rung. She opened it and discovered that her furniture has arrived. She was so happy to see them and offered them breakfast. They declined and told her that they had already eaten. One of them told her that she should have offered an hour ago. They started laughing as she apologized for not waking them up early this morning.

The children were just as excited as she was about the furniture. This is the first time they ever had new furniture. She will purchase those bikes and other toys after she gets her first paycheck. As they brought the furniture in and set it in its proper place, the house took on a new look. It took a couple of hours before everything was placed in its proper place. She and the children are so happy. As soon as they sat down on the sofa the doorbell ranged again. This time when she opened the door, it was her both of her dads, and Mom. She could not believe they were together. They decided to talk to her together for the first time in her life. She felt this was a good time to introduce her dad to his grandchildren.

It took all day to get all of the furniture in place, but Sophie was still beaming. She still needs more pots, pans and dishes. She will get them when she gets paid. She does not plan to go in debt to get the things she needs. She has seen too many people getting laid off. She does not want to run the risk of getting into trouble and not being able to pay her bills. She has to make it on her own, and do not want to ask her family for assistance. They do not even know that she has her own place yet. She will call them as soon as she gets a dial tone. She does not have any utilities turned on yet. They are not opened on weekends and she forgot to go by each location yesterday. She has to wait until Monday, but she is still glad. She wished she held on to the keys. She will ask one of her neighbors to allow her to use their phone to call her mom. She wants a bath before she goes to church tomorrow. She knows her mom will come by and pick her up if she asks. She believes they will be proud of her, especially after she tells them that she is trying to get closer to God.

All of them labeled her as being a heathen because of all the things she was involved in. She was proud of that label because she felt she was big and bad enough to do anything she wanted, and did not have to suffer any consequences from an Almighty God that she did not believe in. She learned to believe that she was a god because it gave her an excuse to say and do whatever she wanted to her friends and family. She just did not care. She did not love anyone, not even her mother. Now she regrets all of the things she said and did. She will ask all of them to forgive her, and she plans to start by asking her mom to forgive her first.

Mary's biological dad gave his children presents and then went back to the truck to get more. She could not believe it. She looked out of the window, and the truck was full of toys. The children ran into the room and put on their shoes. They ran outside to help Granddad. Roy also came in bearing gifts. She felt bad because she does not have anything for them. He told her that she does not have to give them anything, but he would like her to make those pastries that he enjoys eating so much. She hugged him and went into the kitchen to make them. She warned them that they might not be finished until late this afternoon. They said they would help her prepare them. It was nice to see Mom, Dad, Daddy, and Roy, her nieces, her nephews, and her children in the kitchen cooking. She prays that this will occur often. To her, this is truly a new beginning.

Leonora Austin

Chapter Eight

Sunday

Thomas woke up with Jesus still on his mind. He still did not get his answer, but he feels that God will answer him. He decided not to call his fiancé until he gets his answer; he sure hopes God says she is not the one. He does not know if he can live with this woman. He feels bad because he thought he knew her. When he reflects back, he sees it now. Some of the things she said gave him many clues but he overlooked them. He feels dumb. "How could I have been so blind?" he asked himself. He is still trusting in Jesus, and told Him that he will wait for His answer. He has to depend on Jesus.

He decided to go ahead and prepare for church. He is not hungry but decided to scramble some eggs to eat before attending Sunday school. He does not have to pick up Mary because she said she would meet him there. He is still glad that God used him to help her. He will continue to help people no matter what, as long as God says to do it.

This is one of the reasons why he feels that she is not the one. She is an undercover gold digger. She makes a healthy salary, but she wants more money. That is so sad. Well, he has to hurry up, he has an hour to eat, shower and dress. He wants to arrive on early.

Mary stayed up late with her family. She did not go to bed until around 3:00 in the morning, but somehow, she feels refreshed. She already prepared breakfast and woke the children up. She decided to eat after she finishes bathing and is dressed for church. She plans to attend Sunday school today. She wants the children to grow up in the knowledge and love of God. She also wants to know everything there is to know, and she feels that she needs to do whatever it takes because she is so grateful that God has blessed her abundantly. She is living an abundant life.

Sophie's mother arrived early. They talked about God all the way to her house. She felt strange in her mother's house. It felt as if she has not been there in years, but she knows it has been a short time. She was glad that her mom was nice enough to pick her up and allow her to use her bathroom. She knows that she did not have to do it, especially since she mistreated her for years.

The water felt so good, and it was strange trying to envision how she was going to take a shower in the dark. The candles helped but electricity would have been greatly appreciated. After she put all of the furniture in its proper place, it got dark quickly. She was glad that she had a few candles, because if she did not, she would have been in trouble. She thanked God that Mom picked her up. She would rather bathe in the light than in the dark.

After she dried off, she put on one of her new dresses. She had to admit to herself, that she looks good. She is so glad that the expensive shops that she bought the clothes from did not sell hoochie wear. She bought beautiful and tasteful outfits that any mother in church would approve of.

When she walked out of the bedroom, she could tell that her mom was pleased at the way her daughter looks. Her mom started praising God for what He did. She tried and failed, but she is so glad that God can never fail. Her and her daughter looks good and she can't wait to get to the church. They decided to buy breakfast on the way and her dad agrees.

Maggie's family decided to spend the night last night. She had to walk across sleeping bodies to get to the bathroom. After she finished bathing she woke all of them up. "Okay everyone, we need to go to church. We partied as a family, now it is time to worship as a family!" she yelled. They all agreed. All of the women decided to bath first, and told the men to put their temporary beds away. She is glad that the house has three bathrooms. Some of them decided to cook breakfast, while others took a shower or bath. "Now hurry, we do not have much time," she said. They all jumped up and got busy doing what they are supposed to do to prepare for church service.

The children told their mom that they enjoyed Sunday school and learning with the other children. Mary was so glad to hear it. She enjoyed it also. The children asked if they were coming back for Bible school, and she said yes. She was so glad to be there with her family. She could not believe the amount of people who went to Sunday school. There are so many people here, and now she looks forward to worship service, which will start in ten minutes. She looked behind her and recognized Thomas. She smiled but he was not looking in her direction. She looked around the church to see if she recognized others.

The Fullness Thereof

Sophie was glad to be in the house of God one more time. She remembers when she almost died, and if she did, she would have ended up in hell. She comes to church to worship God. She loves feeling His presence. She was glad to be there with her family. As she sat down, she looked around and recognized Thomas. She was glad to see him and wondered if he knew what happened to Eric. She decided not to ask him. She looked around again and saw the rest of Maggie's family coming through the doors of the Church. It was enough of them to fill up several pews. She recognized most of them and knew that they were her family. She waved at them and they waved back with smiles on their faces. Wow, she and Maggie chose to worship at the same church this Sunday. Both of them attended another church Wednesday night. Her mom wanted her to come here, so she is glad she did because she sees familiar faces. She thought she saw the man who sold her the house. He and his wife waved, and she waved back and noticed that it was not him. Everyone is so friendly. She loves this church!

Thomas has so much on his mind. He is still waiting for God's answer. After staring at the floor for a long time, he finally raised his head and saw a beautiful woman walking towards him. He heard a quiet still voice telling him that she will be his wife. He finally got his answer! She looked as if she was looking for a seat. He decided to stop her and said, "Are you looking for a place to sit?" She said she was. He stood up and offered her the small space next to him. She looks nothing like his fiancé. He had to admit, she was not exactly his type but he knows that God knows best.

After talking to the woman that God gave him, Thomas found out that they have the same qualities. He is happy. He will call his fiancé after church to end their relationship. He said a silent prayer and thanked God for everything. If he had walked down the aisle with that woman, it would have been a mistake. It is amazing how someone could fake a personality for years. He is so glad that she showed her true colors. He is well pleased with God's choice.

After the choir sung, the pastor of the church walked up to the pulpit. He decided to go ahead and give them the message from God and told them that they will take up the tithes and offerings afterwards. He said the subject is the Fullness Thereof. He told everyone to turn to 1 Corinthians 10 and start reading beginning at verse 23. He ended at verse 31. Everyone began to read in unison, "*All things are lawful for me, but all things are not expedient: all things are lawful for me, but all things edify not. Let no man seek his own, but every man another's wealth. Whatsoever is sold in the shambles, that eats, asking no question for conscience sake: For the earth is the Lord's, and the fullness thereof. If any of them that believe not bid you to a feast, and ye be disposed to go; whatsoever is set before you, eat, asking no question for conscience sake. But if any man say unto you, This is offered in sacrifice unto idols, eat not for his sake that shewed it, and for conscience sake: for the earth is the Lord's, and the fulness thereof: Conscience, I say, not thine own, but of the other: for why is my liberty judged of another man's conscience? For if I by grace be a partaker, why am I evil spoken of for that for which I give thanks?"* He told everyone to have a seat in the presence of the Lord.

The pastor prayed and repeated the title of the subject, and then he began to preach his sermon. He said, "People are so confused when it comes to living life to its fullness. Some believe that it means getting everything this world has to offer without first asking God if it is what He wants for them. Some believe that partying all night to the point that they are too tired to get up on Sunday morning to go to church is living a full life. They enjoyed their outing, but they are too tired to come to His house to give Him thanks. Some believe that looking at a preacher on television is enough, and it makes them feel that they at least have some sort of religion. What is religion? I'm glad you asked. Religion is anything you believe strongly in. Satanism is religion. Witchcraft is religion. Buddhism is religion. Baptist is also religion. Your child can be your religion because you treat him as if he is your god. Your spouse can be your religion because you would rather worship him rather than your creator. Money can be a religion because you would rather work to make it, than to work on being a good servant for God.

The reason why you get up in the morning is to find another way to live life to its fullness. Not according to God's definition, but according to your own rules. You are too blind to realize that you can only have a fulfilled life if you live a life that is dedicated Christ Jesus, because if it had not been for Him, you would not have a chance to live a fulfilled life. If Jesus is the only way to living a full life, so I need to ask you parents a question. Are you introducing your children to Christ? You simply cannot have a full life without Him.

All things are lawful for me, but not all things are helpful; all things are lawful for me, but not all things edify. Let no one see his own, but each one the other's well-being. Be careful in your interactions with others. People feel it is okay to do whatever you want as long as you don't hurt anyone. How do you know if you are hurting anyone? If your lifestyle is such that it is disruptive to you, it also has an effect on your loved ones. You have been fooled! Everything you do always affect someone else, always. You go out and party all night, and your parents, your wife, your children, your grandparents, or your friends are at home praying that you come home just one more time. God wants you to live an abundant life, but in order to do it, you must include Him in everything you do and want to do. When you are partying at a club, don't fool yourself in believing that He is happy about it. In all you do, it is to glorify God the Father. How can you say you are glorying God by shaking your behind on the dance floor to secular music? How can you say you are glorifying God by drinking to the point of being drunk? Don't you know your body is a vessel of God? How can you tell your children to live a successful life, and they should do as you say and not what you do? You are their teacher! All of us are someone's teacher. I am so tired to people calling me and want me to pray for their family member because he is doing things that are not right in the sight of God. The things that you once did, and now those who saw you doing it, are now they are doing it because you taught them.

Eat whatever is sold in the meat market, asking no questions for conscience's sake; for the earth is the Lord's and all of its fullness. Everything belongs to God, including us. So, let me ask you this question. Where are you trying to build treasure? Down here or up in heaven? Don't you get it? You belong to God, and because He is our creator, you are to worship and thank Him for another day. Do your children see you thanking God? The fullness thereof is all about God. It cannot be found in clubs, in bars, or sin. To experience fullness, you need Jesus. If you want to be rich, you can have it. If you want good health, you can have that to. If you do not get it here, God promise that you will get it in Heaven where it will last forever. You will never have to worry about someone trying to come and steal your property. You don't have to worry about the devil telling you to spend all of your wages you earned in a bar anymore.

If any of those who do not believe invites you to dinner, and you desire to go, eat whatever is set before you, asking no question for conscience sake. But if anyone says to you, "This was offered to idols," do not eat it for the sake of the one who told you, and for conscience sake; for the earth is the Lord's, and all its fullness. Again everything belongs to God, and God's children can have it all. We are to love and treat each other right, but if that person is worshipping or serving other gods, you are to cut that person loose. You are not to have a relationship with someone who is not glorifying your God. You are not to have fellowship with darkness because we are the children of the light.

Let's review the life of Moses. He grew up with the best that this world has to offer. He had the best food, the best education, the best clothes and shoes, and everything else. Moses grew up in a rich house that did not want to have anything to do with the one and only God. Moses made up his mind and gave up all of the riches of this world and chose the riches of Christ instead. The riches that Christ has to offer are everlasting. It will never rust or tarnish. It will never go away. The riches of this world are corruptible and I can prove it. If you spend your last $50,000 today, will you still have $50,000 tomorrow? The answer is no. You will not have those dollars tomorrow. I know what some of you are thinking, what if I invest in a house? What if your house burns down, or if a storm comes your way and cause major damage, will it still be worth the same thing? What if you spend it on a diamond, which is supposed to last forever? I have news for you, if you buy a diamond last year; the price is much lower next year.

Only heavenly treasure goes up in value. God never decrease, He only adds or multiplies. *But if I give thanks, why am I evil spoken of for the food over which I give thinks?* Jesus is still in the saving business. You should at least thank Him for coming down here, dying for you, was buried for you, and rising on the third day, just for you! You should live a life based on that testimony alone. He saved your soul, and one day He is coming back for you.

Be careful of what you do, you can cause another Christian to stumble. Your children, your parents, your family and friends notice more than you think. Your actions can cause them to stumble. I want to talk to you parents who feel that it is okay to do whatever you want. Don't you know that your children are watching and because of it, they will grow up doing the same thing you are doing? When you become old in age, that person who saw you not glorifying God, as you should, will still be out there because you taught them to do it. You taught them that it is okay to work yourself to death trying to get earthly wealth, and when they die before you, you are the first one running down the aisle and asking God why. You may have changed, but those who watched you while you were living it up and trying to live life to its fullness did not change. You caused someone to stumble. You were their example, and now they consider those who are doing right as fools because of your ignorance.

The Fullness Thereof

Therefore, whether you eat or drink, or whatever you do, do all to the glory of God. Give no offense, either to the Jews or to the Greeks or to the church of God, just as I also please all men in all things, not seeking my own profit; but the profit of many, that they may be saved. Everything you do is to point someone to Christ. You are supposed to be the light of the world. The light of the world is not hanging in clubs or bars, or any place that is not glorifying God. Don't tell me that you go to the club to point someone to Christ! I don't believe it, and I don't believe anyone else believes it either.

You see, the Bible tells us that we are not to have fellowship with darkness. We are not to hang with those who do not want to glorify God. We are to tell them about the goodness of Christ, and what He can do for them, but we are not to consider them our buddies. They represent darkness. You can't have it both ways. You will either have a life outside or inside the body of Christ. If it is inside the body of Christ, you will not be consumed with the cares of the world. Check yourself. Your entire life should show someone to Christ. Your behavior should be so different from those outside of the body of Christ, and if it is not, do something about it before it is too late.

It is not too late to change, but we need help changing. The Bible says, *"Be ye transformed by the renewing of the mind."* Our goal is to have a mind like Christ Jesus. Jesus cares about our souls and not about the cares of this world. We are to show someone how to get out of the world. People are looking for direction, and they are looking at you because they believe you got it going on. If you are doing drugs, they will also do drugs because they see you do it, and it tells them that this is the life. Don't let your walk cause others to stumble. Jesus came down through 42 generations and willingly dwelled among people. He did not waver, and although He talked to both Jews and Gentiles, He still lived a godly life. When He was persecuted for lies that others told He still did not change. When they hung Him on the cross and pierced His side, He was not selfish like some of us, but He remained on that cross to save you and me, and endured the shame and pain.

If it was one of us, and if we had the power to get down from off of the cross, we would have. But not Jesus, He died on the cross and before He did, He prayed and asked the Father to forgive all of us. After He hung His head, he thought about those who did not hear the gospel, and descended to hell and preached to the lost. So many believed and their family and friends saw their loved ones walked the earth one more time. He was buried and rose on the third day according to scripture. Do you know that He got out of that grave to save us? We are not worthy of Jesus! His death made it possible for all of us to live an abundant and fulfilled life. He made it possible for all of us to live forever! You only need to believe on Him to get all that He promises. Is there anyone who wants a fulfilled life? The doors of the church are now opened. Is there anyone?"

Thomas went up for prayer. Sophie, Maggie and others went up crying. Mary and all of her family went up, some for prayer and some to dedicate their lives back to Jesus. This was the first time that most of them heard about Jesus. They answered God's call to come out of the world, and others who were released from bondage asked for strength to stay out.

All of them are looking forward to living life to its fullness. After seeing demons and living a destructive life, most of them know that there is no life outside of Jesus. He died for them, and so they are to die to their old way of life and live for Him.

This week has been an eye opening experience for all of them, and starting today, they will give God thanks in all that they do. He gave them a new life, and now they will truly live life to its fullness. A life dedicated to Christ Jesus, their Mentor and their Savior. All of them asked and received the Holy Spirit that very day. They thought they felt His presence before, but this was more powerful. All of them were on one accord. For the first time in their life, they have the joy that can only come from God. Mary said aloud, "Thank you Jesus, thank you God!" and everyone joined in and praised God for many hours and they rejoiced as the Holy Spirit came through there like a mighty rushing wind!

Leonora Austin is available for speaking engagements and/or personal appearances. For more information you can send an email to Leonora at: austin6916@bellsouth.net

ADVANTAGE BOOKS™
PO Box 160847
Altamonte Springs, FL 32716

To order additional copies of this book or to see a complete list of all **ADVANTAGE BOOKS™** visit our online bookstore at:

www.advbookstore.com

or call our toll free order number at:

1-888-383-3110

Longwood, Florida, USA

"we bring dreams to life"™
www.advbookstore.com

Printed in the United States
69889LV00005B/64-93